THE PASTOR'S BIBLE STUDY

VOLUME ONE

A NEW INTERPRETER'S®
BIBLE STUDY

THE PASTOR'S BIBLE STUDY

VOLUME ONE

A NEW INTERPRETER'S® BIBLE STUDY

Abingdon Press
Nashville

THE PASTOR'S BIBLE STUDY
Volume One
A NEW INTERPRETER'S® BIBLE STUDY

Copyright © 2004 by Abingdon Press

This book is printed on acid-free paper.

Cataloging-in-publication information applied for with the
Library of Congress

ISBN 0687043646

04 05 06 07 08 09 10 11 12 13 — 10 9 8 7 6 5 4 3 2 1

MANUFACTURED IN THE UNITED STATES OF AMERICA

Contents

Contributors

David Albert Farmer, General Editor, is also the author of this publication's five-week study, "Unselfish Prayer." He earned a Ph.D. in New Testament Theology, is an ordained Baptist minister who taught preaching in seminary, and presently as an adjunct professor of humanities at Wilmington College. Dr. Farmer has served seven congregations and is now the pastor of Silverside Church in Wilmington, Delaware. He was editor of *Pulpit Digest* for eighteen years and *The African American Pulpit* for three years. He is the author of *Teaching Sermons on the Love and Grace of God* (Nashville: Abingdon Press, 1997*), Basic Bible Sermons on Hope* (Nashville: Baptist Sunday School Board, 1992)*;* he is the coeditor of *And Blessed Is She: Sermons by Women* (San Francisco: Harper & Row, 1990), and contributing author in *The Storyteller's Companion to the Bible: Judges–Kings* Volume Three (Nashville: Abingdon Press, 1992).

Warren Carter is the author of fifteen Bible studies on the Gospel of Matthew, the gospel covered by Year A of the lectionary. A native of New Zealand, he earned a Ph.D. in New Testament from Princeton Theological Seminary and is the Lindsey P. Pherigo Professor of New Testament at Saint Paul School of Theology in Kansas City, Missouri. He has published several books, including: *Matthew: Storyteller, Interpreter, Evangelist* (Peabody, Mass: Hendrickson Publishers, 1996), *Matthew's Parables: Audience-Oriented Perspectives* (Washington, D.C.: Catholic Biblical Association of America, 1998), *Matthew and the Margins: A Sociopolitical and Religious Reading* (Maryknoll, N.Y.: Orbis Books, 2000), *Matthew and Empire: Initial Explorations* (Harrisburg, PA: Trinity Press International, 2001), and *Pontius Pilate: Portraits of a Roman Governor* (Collegeville, Minn.: Liturgical Press, 2003).

Mary Donovan Turner is the author of ten Bible studies on Isaiah 1–39. She earned a Ph.D. in Old Testament from Emory University and is the Carl Patton Associate Professor of Preaching at the Pacific School of Religion in Berkeley, California. She has served congregations as an ordained Disciples of Christ minister. Her books include *Saved from Silence: Finding Women's Voice in Preaching* (St. Louis, Mo.: Chalice Press, 1999) and *The Storyteller's Companion to the Bible: Prophets I* (Nashville: Abingdon Press, 1996). Her writings also appear in *The Christian Century, Interpretation, Lectionary Homiletics, Word and Witness,* and *Setting the Table: Women in Theological Conversation.*

Richard Wallace is the author of ten Bible studies on grief. He earned a Th.D. from Luther Seminary in St. Paul, Minnesota, where he is now the associate professor of pastoral care. An ordained minister in the Evangelical Lutheran Church in America, he has served congregations in Georgia, California, and Minnesota. He speaks frequently on grief, violence, abuse, recovery, and African American culture.

Thorwald Lorenzen is the author of five Bible studies on power for Christian living and five Bible studies on liberating discipleship. A native of Germany, he earned a Th.D. in New Testament from the University of Zurich while studying with Eduard Schweizer. He is the pastor of Canberra Baptist Church in Canberra, Australia, following many years as a professor of systematic theology and theological ethics at the International Baptist Theological Seminary in Rueschlikon, Switzerland. He is the author of *Resurrection and Discipleship: Interpretive Models, Biblical Reflections, Theological Consequences* (Maryknoll, N.Y.: Orbis Books 1995) and *Resurrection, Discipleship, Justice: Affirming the Resurrection of Jesus Christ Today* (Macon, Ga.: Smyth & Helwys, 2003).

Foreword

In response to the needs of hardworking pastors, and bolstered by thorough research about the practices of congregations, Abingdon Press envisioned a new tool for supporting pastors in their ministry. Most pastors teach at least one midweek Bible study; some teach two. *The Pastor's Bible Study* will be published annually and focus exclusively on helping the pastor prepare for these important study and learning opportunities.

Some of the finest scholars, preachers, teachers, and thinkers to be found anywhere in the world have pooled their skills so that the volume you hold could be published, and its format reveals that these authors have written expressly for pastors and others who teach Bible studies. I trust that you will find this book extraordinarily helpful and that acquiring a copy annually will become a regular part of what you do each spring to build your ministry support library.

It has been my privilege both to edit and contribute to this exceptional resource. I am honored to be in the company of the team of writers who made this volume possible, a team that includes:

♦ Dr. Warren Carter, professor of New Testament at Saint Paul School of Theology in Kansas City, Missouri. He continues for us the excellent commentary work he did on Matthew's Gospel in *The New Interpreter's Study Bible*. His juxtaposition of the Roman Empire with the empire (kingdom) of God will astound you.

♦ Dr. Mary Donovan Turner, professor of preaching at the Pacific School of Religion in Berkeley, California. She brings her gifts as a Hebrew scripture scholar, preacher, and preaching professor to her enlightening study of First Isaiah. Dr. Turner pays special attention to keywords of the prophet and to key events during the time of his ministry in order to get to her exceptionally helpful commentary.

♦ Dr. Richard Wallace, associate professor of pastoral care and counseling at the Luther Seminary in St. Paul, Minnesota. On the heels of his own loss and bereavement, Dr. Wallace prepared his set of lessons, "Healing in Grief." He deals with several types of grief and discusses the healing possibilities of each one.

♦ Dr. Thorwald Lorenzen, pastor of the Canberra Baptist Church in Canberra, Australia. Not long ago he left the seminary classroom, where he taught systematic theology and theological ethics for many years in Switzerland. Dr. Lorenzen has written two study units for us that both relate to practical matters of discipleship.

An abundance of further information, including session outlines, PowerPoint™ slides, and exciting graphics, are available to you on the CD-ROM that is included with your purchase of volume one. The teaching helps we offer will support you in your teaching efforts.

I have done some test runs of certain segments of the material with some of the smart and faithful people who call me their pastor, the members of Silverside Church in Wilmington, Delaware. They gave their emphatic approval. I express my appreciation to them for yet another way in which they have affirmed me as I encourage them on their spiritual journeys.

I also express abiding gratitude to Diane and Victorio Hoskins of Baltimore, Maryland, former parishioners of mine, whose unfailing friendship and other acts of support have made a lasting impact on my life as preacher/pastor/teacher. I have done my part of the work on this volume in honor of them.

The staff of Abingdon Press, especially the division of Bibles, Reference, and ePublishing, has made this volume possible. Their untiring commitment to meeting the professional needs of pastors and local congregations in all denominations, along with their excellence in every phase of the editing and publishing process, have not only inspired me and the other writers with our tasks but have also brought into being the first of many volumes of *The Pastor's Bible Study* that you will both treasure and use again and again.

David Albert Farmer
Wilmington, Delaware

Introduction

The Pastor's Bible Study is the latest series offered in a line of *The New Interpreter's Bible* products to provide the best in scholarship for the service of the church. Designed to help pastors lead Bible studies for their congregations, this series is intended to enhance the study, teaching, and preaching of the Scriptures.

The results of a recent study conducted among nearly one thousand pastors (male and female) from over three hundred different churches (urban, suburban, small town, and rural) of various denominations (United Methodist, Presbyterian, Baptist, Lutheran, United Church of Christ, and others) show that 76% of the pastors regularly teach a Bible study. Most teach an average of five times per month to an adult group. Over 51% regularly offer a Bible study to more than one adult group. Over 24% of the respondents have a group that meets on Wednesday evenings and another 24% have another weekday evening group. Additionally, most pastors are asked to teach a Sunday school class. In their teaching ministry, 58% have some type of teaching agenda or philosophy to communicate or implement. On average, it takes pastors approximately four hours to prepare to teach a Bible study.

The Pastor's Bible Study is intended to help pastors meet their teaching responsibilities. Each volume will include six studies written by recognized biblical scholars, professors of preaching and pastoral care, and outstanding pastors and church educators. The six studies will include:

♦ Fifteen sessions on one of the four Gospels

♦ Ten sessions from an Old Testament book frequently cited in the lectionary

♦ Ten sessions on a special topic of interest to the teaching pastor (e.g., pastoral care, faith and practice, social justice)

♦ Three studies of five sessions each on relevant themes for the pastor (e.g., practical issues, inspirational themes)

Whether your study group meets for thirty minutes or an hour, for four weeks or the entire year, the flexible structure of *The Pastor's Bible Study* will meet your preparation needs. Its versatile design is also useful whether you choose to follow the lectionary, the canonical order of the Bible, or a key biblical theme on the Christian life.

As you prepare to lead your Bible study, look for the useful sidebars to the text that will help you provide a meaningful study experience for participants. **Teaching Tips** has ideas that will facilitate class discussion in a variety of creative ways. **Sources** will provide you with resources for further study derived from the lesson studies. **Study Bible** sidebars will indicate points of integration with *The New Interpreter's Study Bible*.* Finally, **Reflection** questions will foster participation, generate group and individual study, and encourage interaction with the biblical text.

Supplementing the six studies and sidebar helps in this volume is a CD-ROM containing valuable data and suggestions for classroom use, such as:

♦ A video introduction by the general editor

♦ The full text of *The Pastor's Bible Study: Volume One*, completely searchable

♦ An outline of each lesson

♦ PowerPoint™ slides

♦ Supplementary material that can be customized for handouts and screen and video viewing

It is our hope that *The Pastor's Bible Study,* our newest in a line of *The New Interpreter's Bible* products that provides scholarship for the church, will help you, the pastor, lead Bible studies in your congregation, in order to advance and increase the study, teaching, and preaching of the Scriptures.

---

*Note: *The Pastor's Bible Study* frequently cites material
from *The New Interpreter's Study Bible,*
the recommended textbook for study participants.

THE GOSPEL OF MATTHEW

A STUDY BY

WARREN CARTER

Warren Carter is Lindsey P. Pherigo Professor of New Testament at Saint Paul School of Theology in Kansas City, Missouri.

Introduction

The Pastor's Bible Study on Matthew

Matthew's Gospel is emphasized during Year A in Christian worship in congregations that choose to follow the three-year lectionary. The lectionary is one factor in choosing the texts for the fifteen Bible studies that follow. The pastor may choose to connect the substance of proclamation with Christian education during a midweek Bible study.

The other factors in choosing the texts for studying Matthew over fifteen or more weeks are seven presuppositions about Matthew's Gospel.

1. The Gospel's Plot

Matthew's Gospel unfolds through six sections.

- ♦ 1:1–4:16 introduces Jesus and his commission.
- ♦ 4:17–11:1 Jesus carries out his commission with three types of actions.
- ♦ 11:2–16:20 focuses on responses to Jesus' actions and words.
- ♦ 16:21–20:34 introduces a new piece of the commission, his death in Jerusalem.
- ♦ 21–27 Jesus enters Jerusalem, conflicts with the elite, dies.
- ♦ 28 God raises him back to life.

A coherent "big picture" should be emphasized because Bible students often struggle to understand the overall gospel story if they are not connecting individual stories to the larger, unfolding plot. The developing story is very important for interpreting Matthew.

2. The Situation of Matthew's Gospel

Matthew's Gospel was probably written in the 80s

Sources

These presuppositions come from my previous scholarly work in Matthew and from leading many adult Bible studies with various church groups. This material is consonant with my comments and notes on Matthew in *The New Interpreter's Study Bible* (Nashville: Abingdon Press, 2003), 1745–1800; with my commentary, *Matthew and the Margins* (Maryknoll: Orbis Books, 2000); and with the collection of studies in *Matthew and Empire: Initial Explorations* (Harrisburg: Trinity Press International, 2001). Further discussion and support for the positions presented in this material can be found in these resources, especially *Matthew and the Margins*.

CE from and for a small community of disciples who were probably located in Antioch in Syria. Matthew's community occupied a socially marginal location in relation to two centers of power.

One center of authority was a synagogue community to which it had belonged and with which it was now in considerable tension. In dispute were claims that, after the destruction of the Jerusalem temple in 70 CE, God's saving purposes (1:21-23), forgiveness (9:1-8; 26:28), presence (1:23; 18:20; 28:20), reign (4:17), and will (5:17-48) were revealed in Jesus.

A second center of power concerned the pervasive Roman Empire, whose presence was quite visible in Antioch, the capital city of the Roman province of Syria. According to the Gospel, the world constructed by the Roman Empire was contrary to God's purposes (20:25-28), controlled by Satan (4:8), and under God's judgment (24:27-31). God is in the process of establishing God's reign, which is a just and life-giving world.

3. Daily Life in the Roman Empire

The story of Roman times is a tale of two worlds—comfortable for the elite, desperately difficult for the rest. Societal structure was vertical and hierarchical, dominated by the ruling elite who comprised about five percent of the population. This elite group systematically exploited rural peasants and urban artisans for its own benefit through taxes, tributes, rents, loans, and foreclosures. In such circumstances many suffered from inadequate food supply, poor nutrition, overwork, poor health, poverty, dislocated households, overcrowding, and anxiety. In Antioch, there was little protection against natural disasters like flooding, earthquakes, or fire. Rome justified this world with claims of being chosen by the gods (e.g., Jupiter) to manifest the gods' will, presence, blessings, and well-being. In reality, that meant subjugation to Rome's military and taxation power, represented in Antioch by troops (three or four legions), images, statues, buildings, coins, governing personnel, and local elites who shared power with Rome.

> ## Study Bible
>
> See the *NISB*, 1745-47 for background information on the Gospel of Matthew.

4. Matthew as a Word of Address to this Context

Matthew's good news is that God's saving presence and reign are manifested in Jesus. What difference does it make that the language of the kingdom, reign, or empire of God is the same language that is used for Rome's empire? What happens when there is a clash of empires that represent vastly different visions of human society? Why does Jesus perform so many healings? Why do disciples pray for God's will to be done on earth as it is in heaven?

5. Reading is Hard Work

These contexts of synagogue disputes and of the realities of the Roman imperial world matter in our reading of the Gospel. Matthew, like any author, assumes our knowledge and experience of these contexts in every verse. He does not stop and explain things with sidebars. He expects us, as readers, to supply what is assumed. The absence of such knowledge and experience is a major reason that many people find the biblical material difficult to engage. It was not written in our world; it assumes understandings and experiences that we do not have. We can, of course, connect across the millennia in some ways with this text, but in doing so we miss so much. Moreover, our experiences will always dominate the interpretation and thereby overwhelm what the text might want to put on our agenda.

Interpreting biblical texts means engaging in a conversation with them. It involves a fusing or interplay of the ancient worlds with our own. If you have traveled and encountered another culture that does not speak your language, you have been surprised by the physical and mental fatigue that you experience by the end of the day. Communicating with strange language and customs is exhausting.

Reading this Gospel is not a monologue, a one-way street from the reader to the text. We work at understanding the Gospel and its world, thereby allowing it to have voice in the conversation. You will locate some of this knowledge in the comments in each of the fifteen studies, and I will refer you to studies (my own and others) for further depth.

Reflection
Kingdom of God

Ask the members of the class what the kingdom of God means to them. Facilitate discussion, then explain that this phrase will be crucial in the Bible studies ahead.

---

6. Bible Study: Formation of Disciples

While we are very interested in the synagogue tensions and the Roman imperial realities that shaped the world that left its mark on every verse of the Gospel, we must avoid getting stuck in the past. Matthew is, of course, our Gospel. It is part of our canon in which we listen for God's word of address to us. We are not interested, then, only in information (though that is important), but also in formation as a disciple of Jesus. I know from various teaching experiences that, as people come to understand these texts and bring them into conversation with their own lives, discipleship formation takes place.

Matthew raises profound questions about our commitments and priorities. The Gospel is very concerned with a lived and faithful discipleship that participates in God's saving purposes. It expects disciples to embody God's merciful, just, and life-giving agenda. That agenda often puts us at odds with dominant values in our society and even, sometimes, in our churches. The quest for wealth and status, the pursuit of comfort, the blessing of our own agendas, the insulation from the harsh realities of our society and two-thirds of the rest of the world—these are a few of the values that conflict with the values of God's kingdom. The question that constantly confronts us as readers is, "What does God's saving justice look like in our world and circumstances?"

7. Studying and Living in Communities of Discipleship

The group context in which we wrestle with these difficult questions is very important. Together, as people committed to Jesus and to each other, we can understand the information about the Gospel's world, ask and explore the hard questions of its implications, share our struggles, support one another's and the group's efforts at living faithfully, and thereby sustain an alternative community of discipleship until the completion of God's purposes. Matthew would be well pleased.

Session 1

The Family Album

Welcome to the much neglected and much misunderstood, but very rich and important, beginning to Matthew's Gospel. Our movie-watching and book-reading experience tells us that the beginning of a story is enormously important. A genealogy is probably not our idea of an attention-getting and gripping start. So our first task is to understand the three functions of this genealogy at the outset of Matthew's Gospel.

First, the genealogy establishes a theological agenda that provides an interpretive framework for the whole Gospel. God is the unnamed main character. The genealogy evokes God's good and life-giving purposes for the world. It offers a selective account of God's relationship with Israel (neither Moses nor the prophets are included) into which it sets the origins and identity of Jesus and his followers.

That theological focus may sound strange to us because family trees are usually concerned with lines of biological descent. People spend much time and energy in research to connect those lines. But Matthew does not. The artificial patterning of 3 x 14 generations, the lack of match between the number of generations and the likely time periods (verses 2-6*a* cover approximately 800 years and verses 6*b*-11 cover 400 years, both with fourteen generations [14 x 40 years = 560 years]), the false link of Salmon and Rahab in verse 5, and omissions of generations from verses 8 and 11, indicate that the genealogy's intent is not the identification of biological links.

The genealogy is more like a family photo album.

Study Bible

For further discussion of Matthew's genealogy, see *NISB*, 1748-49.

Reflections

Why begin the Gospel with a genealogy?

1. How is the genealogy structured? Observe 1:1, 17, and the three main sections (1:2-6*a*, 6*b*-11, 12-16).

2. Elaborate God's purposes that are identified by the three big figures and events and emphasized by the summary of 1:17: Abraham (divine promises in Gen 12:1-3; 15; 17), David (vision of kingship in the royal Psalm 72), and Babylonian exile. Study the latter event and its theological interpretations: God's use of Babylon to punish the people (Deut 4; 28; 2 Kings 21–25; Jer 25); God's punishment of Babylon and deliverance of the people back to the land (Isa 44:28–45:8; 47–48; Jer 31; Ezek 34).

3. Why include both "good" and "bad" kings in verses 6-11? Compare the participation (or nonparticipation) in *(Continued on page 8)*

7

An unspoken narrative accompanies every picture. Every name in this genealogy evokes a story of encounter with God. The listing of names assumes that readers will elaborate the stories from their knowledge of the Scriptures, thereby filling out God's workings and purposes. Therein lies the difficulty for many contemporary readers who often do not have that knowledge. Engagement with the genealogy requires that we help people gain such knowledge.

Another context familiar to Matthew's audience is very important. Roman imperial theology claimed that Jupiter chose Rome to manifest the gods' will and blessing throughout the earth. Matthew's focus on God's purposes counters any such claims, contests them, and declares a subversive alternative. God's purposes are displayed through Israel and Jesus, not Rome. They are purposes for life, not for death; for all people, not the privileged elite.

The opening verse ("the book of the origin," author's trans.) evokes the earth's origin in God's life-giving act (Gen 1). God declares to Abraham that, through him, God will bless all the nations of the earth (Gen 12:1-3), a promise elaborated in the covenant blessings of Deuteronomy 28–29, which include fertility, food, health, and safety. The kings from David's line represent God's good purposes (Psalm 72). The genealogy demonstrates that God's purposes widely embrace Gentiles (Ur, Babylon) and Jews (Israel, Judah), men and women (five in 1:3, 5, 16), the celebrated (Abraham, David) and the nobodies that even tradition has forgotten (1:3b-4, 13-15), the powerful (kings) and those on the cultural margins (the women), those who embrace and resist God's purposes (Babylon), and the faithful and the faithless.

Throughout, it shows God's faithful efforts to be with God's people and to enact God's purposes. God chooses David and his line (2 Samuel 7) to be kings who represent God's life-giving reign marked by justice and protection for the vulnerable. David's importance is also underlined by the use of the number "fourteen" to structure the generations. The numerical value of the consonants in David's name in Hebrew

(Continued from page 7)
God's purposes of David (e.g. 1 Sam 16; 2 Sam 5, 7, 11–2), Hezekiah (2 Kgs 18–20; 2 Chr 29–32), Manasseh (2 Kgs 21:1-18; 2 Chr 33:1-20), and Josiah (2 Kgs 22–23:30; 2 Chr 34).

4. How does the inclusion of women in the geneology elaborate God's purposes? Examine the accounts of each of the women: Tamar (1:3; Gen 38), Rahab (1:5; Josh 2), Ruth (1:5; Ruth), the wife of Uriah (Bathsheba, 1:6; 2 Sam 11–12).

5. Select and elaborate several other names from the geneology, in terms of their relationship with God and their place in the history of God's people.

6. Our biblical traditions have no other references or little information for many of the names in 1:13-15. What do you make of this?

7. Here at the outset of the Gospel, what is the impact of locating Jesus in this rapid review of God's interaction with Israel? What does the genealogy contribute to the Gospel?

8. How does the genealogy, with its cast of both likely and unlikely characters, speak to the ways that we regard people in and outside of the church community?

adds up to fourteen. But most of the kings named in 1:6*b*-11 did not live up to their calling. Even human sinfulness is caught up in but cannot derail God's purposes. Nor is God bound by human structures such as imperial power (Babylon), patriarchy (the women), and primogeniture (Isaac not Ishmael; Jacob not Esau). God will not be put into human boxes.

The presence of the women underlines God's inclusive and unconventional ways of working. The naming of Tamar, Rahab, Ruth, the wife of Uriah (Bathsheba), and Mary disrupts the pervasive and patriarchal "'A' was the father of 'B'" pattern (which occurs thirty-nine times). These women have Gentile origins or connections. They occupy unconventional sexual roles (Tamar [and possibly Ruth] acted as seducer; Rahab was a prostitute; Bathsheba committed adultery; Mary was a pregnant virgin). They threaten conventional patriarchal structures. They occupy socially marginal and culturally powerless positions in which they exercise initiative and participate in God's purposes.

Second, the genealogy sets followers of Jesus within these divine purposes, committing us to God's agenda of blessing all the peoples of the world. This agenda defines our identity and determines our purpose in relation to God's intention, to Jesus, and to a world that so often does not welcome God's life-giving, just, and merciful ways. This agenda strengthens and shapes a way of life in the midst of circumstances and cultural values that are often contrary to God's purposes.

By locating followers of Jesus in relation to God's purposes, the genealogy begins a process that will continue throughout the Gospel. Constantly, the Gospel encourages its readers to see the world through God's eyes, in terms of God's purposes. Jesus' words and actions raise questions about things that are so often taken for granted. Hunger and disease, so common in Matthew's first-century world (and our own), are revealed to be completely at odds with God's will to bless all people as seen in Jesus' transformational healings and feedings. Jesus questions "normal" human preoccupation with "living to shop and shopping to live," advocating God's agenda of seeking first God's reign and justice (6:33). He rejects the usual ways of

---

Reflections
The Genealogy, Jesus, and the Church

The genealogy locates Jesus and his followers in the purposes of God to bless all the nations of the earth (Gen 12:1-3).

1. The genealogy offers twenty/twenty hindsight about God's workings. How do we recognize and encounter God's presence in our individual lives and in our church life? Or are we more familiar with God's absence from our lives and world?

2. How do we participate in God's purposes to bless all the nations? How do God's purposes shape and challenge our lives?

3. We can be both reticent and over-eager to claim to know and participate in God's purposes. What examples, encouragement, and cautions does the genealogy offer?

4. Create your own faith "genealogy," including family, friends, and other persons who have influenced your journey. Continue by listing your own faith "descendents"—those to whom you have taught the faith. How have your "ancestors" worked with God's purposes? How have you?

domination as contrary to God's purposes. Instead, humans are to seek each other's good (20:25-28). From the outset, the Gospel encourages us to question our world in relation to God's purposes, creates tensions with cultural norms, and requires actions from us that are consistent with and expressive of God's purposes.

A third function of the genealogy is its narrative function. It frames the whole story of Jesus in terms of God's purposes. These purposes will assess all subsequent words, actions, characters, relations, and institutions that appear in the story. It provides lenses through which we can understand what Jesus is about. It shapes our understanding of discipleship. It puts these enormous questions of identity, purpose, and way of life on our agenda from the outset.

God's Grace and Jesus' Life's Work

Paul would call it grace. Matthew tells a story that displays God's life-giving initiative and intervention through angels, the Spirit, and faithful humans. The "origin" of Jesus is undoubtedly God's work, gracious and disruptive, life-giving and dangerous. This divine act gets Matthew's story under way.

Verse 18 often contains a misleading translation, "birth," but Matthew's interest is more with Jesus' conception. The word often translated as "birth" is the same word used in 1:1 in the phrase "the book of the origin/genealogy." The Greek word "genesis," the beginning or origin, evokes the creation story. In Jesus' conception, God begins a new creation that will transform all things. For Matthew, several centuries before orthodox Christology is formulated at Nicea in 325 CE, Jesus' origin or beginning is found, not in heaven, but in his conception as a result of God's activity.

God's initiative is indicated four times. Verse 18 locates Mary's pregnancy "before they lived together." It also identifies the Holy Spirit as the agent. Verse 20 repeats the point but gives it authority as the revelation of "an angel of/from/ belonging to the Lord." Verse 25 indicates the absence of sexual relations.

God's concern with conception and the womb is widespread in the Hebrew Scriptures (see Reflections #2, this page). Claims of conception by some sort of divine interaction with a woman are not unique to the Christian tradition. Such stories accompany powerful figures like Alexander the Great, Romulus, and the emperor Augustus, all of whom carried out imperial agendas on behalf of gods. Matthew's story about

Lectionary Loop

Fourth Sunday of Advent, Year A

Reflections

God, Mary, and Jesus

The scene emphasizes God's initiative by highlighting God's activity in the womb.

1. Identify the ways that the passage (1:18-25) presents Mary's conception of Jesus as God's work.

2. Such divine activity in the womb is common in the Scriptures as a means of accomplishing God's purposes. Study Gen 16; 21; 25:19-26; Ps 139:13-18; Jer 1:5.

3. The Spirit carries out God's purposes in the conception of Jesus. Explore the role of the life-giving, powerful Spirit in scriptural traditions: creation (Gen 1:2), empowering leaders (Gideon, Judg 6:34), deliverance (Isa 61), and the people (Ezek 36:27; 37:5).

4. Of what significance is it that Jesus' origin is presented in relation to these traditions of both God's activity in the womb and of the Spirit's activity?

5. In what ways do you see the Spirit at work in the church universal? In your church? In your life?

Jesus thus locates him among the greats who enact divine work. But it also makes a distinctive claim about the nature of divine activity and where it is located, resisting conventional wisdom. God's activity is not located in the great and mighty—the powerful Romans who subdue peoples and land to secure their own wealth at the expense of the rest. That is not God's way. Rather, it is located in Jesus, born of peasant parents in this dangerous world, subjected to the power-hungry destruction wrought by King Herod and his allies (Matt 2).

In this regard, Jesus' Davidic connection is very important. Verse 16 raises a question about how Jesus might be "son of David" by identifying Joseph as "the husband of Mary" but not as the father of Jesus. By using a feminine relative pronoun, verse 16 has clearly linked Jesus with Mary only: "of whom (Mary, not Joseph) Jesus was born." Verse 20 reasserts the connection when the angel addresses Joseph as "son of David." In naming Jesus, Joseph assumes paternity and incorporates Jesus in the Davidic line.

This connection matters because it is one of several ways in which the scene establishes Jesus' significance. As a descendant of David, he is identified with kingship in order to represent God's just and life-giving reign (Psalm 72; Deut 17:14-20). This reign conflicts and contrasts significantly with Rome's very different rule (see 20:25-28) because it envisions a very different social order that enacts God's justice and blessing. Conflict with Roman-sanctioned rule in the person of King Herod will be evident in Matthew 2.

Further, 1:21 identifies Jesus' job description or life's work. Frequently, the concept of sin is "spiritualized" and understood only in personal and individual terms. But God is not interested in redeeming us from only some sins; nor does God spiritualize sin. God's redemption extends to all that is contrary to God's good purposes, including structural or societal sins. For Matthew, that includes an imperial system utterly contrary to what God intends. If the current world was ordered according to God's purposes it would not need saving. The verse evokes several traditions of God's

Reflections
Jesus' Commission

The conception story in 1:18-25 establishes Jesus' commission or life work by evoking and associating him with key figures and events in Israel's history.

1. In 1:21 Jesus is commissioned to save "his people" from sins. How does Psalm 130, echoed in 1:21, elaborate his commission?

2. In 1:23 Jesus is commissioned to manifest God's presence. How does the narrative of Isaiah 7–9 clarify his commission?

3. How does the Royal Psalm 72 and the promise of 2 Sam 7:5-17 elaborate Jesus' identity as son of David?

4. Matt 1:21 identifies Jesus' mission. What is the church's role in that mission today? What sins (personal, structural, societal) can we identify?

5. How do we, as individuals and as a church, participate in God's purposes to save us from these sins?

saving work: The name "Jesus" is the Greek form of the Hebrew name "Joshua," the one entrusted with completing the redemption from Egypt. Likewise, 1:21 echoes Psalm 130:8, a psalm that celebrates God's redemption of the people. Jesus will enact this task in his words, actions, death, resurrection, and return.

Verse 23 adds another dimension of Jesus' mission in its citation of Isaiah 7:14. Isaiah's chapters 7–9 are concerned with the threatening efforts of Israel and Syria to force Judah to ally against Assyria. The prophet announces that a child whose birth is imminent (perhaps Hezekiah) signifies God's presence with the people and a reversal of their fortunes. On the basis of analogous situations of Isaiah's and Matthew's audiences (imperial control), the citing of Isaiah 7:14, and evoking of its larger context interprets Jesus' mission as manifesting God's saving presence. This is good news for many but bad news for Rome. How Jesus accomplishes this task will be unveiled through the Gospel. Eschewing violent or military action, he will employ nonviolent actions and words to enact God's saving presence and reign.

Joseph and Mary play vital roles in this divine initiative. Matthew pays almost no attention to Mary, unlike Luke's more extensive focus. Her plight, though, is desperate. The divine action has placed the pregnant, unwed Mary in a very vulnerable and culturally marginal location. There are death sentences on unfaithful mothers and curses on children from adulterous relationships (see Reflections #2, this page). Yet God is doing gracious work.

Joseph, though, is on center stage, challenged by yet compliant with the divine will. The challenge comes in standing by the pregnant Mary. Verse 19 describes his intentions when he knows she is pregnant but before the angel reveals its cause. Since he has not slept with Mary, her pregnancy most probably results from a violation of their betrothal (contract to marry). This is a serious breach of societal values requiring action (Deut 22:23-27). Joseph's plan is a quiet divorce. Compliance with the divine will means an act that goes against the grain. The angel announcing God's will

Reflections
Joseph and Mary

They are not labeled disciples; no disciples will be called until 4:18-22. But Joseph and Mary exhibit qualities of discipleship.

1. What characteristics of discipleship do Joseph and Mary exhibit in 1:18-25?

2. Using the Apocrypha, (beginning on p. 1357 in the *NISB*) read more about the counter-cultural and difficult thing God asks Mary to do. There is condemnation of unwed mothers in Sir 23:23-27, and of children born into adulterous relationships in Wis Sol 3:16-19; 4:3-6. How does God's gracious work challenge our rush to judgment?

3. Follow Mary and Joseph's story into chapter 2, especially 2:13-25.

4. What connections do you see between this Joseph and the story of another Joseph who, though in danger, journeys to Egypt and is kept safe by God (see Gen 37, 39–47, 50)?

5. What are the implications of this depiction of Mary and Joseph for contemporary discipleship? In what ways is God's agenda at odds with contemporary values and societal practices and structures e.g., the use of power, the quest for wealth, and the worship of God? Does God's agenda place contemporary disciples on the cultural margins?

requires the counter-cultural act of marriage. Like a model disciple, Joseph enacts the divine will even though it is contrary to conventional wisdom and places him on the cultural margins. Jesus' teaching will constantly place disciples in this position. But as the scene makes clear, it is precisely there, on the cultural margins, that God's life-giving purposes are enacted. Matthew 2 will continue the theme, showing the resistance of Rome's puppets—Herod and his elite allies— to God's workings.

Joseph's trusting obedience (1:24) prepares the way for his crucial role in Matthew 2. Threatened by Herod's efforts to wipe out God's saving purposes, Joseph receives divine guidance and protection via angels and dreams. Reenacting the sojourn of another Joseph in Egypt and deliverance of a people, he serves the vulnerable child "and his mother" (2:13-15), ensuring their safety from Herod and his son, Archelaus, who succeeded him.

John: Baptizing Prophet

Our "slice-and-dice" approach to the Gospels often pays little attention to the way in which the gospel story unfolds. The issue of connection is especially important for this passage since it introduces a new character and jumps several decades from the infant Jesus of Matthew 2 to the adult Jesus who comes to John for baptism in 3:13-17.

The scene develops two themes from chapters 1-2. First, it continues to define Jesus' commission. We know from 1:21-23 and 2:15 that Jesus is commissioned as God's chosen agent ("son") to manifest God's saving presence. John announces Jesus' coming as the enactment of God's eschatological purposes of judgment and salvation (3:11-12). Jesus' ministry will bless some and destroy others. Second, the scene continues the conflict in Matthew 1-2 between the centers of power (Herod and his allies) and the cultural margins (Joseph and Mary, the magi) where God's purposes are encountered. John appears in the wilderness away from the urban centers of power. He is a prophet and is not sanctioned by the temple. He attacks representatives of the elite, Jerusalem leaders who maintain and benefit from the current social order. John will subsequently pay for such attacks with his life (4:12; 14:1-12).

John's prophetic identity is crucial for understanding this character. The scene constantly echoes prophetic images in John's message (repentance), sign-action (baptism), clothing (Elijah), and language. Often the Hebrew prophets are misunderstood as visionaries, detached from society, who mysteriously

Lectionary Loop
Second Sunday of Advent, Year A

Study Bible
See Warren Carter's *Matthew and the Margins* (Maryknoll: Orbis Books, 2000), 90-101; see also the "Excursus: Prophets and Sign-Acts," *NISB,* 968.

predict the future. While prophetic material contains visions and predictions, these forms do not comprise its center. Primarily, the prophet is very much a societal participant and is charged with discerning and announcing God's perspectives and purposes in relation to particular situations. Frequently that divine perspective is one of critique of current socio-economic, religious, and political practices. Prophets warn, call for change, and declare God's salvation and/or judgment. There may, of course, be future consequences, but the prophet's attention is on formulating God's word-of-address for the present in which the prophet is located. Socio-political analysis and divine purposes intersect. The prophet is a forthteller more than a foreteller, a proclaimer more than a predictor. John appears in this tradition.

John's prophetic identity pervades the scene. Verse 1 introduces him with reference to his proclaiming activity. His message will be elaborated in verse 2; its accompanying sign-action of baptism will be featured in verse 6. Verse 1 locates him in the wilderness, an enormously significant location in biblical traditions. Primarily, it is the place of salvation and testing for God's people in the exodus from Egypt. Both elements are important for John's role. But also very important is the wilderness' distance from centers of urban control such as Jerusalem and its temple. As chapter 2 has demonstrated, and as 3:7-10 confirms, elite control extends a long way. But away from such centers, on their margins, and apart from the temple controlled by the powerful and wealthy high priestly families, people encounter God's purposes (3:5).

Verse 2 identifies John's message. Like numerous prophets before him (Jer 3:11-4:10; Ezek 18:30-32; Amos 4:6-13), John calls for a turn-around, a return to faithful covenant relationship with Israel's God of justice and mercy. Clearly, the status quo under Roman rule does not accord with God's purposes and does not enact God's reign. Two empires are in conflict and at odds with each other, with vastly different commitments and structures.

Verse 3 provides scriptural context and confirmation

Reflections
John as Prophet

How does the depiction of John draw on prophetic traditions, and how does it add to the presentation of Jesus?

1. What is the significance of locating John's ministry in the wilderness? Review the prophetic wilderness traditions in Numbers 11–12; 1 Kgs 19:4; Hos 2:14.

2. Compare the prophetic demand for repentance (a turn-around) in Isa 1:11-20; Jer 3:11–4:10; Hos 2:1–3:5; Amos 4:6-13.

3. Compare John's way of dressing with Elijah's appearance in 2 Kgs 1:8 and his sign-action of baptism with Isa 20:1-4; Ezek 4:4-8; Hosea 1.

4. Compare John's identity and social location with those prophets who preach against the elite: Amos 1:1; 7:10-17; Mic 6:3-15.

5. What does John's identity, social location, and role have to say to the identity, social location, and role of the church?

6. What are the challenges and opportunities for churches on the margins? In the cultural center? Which is your church? How are we responding to God's call?

for John's identity and message. The citing of Isaiah 40:3 evokes another imperial context from which God effects deliverance. Its citation locates John in God's saving purposes, the setting free of the people from Babylonian imperialism. As it was for Babylon so it will be for Rome.

Not only does John talk like a prophet, he also dresses like one, resembling Elijah (3:4; compare 2 Kgs 1:8; see also Matt 11:14; 17:11-13 where John is Elijah). Like Elijah's struggle with Ahaz, Jezebel, and Baal, John is in a life-and-death struggle for God's purposes against destructive elite ways that are contrary to God's wishes. His diet, appropriate to the wilderness, also signifies his commitment to God's purposes. He trusts God (as Jesus teaches, 6:25-34), rejecting the extravagant lifestyles of the powerful and wealthy. John's asceticism is commended by Jesus (11:7-9).

Verses 5-6 narrate extensive (hyperbolic) positive response to John's proclamation from Jerusalem (contrast 2:3), Judea, and the region of the Jordan. The reference to the Jordan significantly links John's baptism with the river through which the Israelites passed after the exodus from Egypt, as they entered the promised land (Josh 3:14-17). As with the Isaiah reference in verse 3, John's liberating activity is connected to major events in which God's salvation from imperial powers was experienced. Numerous prophets accompanied their message with a sign-action (Hosea 1; Isa 20:1-4; Ezek 3:1; 4:4-8); John uses baptism. The precise link between baptism and sin is not made clear. There is no reference to forgiveness (associated in Matthew with Jesus; contrast Mark 1:4), suggesting that the baptism expresses a turning from sins in anticipation of "the way of the Lord," the reign or empire of God that John manifests (3:2-3). Again, John's bypassing of the Jerusalem Temple should be noted.

Verses 7-10 provide an example of John's preaching against the elite. In contrast to those who respond positively in 3:5-6, elite leaders from Jerusalem come against (a preferable translation) John's baptism. It is customary for us to think of Pharisees and Sadducees as religious leaders, but in this first-century world, reli-

Reflections
Prophetic Church

The church has long understood itself to have a prophetic role in our society. What does that look like in our circumstances?

1. How might we apply John's words (Matt 3:7-10) to our own circumstances? Consider some issues such as war, personal and corporate morality, and the role of work and wealth in our materialistic society. To what sort of lifestyle are rich Christians, in an age of hunger, entitled?

2. What actions might this word require of us in our lifestyles? Our congregations? Our society?

3. What individuals in the last 100 years have behaved like prophets, and how do they enact the gospel (*e.g.*, Martin Luther King Jr., Mother Teresa, Bishop Desmond Tutu, Mahatma Ghandi, Jimmy Carter, Daniel Berrigan)?

4. Why are we cautious about referring to individuals as prophets and prefer, instead, to generalize about a collective prophetic church? What advantages and disadvantages does such an approach offer?

5. What are the consequences of our communal prophetic identity and role?

6. John works outside established religious roles (priests) and institutions (temple). How and when might the contemporary church be an obstacle to God's saving purposes? How and when is our church an obstacle and/or participant in God's saving purposes?

gion was not separated from societal and political matters. Both of these distinct groups presented very different visions of society. The Jewish historian Jose-
phus locates both groups as part of the leadership
group in Jerusalem, interested in maintaining the societal status quo. Here, despite their differences, they are
allied against John (and God), just as in 2:4 the chief
priests and scribes, also part of the Jerusalem leadership group, are allied with Herod against Jesus (and
God). These two chapters thus present the entire leadership group allied with each other, despite significant
differences, against John, Jesus, and God. John
rebukes them for their reliance on their ethnic-cultural
heritage, and neglect of living faithfully.

John's prophetic work concludes in verses 11-12
with testimony to Jesus and a warning to those who
have received his (John's) message. According to
John, Jesus' mission involves salvation and judgment.
Salvation/purification and destruction are denoted by
both Spirit (Jer 4:11-16; Ezek 36:25-28) and fire (Mal
3:1-3; Matt 13:40-43). Some will be blessed, and some
will be destroyed both in Jesus' ministry and in the
eschatological judgment. But there is no complacency
for those who have responded to John. His baptism
guarantees nothing. Ongoing participation in God's
purposes, encountered on the cultural margins and
opposed to the way of life sanctioned by the status quo,
is necessary.

Jesus' Ministry

In closing the first section of Matthew's Gospel, 4:12-16 sums up key themes asserted in the first four chapters. In beginning the Gospel's second section, 4:17-25 narrates the start of Jesus' ministry, introducing significant ways in which Jesus carries out his God-given commission that will be elaborated upon in subsequent chapters.

One of the main emphases in 4:12-16 is the conflict between Jesus/John and the imperial context that is contrary and opposed to God's purposes. The reference to Babylonian exile in 1:11-12, the struggle with Herod (chapter 2), and the reference in 4:8 to the devil's control of all the empires of the world have underlined this theme. John's arrest is mentioned in verse 12 but not explained until 14:1-12, when the consequences of his challenge to Herod Antipas are narrated.

Likewise, Jesus' commission and context are framed in terms of challenge and conflict. Jesus' withdrawal to Galilee is not escape into safety but engagement with a dangerous situation since Galilee is the territory of Antipas, Rome's puppet ruler or tetrarch. But therein is the problem that verses 13-16 indicate. Galilee is described in a series of terms that recall God's removal of this land from Canaanite overlords, making it a gift to the people of Israel. Twice it is identified as "land of Zebulon, land of Naphtali," names that evoke the tribal allocation of the land God had promised to Abraham, shown to Moses (Deut 34:1-4), and apportioned by Joshua (Josh 19:10-16, 32-39). This is land that should recognize God's sovereignty

Reflections
Jesus' Identity

1. What do these opening chapters establish about Jesus' identity and commission? See 1:17, 21-23; 2:15; 3:13-17.

2. How does the image of light/darkness sum up Jesus' identity and commission as it has been established in 1:1–4:16? What do these images connote about God's purposes? Review the use of darkness for slavery in Egypt (Exod 10:21-23) and exile in Babylon (Isa 42:7; 49:9), and light for God's saving presence (Exod 14:20; Ps 27:1; Isa 42:6-7; 49:6-10).

   Study especially the circumstances and situation of Assyrian imperial aggression in Isaiah 7–9 that Matthew evokes here.

3. In what ways are the darkness and death of imperial powers made manifest in today's world? What evidence do you see of the light of God's saving purposes in the midst of this darkness and death?

but is now subject to Roman claims. Matthew challenges Rome's legitimacy by evoking God's purposes.

The citation from Isaiah 9:1-2 continues the challenge. "Galilee under the Gentiles," possessed by the Gentiles, is "across the sea" (author's trans.; NRSV, "beyond the Jordan"), a phrase used in the exodus and occupation narratives to refer to God's promised land (Deut 3:20, 25; Josh 1:15; 22:4). In Isaiah's time, the passage referred to Syro-Israelite and Assyrian imperialism, from whom God promises deliverance if the people trust God. In Matthew's time, the imperial power is Rome, who had freshly asserted control of Galilean land after the victory of 70 CE. Either way the message is the same: God opposes imperial power; God uses it to punish; God frees people from it. The world under sinful imperial power is darkness. In the biblical tradition, the image denotes slavery in Egypt and exile in Babylon into which comes God's light or saving presence (see Reflections #2, previous page). While Roman propaganda described the emperor as light, here God's saving presence is manifested (as we know from 1:18-25) not in the empire but in the ministry of Jesus (1:21-23). In this way Jesus enacts the scriptures as the agent of God's life-giving and light-bringing purposes.

But while this first section (1:1–4:16) has established Jesus' identity and commission, as well as the context of sinfulness in which he will enact his commission, Jesus has not yet done anything. Of course he has been baptized, thereby "owning" his commission (3:13-17), and he has resisted the devil in the temptations, refusing to take any directions from the devil since he (Jesus) is God's agent or son (2:15; 3:17). But he has not publicly carried out his commission. The first section establishes his identity and commission, ensuring that we as readers know *who* Jesus is as God's agent, but it also raises a question: *How* will Jesus carry out his commission?

The scene in 4:17-25 begins Jesus' public ministry and, in summary form, identifies three ways in which Jesus carries out his commission to manifest God's saving presence.

Reflections
Reign of God

Jesus announces "the reign of the heavens," "the empire of God" (4:17).

1. This phrase draws on Scriptural traditions about God's kingship, in which God asserts divine rule among humans. Examine Psalms such as Pss 8, 72, 75, 76, 103, 118 for visions of the impact of God's reign.

2. Jesus' words and actions in 4:18-22 and 4:23-25 demonstrate God's reign. What do the two scenes demonstrate about God's reign? What is affirming, challenging and troubling about the call of the fishermen? How do we encounter God's call in our lives?

3. The command to "fish for people" in 4:19 establishes disciples as a mission community that participates with words and actions in God's mission in the world. How do we carry out this mission? Identify the tasks, challenges, obstacles, opportunities, resources, and rewards of mission. Think specifically about your congregational mission.

4. What particular challenges does a pluralistic, multi-religious world present to a church called to participate in the mission of God? What is your church doing, or what can we envision doing, to respond to these challenges?

1. Jesus' words announce the reign or empire of God (4:17).
2. Jesus forms an alternative community of disciples committed to God's rule (4:18-22).
3. Jesus begins to transform the Roman-dominated world, teaching people about God's saving purposes and demonstrating those purposes by healings and exorcisms (4:23-25).

The subsequent chapters will elaborate these three means. In Matthew 5–7 (the Sermon on the Mount) and Matthew 10 (instructions about mission), Jesus' teaching does formational work, shaping the alternative community of disciples. In Matthew 8–9, he does transformational work with actions that manifest God's saving presence.

The one-liner that comprises Jesus' first public words in 4:17—"Repent for the empire/reign of the heavens is at hand" (author's trans.)—announces the central claim of Jesus' ministry. How are we to understand Jesus' announcement? Various studies have shown that the meaning of "empire/reign of the heavens" is not tightly fixed in Jewish traditions (where it does not often appear). The phrase refers to Israel's covenant God, the Lord or King, acting faithfully and powerfully on behalf of God's people for their well-being.

Matthew provides a more specific definition for the phrase in two ways. Partly, the subsequent narrative will elaborate the term from Jesus' words and actions. But already, the previous chapters have provided a framework for understanding the term. In 1:21-23, Jesus' mission of manifesting God's saving presence is defined. He has embraced God's job description for him in the baptism and temptation (3:13–4:11). He is light in the darkness of a world filled with powers making false claims of sovereignty (4:12-16). Hence, in announcing God's sovereignty or reign, he declares that God's saving presence is at hand. The phrase expresses his commission.

What does God's empire look like? The language

itself provides an initial clue. The term usually translated "kingdom" or "reign" is the same term that is used to refer to Rome's empire. Empire is, of course, a claim of ownership, of sovereignty, of the right to order the world and human interaction. By definition, empires do not tolerate competition! The use of this language for Jesus' ministry indicates that conflict with Rome's empire and claims is inevitable. In Jesus, God—the creator of the world—asserts a claim of ownership on the world and human beings. Some will gladly acknowledge God's rule; others will defend the unjust status quo.

The next scene, 4:18-22, provides an example of God's reign. Jesus claims the loyalties of four fishermen. His call disrupts their daily routine, their priorities, and their social order. (Think about what Zebedee might have said when his workforce walked out!) It disrupts their economic participation in the empire. Rome claimed to control the yield of the sea. It issued contracts for catches of a defined size, and it taxed the catch. Jesus calls them to put their time and energies into a different sort of fishing, one that enables people to participate in God's purposes. He also calls them into new relationships as part of a new community (12:46-50) and into a life-long process of learning how to live, not by cultural norms, but by God's very different agenda. In the midst of the Roman Empire he forms an alternative community that embodies and witnesses to God's empire.

The final scene offers another vignette of what God's empire looks like (4:23-25). We will return to healing in a subsequent study. (See Session 7; also *Matthew and the Margins*, 123-27.) God's empire is transformative and life-giving, undoing the damage that the imperial world does, and enacting the wholeness that God desires for all people.

Life Shaped by God's Reign

How do the Sermon on the Mount (Matthew 5–7) and the beatitudes in particular (5:3-12), contribute to Matthew's unfolding story? Some have seen them providing impossible ideals, convicting of sin, laying down rules for disciples ignorant of God's will, persuading reluctant disciples to do God's will, or providing discernment to recognize God's will. In their narrative context, they are better seen as providing examples or visions of God's reign that shape the identity and lifestyle of disciples, and empower them to live out their commitment to God's transforming reign and justice. Having called disciples in 4:18-22 and begun preaching "the gospel of the empire/reign" (4:23), Jesus now forms the communal identity and lifestyle of disciples. That is, the Sermon is about being church.

Central to the Sermon is God's empire/reign or kingdom (5:3, 10, 19, 20; 6:10, 33; 7:21). The Sermon illustrates the kind of world God's reign creates. Foremost is its alternative and disruptive quality that contests the primary commitments of Rome's world. God's reign creates a world of righteousness or justice marked by restructured societal relationships, new practices, and access to adequate resources for all people (5:6, 10, 20; 6:1, 33).

The Sermon takes place on an unidentified mountain. The phrase "he went up the mountain" in 5:1 is used nine times to refer to Moses going up Mt. Sinai to receive the Decalogue (Exod 24:12, 13, 18), and six times to the nations gathering at Mt. Zion at the final establishment of God's purposes to learn of God's ways

Lectionary Loop

Pentecost, Year A and Fourth Sunday After Epiphany, Year A

Reflections

The Sermon

The introduction to the Sermon on the Mount "frames" Jesus' teaching as a revelation of life shaped by God's reign.

1. How does the Sermon on the Mount in Matthew 5–7 build on what happens in 4:17-25?

2. What is the significance of the mountain location (5:1)? Examine the significance of the phrase "going up the mountain" in Exod 24:12, 13, 18, and Isa 2:1-4.

3. The beatitude form expresses God's favor or blessing on particular situations. Check out Pss 1:1-2; 119:1-2.

4. What is the significance of choosing this beatitude form for the nine statements of 5:3-12?

(Isa 2:1-4). That is, the mountain is a place for the revelation of God's purposes and for the formation of communities committed to those purposes.

Nine beatitudes begin the Sermon (5:3-12). This way of talking was widely used in the Greco-Roman world and in Jewish wisdom and apocalyptic texts. Beatitudes are not concerned with human feelings and emotions (the dreadful "Happy are" translations), or individual attitudes (the "Be-Happy attitudes"). Rather, they announce God's approving perspective, God's favor on certain situations and actions (Ps 1:1-2), both present and future, when God reverses and transforms current injustice and distress. They reassure people experiencing those situations that God's favor rests on them.

These declarations of favor also function to identify and thereby exhort human actions consistent with God's favor. If God favors merciful actions and will reward them, disciples are exhorted to do mercy. The beatitudes thus identify actions characteristic of the community of disciples. The actions and situations that God favors are the hallmarks or defining practices of disciples. These situations (being poor) and practices (being merciful) are commonly not those valued by the Roman elite. Hence there is a counter-cultural quality to the community of disciples that contests and challenges the status quo.

The beatitudes divide into two groups. The first four (5:3-6) concern situations of oppression and distress in which God's favor is already found in the ministry of Jesus, and for which there will be future transformation in the completion of God's purposes. These beatitudes are linked by the letter "π" in Greek (pī; the English equivalent is the letter "p"). David Garland paraphrases the first four beatitudes: "Blessed are the poor in spirit, the plaintive, the powerless and those who pine for righteousness." These four beatitudes are shaped by Isaiah 61:1-3, and conclude with a reference to righteousness (5:6).

The first four beatitudes identify God's just transformation of the destructive socio-political, economic, and religious consequences of Roman rule. The phrase "poor in spirit" is not to be spiritualized as a figurative

Reflections
The Beatitudes

These sayings identify God's reign at work, envisioning a way of life in which disciples are to participate.

1. Explore the links between the beatitudes and key Scripture texts to identify those whom the assertion of God's reign blesses: Isa 61:1-4; Matt 5:3 and Ps 10 (also 77:1-10); Matt 5:5 and Ps 37; Matt 5:8 and Ps 24. What contexts do the Scripture passages address?

2. What claims do these Scripture passages make about God's saving actions and how people live?

3. What insights do they offer in elaborating the beatitudes of 5:3-6 and 5:7-12?

4. How does your church live out the challenge and call of the beatitudes?

5. As First Church of Salt and Light (5:13-16), what is your job description in 5:3-16?

6. Which of the beatitudes are you most drawn to or is expressed in your life choices? Which is the most difficult for you?

form of poverty (those who do not enjoy praise songs or the humble). They are the literal poor. The "in spirit" intensifies their poverty rather than spiritualizing it. Not only are they poor and powerless, their very spirits are crushed and destroyed by the elite's exploitation. There is no hope, no way out, no relief from the desperate daily struggle to survive. Even God seems to have forgotten them (Ps 10:1-13). These are precisely the people of 4:18-25, people trapped in and damaged by an oppressive situation over which they have no control. There is no hope of change unless God intervenes, as Jesus does, announcing God's reign and forming an alternative community that seeks justice (6:33), that knows wholeness and healing. A process of reversal, the expression of God's blessing, is under way.

The three subsequent beatitudes elaborate the people's distress and God's transforming work. Those who mourn are represented by Rachel in 2:18, mourning the destruction wrought by Assyria, Babylon, and Rome's crony, Herod. Their comfort comes in the establishment of God's purposes. The meek are not wimps, but are defined (by Jesus' citation of Psalm 37:11, 22, 29) as the powerless poor who are to trust God to deliver them from "the wicked." Inheriting the earth means access to the basic resource of land that is presently under elite control. The meek ones hunger for justice, transformed societal relationships, and access to life-giving resources. They will not be disappointed at the completion of God's purposes.

The second group of five beatitudes (5:7-12) moves from the circumstances that God is reversing to human actions that cohere with and enact God's good purposes. There is a partnership between God's action and the communities of disciples.

The merciful are those who imitate God's fundamental way of acting in the world. Mercy is not a feeling but the community's practical kindness to those in desperate circumstances (see 25:31-46). The pure in heart are, as Psalm 24:4 indicates, those who exhibit integrity between internal commitment to God and an external way of life (contrast the "hypocrites" who play a false part, 7:1-5, 15-27). The blessing on peacemakers is very polemical. Rome boasted of its gift of peace (*Pax Romana*). The term was, in fact, shorthand for the imposition of Roman order that benefited the elite at the expense of the rest. This way of life is at fundamental odds with God's purposes of peace or wholeness that concern all people in right relationship with each other and God (see Psalm 72). The beatitude blesses transformative and nonviolent resistance to Rome's order. The next beatitude recognizes, though, that such resistance always brings a backlash. However, as the second line of each beatitude makes clear, such ways of living, such characteristics of the community of disciples, the church, result in divine approval and participation in God's good purposes.

Two more images of the church follow in 5:13-16. Salt does flavoring, purifying, and transforming work. Light, already used in 4:15-16 to describe Jesus' mission of manifesting God's saving presence and reign, now describes the lifestyle and mission of the community of disciples, the church.

Three Acts of Justice

This section of Matthew explains in 6:1 how disciples should live. The word often translated "piety" is the same Greek word that is translated "righteousness" or "justice" in 3:15, and 5:6, 10, 20, and 6:33. Righteousness or justice is a central characteristic of disciples. It comprises doing what God requires, acting faithfully in relationship to God and God's purposes. As the beatitudes have made clear (5:3-16), and as the three examples in 6:2-18 will elaborate, God's purposes involve restructured societal relationships and just access to life-sustaining resources for all.

Verse 1 establishes the basic principle. Disciples should live out this just way of life, not for public approval, but for God's approval. The first-century world was significantly shaped by values of honor and shame. Public actions, especially displays of beneficence by wealthy elite citizens (funding a food handout, building a statue, financing a festival), were "honorable" actions, enhancing their power and societal status. Disciples do not imitate this value system. We live in faithfulness to God's purposes. This emphasis matters because the three acts of justice or righteousness elaborated in 6:2-18 (as well as through the whole of the Sermon) challenge rather than enhance existing societal patterns. In order to sustain the faithfulness of an alternative way of life, we need to be clear about the one for whom we live.

The first act of justice concerns giving alms or performing acts of mercy (6:2-4; cf 5:7). The action is assumed ("when you …") as a normal part of Jewish

Lectionary Loop

Ash Wednesday, Year A

Reflections

Acts of Mercy, Prayer, and Justice

1. How are acts of mercy to be performed and not performed (6:1-4)?

2. Compare Jesus' teaching with your/our societal ways of performing mercy.

3. In what ways could the acts of mercy performed by you and your church be more consistent with Jesus' teaching? What would be the cost? The benefit?

faithfulness (Prov 25:21-22). The focus is on *how* the acts of mercy are performed. The scene contrasts with "how not to do it," which is presented first in 6:2. Blowing a trumpet is a caricature; no historic evidence exists for such actions accompanying almsgiving. The tone is hyperbolic and polemical, resulting from the strained relationships between Matthew's community and the rest of the members of the synagogue. Again, the issue is one of public display and honor gained or enhanced through virtuous actions performed before others. Such actions maintain the status quo of the "haves" (5 percent) and the "have-nots" (95 percent).

Instructions on how to do it follow in 6:3-4. Acts of mercy are normal, unspectacular, uncalculated parts of discipleship. Mercy toward fellow sufferers is done, not for self-interest, but as part of faithful relationship with God. It does not maintain a hierarchical society but seeks its just transformation by enacting God's justice that provides adequate resources for all people.

The second act of justice concerns prayer (6:5-15). Two scenes depict the practices of discipleship. In 6:5-6, the manner of prayer is contrasted again with a false practice. Prayer is not about public performance (the theatre metaphor continues in the language of "hypocrite," an actor or one who plays a part). It is about faithful relationship with God.

In 6:7-15, the practice of prayer is contrasted with a false theology. The pattern of Gentile prayer is (unflatteringly) presented as requiring the right choice and number of words (6:7). Implicit in this description is the type of god being addressed. The gods mentioned in verse 7 are fickle, unknowing, uncaring, and vain, manipulated by repetition and verbal quantity. Of course, many Gentiles would not agree, but polemic is not especially interested in accuracy or fairness.

By contrast, disciples engage in prayer to a God who knows and cares for us (6:8). Such prayer is not about manipulating a deity, but about aligning oneself with God's will and purposes for the world. The Lord's Prayer sets out these purposes (6:9-13).

Two questions dominate the Prayer's interpretation. How is the Prayer answered—by God's actions alone

Reflections
Praying and Living Justly

1. Prayer is often a mystery and a challenge for us. Jesus' teaching addresses two issues in 6:5-6 and 6:7-15. What are they?

   On Matt 6:5-15, see NISB, 1757. Are these challenges that you experience? Identify your own particular joys and challenges in prayer.

2. Work through the Lord's Prayer, petition by petition. What are we praying for in each petition? How does Ezek 36:22-37 clarify the first three petitions?

   On Ezek 36:22-37, see NISB, 1210-11.

3. In praying for God's reign, how will we recognize it? Review 4:17-25 and 5:3-16.

4. How is praying for "daily" or "necessary" bread (6:11) affected by having too little or too much?

5. How might the people's testing of God—when God seems to do nothing to provide water for the people in Exod 17:1-7—help in understanding the petitions in Matt 6:13? *On Exod 17:1-7, see NISB notes, 111.*

6. When thinking about the Prayer as a whole, what roles do God and disciples, and the future and the present play in how and when these petitions are answered?

or through the lives of disciples? And when is the prayer answered—in the present or in the future? I would suggest that God answers through God's actions and through the lives of disciples, both now and in the future completion of God's purposes. The prayer enables, rather than displaces, discipleship faithful to God's purposes.

The opening address defines the relationship of prayer. The language of "Our Father" defines the disciples as part of a community marked by vulnerability and threat. The plural pronoun "our," repeated in verses 11 (twice), 12 (four times), and 13 (twice), sets all who pray on the same footing before God. Gender, wealth, status, etc. make no difference. Relationship to God, not cultural markers, defines this community. The language of "Father" (referring to God, not to Jupiter or the emperor as "father of the fatherland") further identifies those who pray as a community of children. Children in the ancient world were regarded as dependent, marginal to centers of power, vulnerable (with high mortality rates), and a disruptive threat to social norms and acceptable behaviors. Children were understood to be unpredictable and threatening because they were not yet socialized into conventional roles. In these ways, the community of disciples is a community of children.

The first three petitions focus on doing God's purposes(6:9b-10). Hallowing or sanctifying God's name involves doing God's will (Lev 22:31-32). In Ezek 36:22-37 God's name is dishonored or shamed by the people's disobedience and punishment in the Babylonian exile, but is honored as God liberates the people. God's name or God's saving purposes are honored in Jesus' mission (1:21-23). But God's name is also honored as disciples live in accord with God's purposes. The parallel petition, "Your kingdom/empire come," expresses a similar desire for God to accomplish God's life-giving and just purposes. Jesus enacts this mission (4:17), as do disciples (10:7-8). This is the doing of God's will, the third petition.

The fourth petition requests God's provision of what is necessary for existence. (As to the difficult word translated as "daily," see Prov 30:8.) It recognizes that often there is not sufficient sustenance available because of human greed, misuse of power, and unjust access to and distribution of resources. Implicit in the prayer is its answer in transformed human communities. For disciples in the western world who often have too much "bread" at the expense of the rest of the world, this is a petition against our greed and incessant quest for "more stuff." It requires appropriate actions of redistribution and disinvestment to ensure enough for the rest of the human family. For those who lack adequate resources, the petition seeks basic survival and community/global transformation.

Forgiveness, a fundamental part of the community of disciples (6:12), enacts the forgiveness encountered from God (6:14-15; see also mercy, 6:2-4; forgiveness, 18:21-35). The petition in 6:13 can be read in several ways, such as a request for help against general temptation or for deliverance from the eschatological woes (see chapter 24). It is more convincing to see it as a petition for God to act to transform the world. The continued existence of evil and injustice provokes doubt as to whether God is doing or can do anything to accomplish God's purposes (Israel's testing God in Exod 17:1-7; Deut 6–8). God can answer by "delivering us from the evil one" (author's trans., 6:13) and completing God's purposes.

The third act of justice concerns fasting (6:16-18). The same point of divine rather than societal approval is made. How is divine approval gained through fasting? Isaiah 58 emphasizes that fasting participates in the struggle against societal injustice and for the doing of God's will.

Study Bible

For further study on the Lord's Prayer, see *NISB*, 1756-57 and *Matthew and the Margins*, 161-70.

Reflections
Fasting and Living Justly

1. The spiritual discipline of fasting receives little attention these days. Why is it so often neglected?

2. What are the benefits of fasting?

3. Jesus commends fasting that occurs, not for public viewing, but in the context of relationship with God. Yet fasting is not an isolated act but is part of a life where worship and work are one. Study Isaiah 58. God commends the people in 58:2a and 2c yet reproves them in 58:1, 2b. They are frustrated in 58:3a that God does not act. What is God's explanation (58:3b-12)?

4. How does this material in Isaiah 58 help to clarify why Jesus introduces the three practices of acts of mercy, prayer, and fasting in Matthew 6:1 as acts of justice or righteousness?

5. What are ways to fast that are consistent with Isaiah's and Jesus' teaching?

6. What, then, is justice and how do we live it?

Healings and God's Reign

Lectionary Loop

Third Sunday of Advent, Year A

This passage begins the third section of Matthew's story of Jesus. Section one established Jesus' identity as God's agent (Christ, Son), chosen or anointed to manifest God's saving presence in a world fundamentally at odds with God's life-giving purposes (1:1–4:16). Section two moved from the *who* question to the question of *how* Jesus enacts his commission (4:17-11:1). It answered that question by narrating his work of proclaiming God's reign/empire, forming an alternative community of disciples, and enacting God's purposes in actions, especially transformational healings. Section three pursues a further question that emerges from section 2, that of recognition and response. Will people recognize the saving presence of God in Jesus' ministry and commit themselves to it?

This opening scene poses this question, and subsequent scenes will display both positive and negative responses. In 11:2, John, who is in prison (see 4:12; 14:1-12), hears about "the works of the Christ" and sends his disciples to question Jesus' identity (11:3). The sequence is important. Jesus' works precede and provoke the inquiry. The question of identity arises out of hearing about his works. Repeatedly, subsequent scenes up to the point of Jesus' crucifixion are going to contrast responses to Jesus' ministry. Some pursue the identity and recognition questions, while others dismiss and resist his claims. (Compare the last scene of this section, 16:13-20; *NISB,* 1776).

Jesus' answer in verses 4-5 is not straightforward. There are no objective criteria to which he can appeal to answer John's question about his identity. First-century Judaism did not have a widespread, universal understanding of a messiah's job description. There were no commonly agreed-upon signs or checklists by which any person could identify the Messiah. In fact, messianic expectations seem to have been held among a minority and were very diverse. Recognizing Jesus' identity and committing oneself to him requires not a checklist, but discernment and faith.

Jesus' response in verses 4-6 rehearses his merciful ministry presented in Matthew 8–9. There he restored sight to the blind (9:27-31), enabled the lame to walk (9:1-8), cleansed lepers (8:1-4), restored hearing to the deaf (9:32-34), raised the dead (9:18-19, 23-26), and preached to the poor (which included most of the population, 9:35). But the list is not merely a plot summary. There are two huge clues that present the Gospel's fundamental claim that God's saving work and reign are being enacted in his ministry.

The first clue is found in the inclusion of passive verbal constructions in the list. Lepers are cleansed. The dead are raised. The poor are "good newsed" (evangelized). Inquiring minds ask the question that the passive construction inevitably raises: by whom? Frequently in the biblical tradition, the passive construction denotes God's action. God's saving presence is being manifested in Jesus' ministry.

The second clue that God's saving presence and reign are being manifested in Jesus' acts of healing comes in the observation that Jesus' summary cites passages like Isaiah 26:19; 29:18-19; 35:5-6; 42:7; 61:1. Pausing over these biblical echoes is very important for understanding the significance of Jesus' actions. Sickness and human deformity were major factors in the ancient world. Not only does this situation reflect the lack of scientific knowledge and appropriate medical interventions, but it also reflects the living situation of much of the population. Roman "justice" meant, in reality, injustice and brokenness for most of the population: widespread poverty, subsistence living, unfair taxation, poor nutrition, overwork, anxiety, disease, indebtedness, social dislocation

Reflections
Jesus' Ministry and Healing

1. Jesus' words in 11:4-5 sum up his healing ministry in 4:23-25 and Matthew 8–9. Work through the subscenes in chapters 8–9 that involve healing (8:1-4, 5-13, 14-15, 16-17, 28-34; 9:1-8, 10-13 [a reference to a physician], 18-26, 27-31, 32-34.

   In each scene, identify (where possible) who is healed, where, how, as well as their response, its impact on their lives, and its impact on others. What does this survey indicate about Jesus' ministry?

2. Jesus' ministry centers on the culturally marginal and the powerless. What sort of challenge and encouragement does this observation present to your church as the light for the world, charged with continuing Jesus' ministry (1:21-23; 4:15-16; 5:14)?

See M. deJonge, "Messiah," in *Anchor Bible Dictionary*, vol. 4, (ed. D. N. Freedman; (New York: Doubleday, 1992), 777–88.

through loss of land or the inability to support a house-hold, urban squalor and overcrowding, societal conflicts, ethnic tensions, and war. We know that all of these factors damage health.

There were numerous centers of healing in the ancient world. Physicians, trained according to various medical theories, attended, more often than not, the elite who could afford them (9:12). Both Hellenistic (e.g. Apollonius of Tyana) and Jewish (e.g. Honi the Circle-Drawer) figures performed healings. Apollonius was an itinerant healer and teacher like Jesus. Shrines or temples for healings by gods and goddesses such as Asclepius or Isis provided access to healings. A payment of a fee and the offering of some sacrifice secured healing favors, celebrated at some shrines with models that represented restored body parts. Surviving written documents attest to an extensive tradition of popular "magical" remedies found in chants, potions, and rituals (see *Matthew and the Margins*, 123-27).

Jesus' ministry of healing, therefore, was not unique. What matters for Matthew is discerning the significance of the healings and the identity of Jesus. In this regard, Jesus' citation from Isaiah in 11:2-6 is crucial in providing commentary on Jesus' actions. Addressing the circumstances of Isaiah's own time under imperial threat from Assyria, and later Babylon, Isaiah depicts the establishment of God's saving reign. God's intervention creates a new world, transforming the exploitative and destructive circumstances under which most of the population live. In creating a just world, God reverses the status quo, bringing wholeness and healing to brokenness and disease, providing abundant food to replace subsistence living and inadequate nutrition (Isa 25:6-10).

Isaiah's vision provides the interpretive framework for Jesus' healings. Jesus enacts God's transformative reign that resists and reverses the world that results from imperial rule. His healings enact God's saving presence now in the concrete circumstances of people's lives and anticipate the full establishment of God's preferences. Thus the healings reveal Jesus' identity as the one commissioned by God to carry out

---

Reflections

Jesus' Healings as Demonstrations of God's Reign

1. How do conditions of empire (excessive taxation, military intimidation, tight control) make people sick?

2. Study the passages from Isaiah that refer to the physical transformation and wholeness that God's reign establishes in overcoming the empires of Assyria and Babylon: Isa 26:19; 29:18-19; 35:5-6; 42:7; 61:1.

3. In the context of the Roman Empire in which Jesus conducts his ministry, what is the significance of his interpreting his healings by quoting Isa 35:5-6? What do his miracles enact? How?

4. The ongoing presence of sickness and suffering in our world—despite wonderful scientific and medical knowledge—is a constant source of "dis-ease" for God's people. What light does this context of Isaiah and Matthew cast on our experiences of sickness, healing, and nonhealing?

these tasks, challenging people to recognize God at work in him.

In 11:6 Jesus speaks God's blessing (favor) on those who recognize his identity and God's saving presence at work through him. The negative construction of verse 6, though, alerts us to the possibility that some will take offense. Jesus bears this out with a section on John's identity (11:7-15). Six questions—underlining John's marginal location (the wilderness), participation in God's purposes, and conflict with the powerful—point to John's identity and mission as a prophet who proclaims God's purposes, notably in Jesus (3:1-12). The point is that to discern John's identity correctly is to discern Jesus' identity. Yet Jesus is not optimistic about widespread recognition. People violently oppose God's reign, defending the unjust status quo (11:12). They misunderstand both John and Jesus (11:18-19). Cities witness Jesus' actions but do not discern his identity (11:20-24). But some—like the vulnerable (the image of "infants" in v. 25) and those weary and burdened from trying to survive in such a world, those marginal to the centers of power—experience God's revealing work (11:25-30).

Reflections

To Recognize John is to Recognize Jesus

1. What is the significance of the six questions that Jesus asks the crowd (11:7-9)? See *NISB*, 1765-66, and *Matthew and the Margins* (Maryknoll: Orbis Books, 2000), 251-52. What do these questions tell us about the ways in which God works?

2. Where do we look to experience God's saving work? How does 11:25-30 inform our search?

3. What is our church's identity? How does it represent the identity of Jesus? Where/how might outsiders experience Jesus among us?

For a study of 11:25-30, see W. Carter, Matthew and Empire: Initial Explorations *(Harrisburg: Trinity Press International, 2001), 108-29.*

Not Enough Food, Too Much Water

Matthew's third section (11:2-16:20) continues to narrate responses to Jesus' ministry. In Matthew 12, his views are in conflict with elite figures over the Sabbath and the vision of social order that the observance of the Sabbath maintains. The elite do not recognize God's purposes in Jesus' words. In Matthew 13, the parable collection elaborates understanding of God's reign/empire, and explains why many have not discerned God's saving reign in Jesus' ministry. It is partly because of human sinfulness, and partly because of the devil's opposition. Nonrecognition also, however, derives from the often elusive, even invisible, way that God's reign is active in the present—like yeast at work in dough, like a tiny mustard seed (13:31-33). The end result, the establishment of God's reign, will be spectacular, and will be bad news for Roman rule (24:27-31). But for the present, God's reign manifested in Jesus is often unnoticed, apparently inconsequential, and seemingly ineffectual. Its discernment, therefore, by disciples is remarkable. It is to be celebrated, like finding a treasure or a pearl (13:44-46).

Despite non-recognition and even hostility (13:53-58; 14:1-12), Jesus continues his task of enacting God's saving presence and challenging people to recognize this presence. He does so in chapter 14 in three scenes: feeding the five thousand (14:13-21), walking on water (14:22-33), and healing the sick (14:34-36). All three actions set God's reign/empire in conflict with life as usual in Rome's world.

As the scene emphasizes (14:13, 15), the feeding

Lectionary Loop
Propers 13 and 14, Year A

Study Bible
For further discussion see *NISB*, 1769-71.

story takes place in a "deserted place/wilderness," which is an insignificant and unimportant place as far as the urban-based elites are concerned. But for the Gospel, as we have seen, such marginal places (like people) are central to God's purposes. God's activity there benefits the non-elite and threatens the elite (2:3-8, 16-18; 3:1-10). The wilderness setting also recalls the liberation from Egypt and God's provision of food (Exodus 16).

Jesus' intervention expresses the compassion that motivates his mission among Galilee's largely peasant population (9:36; 14:14; 15:32). But his compassion accomplishes much. The passage emphasizes his overzealous catering in the abundance of the food that he makes available. All five thousand men plus, women and children (14:21) were filled, and there were twelve baskets of surplus (14:20).

What are we to make of this scene? The feeding of the five thousand powerfully demonstrates God's saving presence as Jesus performs a God-like action that sustains human life. The biblical traditions attest God's commitment to feeding hungry people as well as God's resistance to systems that hinder it (see Reflections #2, this page). Roman rule in alliance with local elites removed food from people through taxation and tribute. Jesus' action protests the injustice of a system that maintains the well-fed elite at the expense of adequate nutrition for the rest.

And what brings about the abundance? Biblical traditions frequently depict the establishment of God's reign as reversing the present inadequate food supply among the poor and eliminating its cause, which is unequal distribution. God's saving presence is experienced in feasting and abundant food. Isaiah depicts a feast that God makes "for all peoples, a feast of rich foods, a feast of well-aged wines" (Isa 25:6-10). Ezekiel anticipates the replacement of present exploitative leaders with a Davidic prince and an age of abundant fertility and plentiful food (Ezek 34:23-31). Presumably all such food is devoid of calories and cholesterol! Jesus' action enacts God's will and anticipates the day when God's reign is established and all

Study Bible

Read the story of God supplying food to the Israelites in the wilderness; (Exod. 16; *NISB*, 110-11).

Reflections
Jesus Feeds the Five Thousand

1. What happens in the scene: Where? Who? How?

2. Examine the passages about God's commitment to feed people with abundant food in the establishment of God's purposes and reign: Exodus 16; Isa 25:6-10; 58:5-12; Ezek 18:5-9; 34:1-10, 25-31. Note also Matt 6:1-4; 12:1-8; 15:32-39; 25:31-46.

3. There are Eucharistic overtones in the language of 14:19 in blessing and breaking the abundant bread and giving it to disciples (cf 26:26). What connections exist between our participation in the Eucharist and the lack of food experienced by people in our world?

4. Contrast the two meal scenes in 14:1-12 and 14:13-21. What does Herod's meal depict? What does Jesus' depict? In Matt 15:32-39 again there is inadequate food. What connections exist between the two scenes? What is the effect of telling a similar story in chapter 15 after 14:13-21?

See NISB, *1775.*

5. Many churches have food pantries or participate in programs for feeding the poor. Why should we, as followers of Jesus, do such things? How might 14:13-21 shape our involvement?

have access to the resources necessary to sustain life.

The next scene, Jesus' walking on water, also manifests God's saving presence (14:22-33). It follows Jesus' prayer in 14:23. (Does 6:9-13 indicate Jesus' prayer list?) And it occurs in the context of the disciples' endangerment from the sea (14:24).

God's control of water and the sea pervades biblical traditions from the outset. In the creation story, God sets the threatening waters of chaos in their place (Gen 1:6-10). In the exodus from Egypt, God opens the sea and drowns the pursuing Egyptian overlords (Exodus 14, before feeding the people in Exodus 16). The return from Babylonian exile is a new exodus with deliverance from the waters (Isa 43:1-21, esp. 2, 15-16). God calms the sea for travelers (Ps 107:23-32; Jonah 1:11-16) and saves people from overwhelming circumstances (Psalm 69). Moreover, God is presented as walking on the water as an expression of God's control over it (Job 9:8 uses the same verb, "walking"; Ps 77:16-20). It should be noted that various Roman rulers attributed control of the sea and possession of its occupants to Rome and its emperor. The poet Juvenal called the emperor Domitian (who was emperor when Matthew was probably written), "ruler of lands and seas and nations."

In contrast, Jesus' walking on the water is a theophany, a revelation of God's rule over creation and the nations. The revelation takes place in Jesus' four Godlike actions:

1. Like God, he walks on the sea (14:26; Ps 77:16-20) and
2. calms the storm (14:32; Ps 107:23-32).
3. He saves Peter from the water. Peter's cry in verse 30 quotes Ps 69:1.
4. He saves Peter by stretching out his hand. God's outstretched hand is the means by which God saves the people from slavery (Exod 3:20; 7:5) and watery adversity (Ps 144:7).

In addition, Jesus' words reveal God's saving presence. Jesus talks in godlike phrases. "I am" is, of course the verb of self-disclosure with which God

---

Reflections
Walking on the Water

Jesus manifests God's saving presence and rule.

1. Explore the rich Scripture texts that are so crucial for this scene:

   a. God's control of water that threatens life: Gen 1:6-10; Exodus 16; Isa 43:1-21; Pss 69:1-18; 77:16-20; 107:23-32; 144:7-8. Note the connections with this scene in Matt 14:29, 30, 31, 32.

   b. The "I am" language of God's self-revelation: Exod 3:13-18; Isa 41:4; 43:8-21. Note the connection with Matt 14:27.

2. What does Jesus reveal in this scene?

3. Note the stories in Exodus 14 and 16 involving water and food that are so crucial in the account of Moses leading the people from slavery to identity as God's people. What is important about the linking of feeding and water stories in Matthew 14? What does this sequence say about Jesus, about God, and about the identity of the community of disciples, the church?

addresses Moses (Exod 3:14) and through which God is revealed to the exiles in Babylon as their redeemer (Isa 43:10-11; 47:8, 10). God and angels use "Fear not" to reassure humans who encounter God's saving purposes (Gen 15:1; Isa 43:1-5). The exhortation, "Do not be afraid," is employed by Moses to reassure the people of God's saving power before delivering them from the Egyptians through the sea (Exod 14:13).

Such revelation of Jesus as the one who manifests God's saving purposes and reign requires response from the disciples. Despite the previous experience of 8:23-27, they do not begin well, being terrified and identifying Jesus as a ghost (14:26). Peter, often the prominent disciple (4:18; 10:2; 15:15; 16:16, 22-23; 18:21), quickly entrusts himself to Jesus' authority (14:29) but equally succumbs to the opposing forces and to fear (as he will again in 26:57-75) and sinks like a rock (14:30) before Jesus saves him (14:31). But "little faith" (also 6:30; 8:26) is better than none and enables the disciples to recognize Jesus' identity, worshiping and confessing him to be God's commissioned agent (son) who manifests God's saving presence and reign, thereby aligning themselves with God's verdict (3:17; 17:5).

(See the next study for more on Peter's role. See also the previous study for more on the healing in 14:34-36.)

Session 9

Cross Purposes

This section of Matthew divides into two scenes. The first scene closes the Gospel's third section with its emphasis on recognizing Jesus' identity (16:13-20). The second scene begins the fourth section with new material concerning Jesus' death and resurrection (16:21-28).

The first scene is set in Caearea Philippi, a city whose very name (and history) attests its active participation in Rome's claims to sovereignty and agency on behalf of the gods. In this place, God's agent and purposes are asserted. Jesus asks the key question (compare 11:2-6) about his identity in 16:13b. "Son of Man" may simply be a substitute self-reference ("I" as in Ezek 2:1), but often the term is used in the Gospel of Matthew to denote interaction with the world (8:20; 11:19; 12:8, 32, 40; 13:37; 16:13; including as eschatological judge 13:41; 16:27).

The disciples' answers locate Jesus in the prophetic tradition (16:14) until Jesus presses and personalizes the question in 16:15 with the pronoun "you." Peter, again the spokesperson (as in 14:28), makes the key confession. This is the first time a disciple has named Jesus as the Christ, though Jesus was introduced in these terms in 1:1, 16-18 (also 2:4; 11:2). The term means "anointed," a recognition that someone has been commissioned for a role in serving God (see Reflections #2, next page). First-century Judaism did not have a standard messianic expectation. Different traditions included those who anticipated a heavenly judge (1 Enoch 46–48), a king who would nonviolently expel Rome (Psalms of Solomon 17), or a priest in

Lectionary Loop
Proper 16 and Proper 17, Year A

Reflections
Who Do You Say That I Am?

Three terms appear in this passage in reference to Jesus, expressing his identity and task of manifesting God's saving presence and reign (1:21-23; 4:17).

1. The term "Son of Man" is used in two different ways in 16:13 and 16:27. Describe the difference between the two usages. Note how they reflect two distinct uses in Scripture. Look at Ezekiel 2–3 (translated throughout as "mortal" in the NRSV) and Daniel 7, especially verses 13-14 in the context of the victory over the four empires in 7:1-12. What does the use of "Son of Man" emphasize about Jesus' identity and tasks? Check also 8:20; 11:19; 12:8, 32, 40; 13:37, 41.

See notes on these references in NISB for further clarification.

(Continued on page 40)

39

the line of Levi (Qumran). Matthew defines what sort of messiah Jesus is throughout the narrative.

Peter's confession elaborates the term with its phrase, "Son of the living God" (16:16). "Son" denoted someone in close relationship with God, chosen for a particular role. Israel is God's son, chosen to witness to the nations (Hos 11:1); kings are chosen to represent God's reign (Ps 2:7). God has named Jesus as "son" in 2:15 and 3:17, so Peter's confession, repeating that of the disciples in 14:33, agrees with God that Jesus is God's agent, chosen to manifest God's saving purposes and reign (1:21-23; 4:17).

In response, Jesus affirms Peter's confession as resulting from God's revealing work (16:17) and commissions this representative disciple to a task (16:18). Jesus will build his church on this rock. The phrase "on this rock" has been much debated. Does Jesus refer to: Peter as representative of every Christian; Peter's faith or confession; Christ; or Peter, the model bishop? In context, a combination of the first two seems most convincing since all disciples make the confession in 14:33. The term "church" appears in the Septuagint for God's people as "called out" to serve God. But the term also has political reference for city assemblies that attended to elite interests in the Roman world. Jesus forms a community that is a counter-society to Roman interests, one that enacts God's purposes.

This community is caught up in a cosmic battle. The "gates of Hades" (16:18) refers to all the destructive demonic forces opposed to God's purposes (4:8; 12:23-28), but Jesus promises that the church will always prevail. The "keys of the kingdom or empire" (author's trans.) given to Peter, the representative disciple, denote authority (cf. Isa 22:20-22) to represent God's concerns in the world. As light (5:14), the disciples continue Jesus' mission through preaching and transforming acts of healing, exorcism, and societal mercy (10:7-8; 25:31-46).

The phrase "binding and loosing" has also been debated. Some see it as referring to community discipline, others to the ongoing task of interpreting Jesus' teaching (entrusted to the whole community, 18:18). Perhaps both are conveyed.

(Continued from page 39)
2. "Christ" denotes one who is anointed or commissioned to serve God in particular ways. Check out Lev 4:3-5 (priests); 1 Kgs 19:16 (prophets); Ps 2:7 (kings); Isa 44:28-45:1 (Cyrus the Persian emperor). For what is Jesus commissioned? See 1:21-23; 4:17; 11:2-6.

3. "Son of God" is a synonym for Christ in verse 16. Like "Christ," the term was used to designate agents of God's purposes in close relationship to God. Review its use in Exod 4:22 and Hos 11:1 (for Israel) and Ps 2:7 (for the king). What aspects of the people's and the king's existence in relation to God's purposes define their identity as "Son/child of God"? In this context and tradition, what, then, does the term "Son of God" highlight about Jesus? See 2:15; 3:13-17; and 14:33.

4. What is the rock (16:18), the foundation of the church? See *NISB* notes, 1776.

5. What is the good news and the bad news in the image of Jesus' promise in 16:18 that the gates of Hades (what are these?) will not prevail against the church that Jesus builds?

Reflections
Peter

Peter has some prominence in the Gospel of Matthew. What roles does Peter play? What sort of disciple is he?

1. Trace the depiction of Peter through the Gospel.
   a. What do you observe from 4:18 and 10:2? And 8:14-15?

(Continued on page 41)

Surprisingly, after all this important confessional and community-building work, Jesus charges the disciples to tell no one about his identity. When was the last time we heard or preached a sermon against witnessing? Why would Jesus say this?

The second subsection (16:21-28) explains the silence. There is more to understand about Jesus' commission. Proclamation of Jesus' identity before 16:21 would be inadequate because it would not include the proclamation of Jesus' death and resurrection. Often the necessity of Jesus' death (he must go to Jerusalem and suffer) is interpreted as God predetermining Jesus' death and sending him from heaven to die. In Matthew, God does not send Jesus from heaven, and his opponents first mention his death in 12:14. Jesus' death is inevitable because violence is the means by which the elite maintain their power and eliminate prophetic challengers (compare Moses, Exodus 14; and Elijah, 1 Kgs 19:1-3). The Jerusalem leaders are not only religious figures. They are also socio-political figures and allies with Rome (the governor appointed the high priest) in overseeing the hierarchical social order that benefits the elite and exploits the rest. Jesus' death must also happen to show the limits of the elites' power. God overcomes the worst that the Roman Empire and its allies can do by raising Jesus from the dead in anticipation of the victory of God's purposes and a just way of life. Peter is unable to understand or accept any of this (16:22-23).

Jesus' death obviously concerns him, but in verses 24-26 he presents it as the model for discipleship, the way of the cross (cf. 10:38). Death by crucifixion was the ultimate form of social rejection. It was a degrading, shameful, and painful means of execution, performed publicly as a social deterrent and as a means of ensuring public compliance with the elites' agenda. It was not used for Roman citizens but for those whom the ruling elite viewed as a threat to the Roman world (i.e., disobedient slaves, rebellious foreigners or provincials, violent criminals, treasonous "citizens").

To call disciples to take up the cross was, then, to ask for four things:

(Continued from page 40)

b. Peter becomes especially prominent in 11:2-16:20. See 14:28-33; 15:15; 16:16-23; 17:1-13; 18:21; 19:27-30.
c. Finally, in the passion narrative: 26:31-35, 57-58, 69-75.

2. Why does Peter fail so badly in 16:21-28 to understand Jesus?

3. What are the implications of Jesus' commission to Peter for disciples today?

4. How does this passage shape the mission of the church universal and of your particular church?

Reflections
The Way of the Cross

1. What is the way of the cross for Jesus? Whom does he offend (12:14; 16:21)? For what does he struggle?

2. How do we commonly understand the image of "taking up or bearing one's cross?" How does examining its use in this passage illuminate those common perceptions?

See the above comments and *NISB*, 1776-77.

3. What does it mean for disciples and the contemporary church?

4. What might it mean for our individual and communal/ecclesial lives to live the way of the cross?

5. What are the ways in which we, as members of the "called-out" community and marked in baptism with the sign of the cross, might sustain one another as we walk this difficult way of the cross and participate in God's work?

1. an active, not passive, engagement with contemporary society;
2. a way of life that manifests God's reign/empire thereby threatening and challenging the commitments and structures of the unjust status quo;
3. an identification with nobodies, with the culturally marginal, such as slaves and outsiders;
4. a willingness to pay the price because, as Jesus' death indicates, the empire always strikes back when contested.

Gaining the whole world counts for nothing (16:26) if this political, social, economic, and religious order is in the devil's hands (4:8) and is opposed to God's life-giving purposes. That is not the way to participate in God's reign.

Verses 27-28 place Jesus' death and resurrection, as well as the counter-cultural life of discipleship, in an eschatological context. The current active, resisting way of the cross anticipates the future completion of God's purposes. The connection and future accountability encourages disciples to persevere in an active but difficult and challenging way of life, knowing that ultimately God's purposes will be victorious. "Son of Man" here embraces traditions of a heavenly judge figure (so Daniel 7; also 1 Enoch 46–48) who vanquishes imperial systems and establishes God's reign, in which disciples participate.

The Community of the Cross

The way of the cross for disciples, which Jesus announces in 16:24, is tough. In Matthew 18 Jesus continues his community formation work, shaping the community of the cross in which disciples embody God's reign and sustain one another. This community of sustaining relationships and practices provides a social order expressive of God's reign/empire in contrast to the societal order of the Roman Empire. Note the four references to God's reign in 18:1, 3, 4, 23.

In 18:1-14 the central image for the community is that of children (18:2, 3, 4, 5), of little ones (18:6, 10, 14). What do these images suggest? In the twenty-first century, we associate children with qualities of innocence, purity, and unlimited potential (though anyone who has parented a two-year-old wonders regularly about all three!). The first-century world associated very different qualities with children. As Matthew's Gospel has shown, children were powerless and vulnerable to the destructive forces of the imperial world: violence, hunger, sickness, death, and demon possession (see Reflections #2, this page). The community of (adult/parental) disciples lives this sort of "childlike" existence.

Significantly, then, the community of disciples is not to imitate the empire's social structure. It is not to be a mirror image of the society defined in terms of hierarchy, power, status, wealth, and political office exercised for the benefit of the elite at the expense of the rest. Rather, the community of disciples is defined in terms of equality (all are children), powerlessness, and

Lectionary Loop
Propers 18 and 19, Year A

Reflections
The Way of the Cross as Alternative Community

The way of the cross is difficult. What role does the church play in both expressing and sustaining this way of life?

1. What sorts of relationships do verses 1-14 exhort for disciples?

2. Check out the scenes involving a "child" and/or children in the gospel: 2:8-16; 8:6; 9:2; 9:18; 14:21; 15:26, 38; 17:18; 18:1-5. What sorts of circumstances are linked with children?

3. Given these associations, what does the image of child/children say about the community of disciples that follows Jesus on the way of the cross?

4. The image of "shepherd" in 18:10-14 displays not only God's care but also models how disciples are to treat each other. Check out the contrasting images of shepherds in Ps 23 (God) and Ezekiel 34 (Israel's leaders).

5. How does the life of discipleship compare to life in our society?

vulnerability. That is where God's empire is evident, contesting the dominant social values and offering an alternative experience of human community. Such a community does not focus on competition and domination. It focuses on not causing each other to stumble (18:6-9) and on caring for each other (18:10-14). Why? Because the empire of God is about God's agenda of justice, life, and blessing for all people. The community of disciples—the church—constituted by God's action, embodies God's purposes. The way of the cross, the way of discipleship, is hard work and is sustainable only through life-giving relationships.

The language of little ones in 18:6-9, 10-14 continues these emphases and contrasts. The image of a stumbling block denotes sinful actions (5:29-30), negative reactions to Jesus (11:6; 16:23, Peter), and those who give up discipleship (13:21). Causing other disciples to stumble has serious eschatological consequences (18:6-9), a warning that underlines the desired social interactions. Also underlining the desired interactions is the parable in 18:10-14. Now framed positively, disciples are exhorted to care actively for (not despise) one another. Active care in this world of peasant and artisan poverty involves the practices outlined in 6:1-18 and 25:31-46. (See notes in *NISB*, 1756-57; 1792-93, and Session 6 above.)

The parable is a significant piece of political polemic. We know that "shepherd" imagery describes God's actions (Psalm 23) and Jesus' kingship (Matt 2:6). But it is also a political image referring to leaders. Ezekiel 34 attacks Israel's leaders for failing to represent God's purposes among the people and for damaging people by depriving them of basic material resources to sustain life (*NISB*, 1207-08). The Roman writer Suetonius said that the Emperor Tiberius rejected a governor's suggestion for extra taxation by saying, "It is the task of the shepherd to shear the sheep not skin them." By contrast to these exploitative scenarios, 18:10-14 presents a shepherd who expresses God's purpose (18:14) of seeking out and caring for the sheep. Such is to be the style of care and vigilance among the community of disciples

Reflections
Conflict and Forgiveness

How do we live with both conflict and forgiveness in the church?

1. Verses 15-20 recognize conflict as normal and inevitable in the church. Why should this be? What is it about God's reign that allows both conflict and peace?

2. Verses 15-20 provide a way of dealing with conflict. Identify the process.

3. In 18:17 the alienated person is to be treated as a "Gentile and a tax collector." Is this a mandate to shun and avoid, or to seek reconciliation? Examine how Jesus treats and talks about such people in 5:43-48; 9:9-13; 28:18-20.

4. Compare the process for dealing with conflict that you have identified in the previous questions with your experiences of conflict in the church. What might be done differently to effect resolution and reconciliation?

5. Verses 21-35 focus on forgiveness. Read the verses carefully. Is "seventy-seven times" in 18:22 an upper limit or an open-ended exhortation to a way of life?

6. In the parable, what does each of the characters—the king; the first slave/official; the second (lower) slave—show about forgiveness?

7. Talk about the process and act of forgiving and being forgiven. Why is it so hard for us? How can we learn this practice both in offering and receiving forgiveness? Are there times not to forgive? Is there a difference between "tough love" and forgiveness; between genuine and

(Continued on page 45)

in protecting one another as God protects them.

The community of disciples is also a community of reproof and restoration (18:15-20). Conflict is inevitable in any human community, but how and if the conflict is resolved determines a community's way of life and survival. One way of dealing with conflict is to do what the Empire does; namely, squash challengers and competing views. By contrast, like numerous other first-century communities, verses 15-20 offer a multi-phase process aimed at reconciliation. Is 18:17 an act of excommunication or an act of recognition that the relationship has been broken? The latter seems more consistent with the conciliatory emphasis and lack of formal process. Being "a Gentile and a tax collector" is not a cause to shun the person, but, as the rest of the Gospel indicates, an impetus to win the person with inclusive love (5:43-48; tax collectors, 9:9-13; Gentiles, 28:18-20). This response, this way of life that expresses God's reign, is ratified by God (18:18-19). Jesus continues to be present with this praying, reconciling, and missionizing community (18:20).

Corresponding with this emphasis on inclusion rather than exclusion (18:15-20) is an emphasis on repeated forgiveness and reconciliation rather than continued conflict and elimination of opponents (18:21-35). The basic point is clear: God requires disciples to manifest to each other the same forgiveness that they receive from God. For such forgiveness, there is no limit (18:21-22). The basic notion of the term "forgiveness" involves "release" from situations of indebtedness and enslavement (e.g., the year of Jubilee or release, Leviticus 25). Forgiveness is about releasing the other and the self from sinful actions that breech relationships, mandate retaliation, and provoke counter assertions of honor.

Forgiveness here involves release from indebtedness. The parable of 18:23-35 employs a typical politics as usual scenario of obligation and indebtedness derived from exploitative imperial politics. Its basic point is clear, yet the connections with 18:21-22 are not without complication. Jesus' teaching requires unlimited forgiveness, but the parable exemplifies the

(Continued from page 44)
cheap forgiveness; between external actions that suggest forgiveness and genuine internal release from alienation, wrongdoing, and pain? What is at stake in our forgiving/being forgiven or not forgiving/being forgiven? What role might spiritual disciplines—such as prayer, study, fasting, service, or participation in the eucharist—play in fostering that vital sense of our solidarity in communal brokenness and vulnerability?

very opposite. The king in the end does not forgive (18:32-34), nor does the "forgiven" slave (18:28-30). And the king takes back the forgiveness that he first offered!

It seems, then, that the parable operates by contrast. The king is not God. The king and his servant exemplify what happens if forgiveness is not the basis for social interaction. If forgiveness is a tradable asset— sometimes offered, sometimes withheld—social interaction continues without any transformation. There is no release from broken relationships. God's purposes, which are outlined in the rest of the chapter, point to different interaction in the community of disciples. How serious is Matthew about this embodiment of God's reign? The last verse (18:35) threatens eschatological judgment for those who do not forgive. In this way, at least, God is like the king of the parable.

It Shall Not Be So Among You

In Matthew 19-20 Jesus walks the way of the cross, literally. He leaves Galilee (19:1) for Judea and Jerusalem, where he will be crucified. On the way, he continues to instruct disciples about the way of the cross (16:24). The journey and the instruction for disciples unify the two chapters. So does the content. Jesus addresses a series of topics associated with households:

19:3-12	Marriage and Divorce
19:13-15	Children
19:16-30	Wealth
20:1-16	The Parable of the Householder
20:17-28	Being Slaves
20:29-34	Jesus Heals Two Blind Men

Several important pieces of information explain the significance of this focus.

First, various traditions in the ancient world (Aristotelian, Stoic, Neopythagorean, and Hellenistic Judaism) understood the household to be the foundational unit of a city, kingdom, or empire. The household was the microcosm of imperial society.

Second, given this crucial contribution of households, these traditions paid great attention to how households should be structured. They identified three key relationships and an important activity. The relationships involved husband and wife, father and children, master and slaves. The activity involved the male's responsibility for economic activity to support the household.

Third, the three relationships were to be structured around the central power dynamic of "ruling over."

Lectionary Loop
(Markan parallels only)
Proper 24 or 29th
Sunday (Mark 10:35-45),
Proper 25 or 30th
Sunday (10:46-52), Year B

Study Bible

See *NISB*, 1780-82.

For elaboration, see *Matthew and the Margins* (Maryknoll: Orbis Books, 2000), 376-410.

Husband was to rule over wife, father was to rule over children, master was to rule over slaves. That is, the household, like society, was hierarchical, patriarchal in that the male ruled over others, and androcentric in that it centered on him and benefited him the most.

Given this widely understood link between an empire and a household, it is not surprising that Jesus' instruction about life that embodies God's kingdom/empire should include instruction on household structures that represent God's purposes. Six times in these two chapters Jesus refers to God's kingdom or empire (19:12, 14, 23, 24; 20:1, 21). But, significantly, Jesus' instructions about households that represent God's reign contest and oppose the standard cultural values and structures. Jesus creates alternative households.

In 19:3-12, for example, instead of endorsing male power over a wife, he enjoins a relationship of mutuality and reciprocity with the image of "one flesh." In 19:13-15, instead of maintaining the dismissal and marginalization of children, he again (see 18:1-5) affirms children as central to God's reign and purposes. In 19:16-30, instead of endorsing the pursuit of wealth, he upholds the needs of the poor and points to God's different future. In Matthew 20:1-16 he gives an example of what this kingdom looks like in that it treats all people equally (20:12), resisting the hierarchical and privileged status of the current imperial order. He addresses the fourth aspect of households, masters ruling over slaves, in 20:17-28.

This section (20:17-28) presents Jesus as a slave and calls disciples to imitate his example in not seeking to dominate others (contrary to societal values) but in furthering their well-being. Jesus' death provides the supreme example. 20:17-19 and 20:28 "bookend" 20:20-27, and provide the basis for interaction within this section.

Jesus again announces his death (16:21; 17:12, 22-23), but in taking the disciples aside and using the plural language "we," he reminds them of their involvement in it. Jerusalem is the center of power, and it is the ruling center controlled by Rome's allies.

Reflections
Jesus' Death

How does Jesus explain the significance of his death?

1. Compare Jesus' five announcements of his approaching death and resurrection: 16:21; 17:12, 22-23; 20:17-19; 26:1-2. What details are highlighted? Who is responsible? (Also check 12:14.)

2. In verses 21-23, Jesus speaks of his death as drinking a cup in response to the mother inappropriately lobbying for positions of prominence in God's reign. What does this image say about his death? Consider the various meanings of the cup image in Isa 51:17-23; Jer 49:12; Ezek 23:31-34; as well as in Pss 16:5; 116:13.

3. In verses 24-28 Jesus speaks of his death as an act of service. How is it an act of service?

4. In verse 28, Jesus speaks of his death as a "ransom for many." What does the image of "ransom" signify in the biblical tradition? Look at Exod 6:6; Deut 7:8; Isa 43:1. From what is Jesus' death a ransom? For what? For whom?

See notes in NISB, *1783.*

5. How do we as a church participate in Jesus' suffering and death? What does a way of life shaped by the cross, a cruciform existence, look like for us?

Jerusalem's leadership embraces political, social, economic, and religious leadership. Jerusalem has not welcomed Jesus previously in the Gospel. In Matthew 2, Herod tries to kill Jesus. In 15:1, the leaders from Jerusalem challenge Jesus. Jesus' teaching and actions present a societal vision that confronts their hierarchical way of life and societal status, power, and wealth. They have too much to lose and cannot tolerate such a challenge. They will deal with Jesus as they have dealt with every other challenger, by killing him. Interestingly, his prediction meets with no response, no sympathy, no support, or even argument from the disciples (contrast 16:22-23).

Societal patterns and cultural values, though, run deep. In stark contrast to Jesus' announcement of suffering, and perhaps picking up on his reference to resurrection, the mother of James and John (see 4:21-22) approaches Jesus respectfully (the language presents her as a disciple) to ask for a favor. Can her sons have places of prominence and power in God's empire?

In response, Jesus offers a cup—his cup. The image of drinking from Jesus' cup is appropriately ambiguous. It denotes suffering inflicted by imperial powers (Isa 51:17-23; Jer 49:12; Ezek 23:31-34) just as Jesus will experience. Yet it also signifies God's salvation (Pss 16:5; 116:13). James and John confidently indicate that they can participate faithfully in both the suffering and the salvation. That is as much as Jesus can offer; places in the kingdom are God's prerogative (cf. 24:3, 36). But the exchange has angered the other ten disciples, perhaps resentful of the lobbying or perhaps fearful that they have missed out.

Jesus' instruction about the way of life created and required by God's reign contrasts their culturally shaped quest for power and prestige (20:24-28). Jesus appeals to their everyday experience of imperial society. Gentile rulers and their great ones (e.g., the Jerusalem leadership) "lord it over" and are "tyrants over" others. Those two verbs summarize the Roman imperial order in which the powerful (employing military, political, economic, social, cultural, legal, and religious means) organize society to exploit the major-

Reflections
Jesus' Death and Discipleship

How does the passage connect Jesus' death and the life of discipleship?

1. Work through the passage, carefully identifying the ways in which the passage connects Jesus' death with discipleship (e.g., "we are going up" —20:18; the question of verse 21 assumes Jesus' triumph; drinking the cup—20:22-23; life of service ["just as"]—20:27-28).

2. What do the images of drinking from Jesus' cup and being servants like Jesus imply for how we should live as disciples?

3. If all disciples are to live as servants or slaves, there are no masters. (Compare with the image of all disciples being children in 19:13-15.) What understanding of power in relationships does the image of being servants convey? Is it a destructive image for some (especially women and the powerless)? What way of life does it create? Elaborate the contrast that Jesus offers in verses 25-26.

4. How does this image impact the patterns and practices of leadership in the church?

ity poor for the elites' benefit. Jesus names this societal reality and in very clear terms announces what is to
shape the way of life of disciples: "It will not be so
among you." The community of disciples is not to be
a mirror image of its society. It is not to take its cues
from the surrounding society. It is constituted by God's
purposes, God's reign. This alternative community
will challenge cultural values and norms, causing tension. Instead of prestige, status, power, and domination, Jesus requires service and humiliation. Slaves,
like children, were powerless, vulnerable, and marginal. Among disciples there are no masters other than
God (23:8-12).

This reversal of values and structures constitutes
Jesus' life and death (20:28). The image of ransom
evokes powerful acts whereby God redeems or liberates God's people (from Egypt, Exod 6:6; Deut 7:8;
from Babylon, Isa 43:1). Jesus' death is a ransom for
many in that it openly reveals the powerful elites' sinful opposition to God's purposes. But it also reveals
the limits of their power. They cannot resist God's
power and keep Jesus dead. God overpowers them in
raising Jesus. God's power is not destructive like
theirs, but life-giving in that it seeks the good of others
(cf. so the image of servanthood, 20:26-27). Armed
with this perception and sharing this power, disciples
live against the grain as an alternative community
committed to God's reign in accord with and in anticipation of the completion of God's purposes. The
final scene (20:29-34) displays God's merciful and
transformational power rolling back the destructive
impact of the imperial world.

An Anti-Triumphal Entry

Having announced that he must go to Jerusalem to die (16:21; 20:17-19), and having journeyed from Galilee into Judea (Matthew 19–20), Jesus now enters Jerusalem, the center of the elites' power. The Gospel's fifth section, comprising Matthew 21–27, narrates how Jesus' death comes about. His challenge to and conflict with the powerful elite unfolds in successive chapters, as Jesus:

♦ challenges the temple powerbase (21:1-17);
♦ condemns it in a series of parables (21:28–22:14);
♦ silences the leadership in verbal exchanges (22:15-46);
♦ curses them in a series of woes (23);
♦ announces that God's eschatological purposes center on him, not the leaders (24–25);
♦ refuses to submit to their authority (26–27)

It is crucial to remember that in Rome's imperial world, so-called "religious" figures (priests, scribes, elders, Pharisees, Sadducees) exercised socio-political roles that sustained and represented the status quo. There was no separation of religion from politics or economics. They exercised power as allies of, and as dependents on, Rome. The Roman governor, for instance, appointed the chief priest. These figures expressed and provided religious sanction for the hierarchical socio-economic order from which they benefited (through temple taxes or tithes) at the expense of the rest. Throughout the Gospel, Jesus has clashed with their societal vision and with their claims to represent God's will for human interaction.

In 21:1-11, Jesus enters Jerusalem. We customarily

Lectionary Loop

Palm/Passion Sunday, Year A

Reflections
Jesus' Entry into Jerusalem

How does this action display God's reign?

1. Jesus' entry evokes several Scripture passages that are crucial for understanding this action.

   a. *Why a donkey?* Check out Exod 4:20; Deut 5:14; 1 Kings 1:33-48; Job 1:3, 14; Zech 9:9.

   b. *Why as a king?* Check out Zech 9–14 (9:9 is quoted in 21:5 but the larger context is crucial); Ps 8; Isa 62:11.

   c. *Why branches?* See 2 Macc 10:1-9.

   See the introductions to 1 and 2 Maccabees in the NISB *and 1 Macc 1:10-3:2 for the historical context of struggle against another tyrant, Antiochus Epiphanes, in the 160s BCE.)*

2. How does Jesus' entry into Jerusalem display his declaration in 20:17-28 (and action in 20:29-34) that human greatness is, in God's purposes, experienced in lives of service for others?

(Continued on page 52)

celebrate this event on Palm Sunday as Jesus' triumphal entry. More accurately we should call it Jesus' "anti-triumphal" entry. That is, like street theater, the scene employs and parodies a number of features of rituals that were observed when an important figure (an emperor, governor, general) entered a city. The most famous of such entry occasions was "the triumph" in Rome that celebrated (with displays of booty and captured soldiers) the return and military victories of a triumphant general. These rituals included a procession with loyal followers (21:1, 7), welcoming crowds (21:8, 10), hymns (21:9), speeches of welcome from local authorities, and worship in the city (21:12-17).

Such entry processions paraded and celebrated values and societal structures of the ruling elite. The elite defined greatness in terms of political and military conquest. Greatness comprised the power to dominate and subject enemies to Roman power. Entry processions provided an occasion to intimidate or overpower the non-elite into recognizing commitments to power, status, and wealth as central to their society. Parades did not honor kindness or the poor. In other words, entry processions upheld the very values and societal structures Jesus has just finished denouncing in 20:25-28. Against domination he has upheld service. Against aggressively pursuing one's own interests he has upheld mutual well-being.

Jesus' entry procession displays the commitments of God's empire. First, verses 2-7 emphasize the donkey. Jesus does not enter in a chariot or on a warhorse. The donkey is associated with royal rule (Solomon, 1 Kgs 1:33-48) including the king who establishes God's just reign in the last days (Zech 9:9, quoted in Matt 21:5). But it is also a lowly beast of burden (Job 1:3, 14), for whom Sabbath rest was stipulated (Deut 5:14), and a symbol of scorn. Some Gentile polemic mocked Jews for worshiping a donkey's head in the temple. It was also associated with the liberation of the exodus (Moses, Exod 4:20). Jesus chooses what is both royal and common, mocked and liberating.

Second, he enters as a king (21:5, 9). He does not represent Rome's rule but God's empire. (See the

---

(Continued from page 51)

How does it contrast with dominant values in the Roman world?

3. Think about parades in our society. What values are and are not upheld and celebrated? How do our parades compare with Jesus' teaching and God's reign?

4. Think about national displays, especially in times of international conflict. In what ways does this text inform or critique national actions?

5. Should the church, as an alternative community committed to Jesus' way of nonviolent resistance, contest national actions that are contrary to God's reign? If so, how?

Reflections
Jesus in the Temple

Why does Jesus attack the temple? It is crucial to understand that the temple is not an isolated "religious" building, but is a central part of first-century Jewish social, economic, and political life; the power base for Jerusalem's ruling elite, and the hierarchical societal structures that they maintain. A good discussion is found in K. C. Hanson and D. Oakman's, First-Century Palestine in the Time of Jesus *(Minneapolis: Fortress, 1998), 131-59.*

1. Verse 13 interprets Jesus' action in verse 12 by quoting two Scriptures (Isa 56:7 and Jer 7:11). Read Isaiah 56 and Jeremiah 7 in full. What is each prophet attacking and why?

2. How does evoking Isaiah 56 and Jeremiah 7 interpret the significance of Jesus' action?

(Continued on page 53)

vision of Psalm 72.) He does not come to fight for and subdue the city (as Rome did in 66-70 CE) but to give life (20:25-28). Instead of the elites' self-interested domination and exploitation, he enacts God's purposes of life and wholeness or peace (healing, food) for all people (male and female, Jew and Gentile, especially the non-elite, 20:29-34; 21:14). Verse 5 combines two crucial Scriptures about God's rule. The citing of Isaiah 62:11 ("Tell the daughter of Zion") evokes God's rescue of Jerusalem from Babylon (539 BCE) and the establishment of God's reign. The citing of Zechariah 9:9 evokes Zechariah 9–14 that celebrates God's victorious establishment of God's reign. Since this is not good news for the ruling elite, few recognize him (21:10), and the elite offer no speeches of welcome. Hostility and rejection dominate (21:15, 23-27).

Third, Jesus does not offer worship in the temple. Instead, like many prophets before him, Jesus condemns this center of elite power. Usual Christian interpretations of this action often, quite honestly, say more about our anti-Semitic prejudices than Jesus' action. His action has nothing to do with empty ritual or the futility of Jews trying to encounter God. Rather, he attacks the exploitative temple economy that used tithes and offerings to sustain the elite at the expense of the rest. Temples were commonly controlled by the elite and were often centers for economic activity such as banking. Verse 13 names their rule as making it a den for robbers. The verse cites both Isaiah 56:7 and Jer 7:11. It is crucial to study both passages. Isaiah 56 sets out a vision of actions committed to justice (56:1), that embrace all people (56:7-8) including the traditionally marginalized (eunuchs; foreigners), and that are contrary to the insatiable and exploitative greed of the condemned leaders (56:9-12). In Isaiah 58, the prophet elaborates further acts of justice (58:5-14). In Jeremiah 7, the prophet condemns misplaced trust (7:1-4) and injustice (7:5-7), for which there will be punishment enacted by Babylon (7:8-34). Again, Matthew is explaining the destruction of Jerusalem in 70 CE as punishment, enacted by Rome, for the elites' rejection of God's purposes.

(Continued from page 52)

3. How do Jesus' actions, interpreted with the help of Isaiah and Jeremiah, interpret the hugely traumatic event of Rome's destruction of Jerusalem and its temple in 70 CE? Also read 22:1-14 with its reference to Jerusalem's destruction added in verse 7 (compare Luke 14:16-24, esp. 14:21).

See notes in NISB, *1786.*

4. Jesus claims in 12:6 to be greater than the temple. How so? Explore 9:1-8; 26:28 (forgiveness); 1:21-23 (manifestation of God's saving presence); 5:21-48 (revelation of God's will). What sort of temple does 21:14-22 depict?

See notes in NISB, *1784.*

5. How does Matthew's critique of temple practices and his assertion of Jesus' identity as greater than the temple inform the practices of the church?

6. In what ways can we as disciples better manifest God's reign/empire in our church life? What hinders us?

In condemning current practices, Jesus, who is greater than the Temple (12:6), points to a different sort of temple. Matthew presents Jesus as the new, post-70 CE temple after Rome destroys Jerusalem's Temple. In him is forgiveness for sins (9:1-8; 26:28), mercy (9:13; 12:7), encounter with God's saving purposes (1:21-23), and revelation of God's will (5:21-48). What does this new temple that honors God's purposes look like? In 21:14 it looks like God's transformational mercy, inclusion, healing, and wholeness, extended even to those who are traditionally excluded (Lev 21:16-24; 2 Sam 5:8). Typically, the marginal children recognize Jesus (for the vision of David's reign, see Psalm 72) while the angry elite reject him (21:15-17). Verse 16 cites Psalm 8, a celebration of God's creation of, and therefore ownership of, this world. In verses 18-22, the new temple comprises, through prayer and faith, a place where God can transform even the centers of power that pursue their own agenda and not God's.

Session 13   Matthew 24:36-44

Being Ready

Matthew 24–25 constitutes Jesus' fifth and final major teaching discourse (chapters 5–7, 10, 13, 18). Often identified as the "eschatological discourse," it engages a cluster of issues related to the disciples' questions of verse 3 concerning Jesus' "coming." When will it happen, and what will be the signs of his coming and of the end of the age? Attempts to interpret the chapter only in relation to the destruction of the Temple in 70 CE, or in relation to future events unrelated to the present, are not persuasive. It is more satisfactory to understand Jesus' words as addressing the entire post-Easter age until his return. The "present" embraces the time from Jesus' ministry until his return. It is where we live.

The two chapters view this present context for discipleship from a particular perspective. They place this lengthy period of time—a time in which the world has changed greatly and humans have accomplished both incredibly wonderful as well as horrific things—in relation to God's cosmic purposes. Like numerous other Jewish texts, these chapters employ the notion of the eschatological woes or the distress that marks the present. Cosmic disasters, wars, increased evil, and great suffering mark the present age. God will powerfully intervene to save and establish God's purposes.

This perspective offers some explanation for ongoing evil in the world. Despite Jesus' revelation of God's reign, God's purposes are not yet established in full. The world, especially its elite leadership under the devil's control (4:8), generally prefers to pursue its own agenda. The perspective also offers hope and

Lectionary Loop

First Sunday of Advent, Year A

encouragement that the present will not continue forever. God will intervene and establish God's purposes over God's creation, making the present distress worth enduring. It also exhorts watchfulness and faithfulness in the meantime. Both are necessary if disciples are to find vindication in God's purposes. The chapters reinforce, then, the identity of communities of disciples as communities that actively resist current societal practices in an alternative way of life. In the meantime, they provide guidelines about active, faithful living for communities of disciples.

Chapters 24-25 divide into nine sections. In 24:1-2 Jesus predicts the temple's downfall, one of the events of the present distress. In 24:3-26 he identifies various tribulations that precede his "coming (24:3). In 24:27-31 he describes the coming of the Son of Man and his victory over all empires, especially Rome. The parable of the fig tree in 24:32-35 emphasizes the need to recognize the signs. In 24:36-44 Jesus refuses to offer any schedule for these events. Instead, he urges vigilance and readiness that consist of attending to God's purposes now. This point is then elaborated in three parables that contrast the faithful and wicked slave (24:45-51), the prepared and unprepared bridesmaids (25:1-13), and the faithful and unfaithful slaves (25:14-30). The final scene (25:31-46) previews the final judgment so that disciples can see the criterion for judgment and live appropriately now focused on God's purposes.

Interestingly, Jesus does not answer the disciples' question about timing in verse 3. That question expresses what has so often dominated Christian discourse about Jesus' coming. We have devoted considerable energy and time to devising schedules and timelines, trying to pin down the "when" of his return. We seem incapable of resisting the temptation to find a timetable, a blueprint, for our future in this material. Jesus does not offer one.

Rather (and not for the first time; compare 18:21-35), Jesus redirects their and our attention from him to us, from his activity to our activity. The issue is not, "When will Jesus come?" but "What will disciples do

Study Bible

On Matt 24-25, see notes in *NISB*, 1789-91.

Reflections
Jesus' Return

How should disciples live until Jesus returns to establish God's good and just purposes for all?

1. Work through verses 3-26. What are the signs of Jesus' coming and of the end of the age (24:3)?

2. Categorize these signs. For example, some are "natural" events. Some pose threats for disciples. Others require actions from disciples.

3. What threatens your discipleship? How is your church doing when it comes to being faithful to the required actions?

4. Is there any encouraging news in 3-26? What disturbs you about these verses?

Reflections
Being Ready

In a society in which people live very busy lives and are interested in immediate results, how do disciples live in anticipation of the establishment of God's good purposes at the return of Jesus?

1. According to verses 37-39, why were people in the time of Noah surprised

(Continued on page 57)

in the meantime? How will disciples live until he comes?" Hence, the "signs" include disciples paying the price for refusing to live on the basis of our society's agenda (24:9-10) and witnessing to the good news of God's empire (24:14; see 4:23). Three parables in 24:45–25:30 urge active and ongoing attention to God's agenda of mercy and justice (23:23). The envisioned judgment scene in 25:31-46 provides disciples with the criterion for judgment; namely, receiving the good news and living it in acts of mercy and justice. There is nothing about passivity, self-centered living, indifference, speculation, self-congratulation, or smug gloating. There is no sense that salvation is one's own ticket out of here. Rather there is a call to faithful, resistant, lived action.

In addressing the issue of schedule, 24:36-44 is an integral part of these two chapters. It follows the descriptions of the time until his coming (24:3-26) and of the coming itself (24:27-31), and of the exhortation to discern God's purposes (24:32-35). Jesus declares that only God knows the timing. It is not even clear that God has a fixed timetable (24:36).

Jesus then offers four examples of how disciples should live in preparation for his return.

1. In verses 24:37-39 he evokes the days of Noah and a scene of people being surprised by the flood. They are not surprised because they were doing evil things. They are surprised because they are distracted from God's purposes by everyday, ongoing life (eating, drinking, and marrying). In and of themselves these are worthy things. Jesus has upheld each one in relation to God's just purposes (see Reflections #2, this page). Disciples must not be ignorant of or distracted from God's future purposes but must live lives in the present shaped by those purposes.

2. Verse 40 provides a second example. Again, the suddenness of the divine activity interrupting daily activity is emphasized. Presumably, one is ready by living in the light of and anticipation of God's intervention.

3. Verses 41-42 provide a third example that is very

(Continued from page 56)

by the flood? Look at the activities named in verse 38. Has Jesus indicated that these activities are evil and wicked? Look at 14:22-33; 15:29-31; 19:3-12; 26:26-29.

2. Gen 6:5-22 has a different take on the time of Noah. What is it?

For discussion of Gen 6:5-22, see NISB, *16-22.*

3. Why are the people surprised in Matt 24:40-41 by God's sudden intervention in Jesus' return?

4. What warning and exhortation does the scenario of verse 43 look like?

5. Which poses more of a threat to your faithful discipleship—rampant evil that tempts you, or the routines and activities of daily life in which you do not see or encounter God's purposes?

6. Why read 24:36-44 during Advent? How does it frame the event of Christmas? Does it have anything to say about how we celebrate and understand Christmas?

7. Often eschatological thinking, a focus on the final judgment and accomplishment of God's purposes, is interpreted as encouraging a do-nothing, "there's no point" lifestyle in the present. How do the rest of these two chapters (the three parables in 24:45-25:30 and the glimpse of the final judgment provided in 25:31-46) oppose such ethical passivity? In light of the exhortation directing the disciples to actively pursue God's justice in the present, how should disciples live?

8. How can we, as disciples in our current societal and ecclesial contexts, maintain a lifestyle of hopeful readiness and active waiting?

similar. There is no rebuke for the two women for attending to their daily needs. But there is exhortation to keep awake and to remain alert for God's intervention.

4. The fourth example also highlights being prepared and taking precautions to be ready (24:43). If the householder knew that the theft was going to happen, he would have lived accordingly. Disciples do know that there will be, at some unknown future time, accountability to God's purposes. And we know from Jesus' teaching how we are to live. Therefore, the challenge and the hope come from living accordingly. Verse 44 states the very point.

"Son of Man" evokes the Daniel 7 image of one who is entrusted with God's reign, ending the present unjust world and establishing God's good, just, merciful, and life-giving purposes.

Session 14   Matthew 26:1-16

Jesus' Death: Four Perspectives

E ven if congregations are used to preaching that follows the lectionary, most members do not often have an opportunity to engage with the passion narrative of Matthew 26–27. Palm Sunday appears (Matthew 21), then, suddenly for most, Easter Sunday (Matthew 28). Only some will attend worship on Maundy Thursday, Good Friday, and other Holy Week services. Hence, attention in bible study contexts to the two passion chapters (26–27) and their rich narrative of the events and characters involved in Jesus' death is very desirable. We will focus on the four scenes that make up these first sixteen verses, but will also emphasize the way the perspective that each offers on Jesus' death runs through the two chapters. Each perspective could provide the basis for a four-week study over the period before Easter.

The New Testament texts attest to the enormous amount of interpretive attention that the early Christian communities gave to Jesus' death by crucifixion. How and why did it happen? What is its significance for Jesus and for his disciples? How does it enact God's purposes? The texts' authors employed scriptural paradigms such as the vindication of the righteous sufferer (numerous prophets; Psalms 22, 69) and the suffering servant (Isa 52:13–53:12) to frame the event. Matthew 26–27 provide some answers to such questions.

The opening scene (26:1-2) highlights one aspect of the multi-dimensional explanations. Jesus' death is not a defeat but is, instead, the enactment of God's purposes as Jesus gives himself to die. The affirmation

Study Bible

See the *NISB*, 770 on Psalm 22, and, the "Excursus: The Servant Songs in Christian Tradition," 1011-12.

Reflections
Jesus' Death (1)

Is Jesus' death a defeat?

1. Look back to Jesus' predictions about his death, 16:21; 17:12, 22-23; 20:17-19. Why "must" he die?

2. Jesus does not evade his inevitable collision with those who oppose him. At various points, he could act to avoid this confrontation in Jerusalem, the center of power. Consider 19:1; 26:20-35; 26:36-46; 26:47-56.

3. Notice the constant links to Passover: 26:5, 17-19; 27:15, 62. What did Passover celebrate? (Read Exodus 12–15, *NISB*, 102-110.) How does the Passover story of God setting the people free from Pharaoh interpret Jesus' death and resurrection?

4. Churches often emphasize the celebration of Easter Sunday. What is lost in not giving equal attention to the events leading up to Easter Sunday (e.g., Maundy Thursday and Good Friday)?

that God is doing something special in this event is by no means self-evident. The cross was a brutal means of execution, an instrument of Roman domination. The traditions affirmed that one who was hung on a tree was cursed (Deut 21:23). To discover God at work in such circumstances is an amazing affirmation, yet one informed by and consistent with various parts of the Biblical tradition. In apparent defeat and powerlessness, God accomplishes God's purposes (as in the exodus from Egypt and return from Babylonian exile).

In verses 1-2, Jesus repeats four previous predictions of his imminent death (16:21; 17:12, 22-23; 20:17-19). He appears in control as he embraces the inevitable consequence ("must … be killed," 16:21) for any prophetic figure that challenges an unjust status quo. As exemplified by Moses, Elijah, Isaiah, and Jeremiah, to confront power is to provoke retaliation. Yet he remains faithful to his commission to reveal God's transforming, saving purposes. He sets out for Jerusalem from Galilee (19:1). He is not deterred by unfaithful disciples (26:20-35), or by the struggle with the consequence of his mission at Gethsemane (26:36-46). He does not resist arrest either by fleeing or calling in angelic strikes (26:47-56). He is not intimidated into denying his mission by displays of power, physical torture, or verbal abuse (26:62-27:44).

This first scene also points to God's larger agenda and hints at the resurrection to follow in chapter 28. These events occur at Passover, a context that will be regularly evoked throughout (see Reflections #3, this page). Of course, Passover celebrates God's victory over the apparently insuperable Pharaoh. God is in the business of thwarting imperial power; of bringing new life from death; of showing that, despite its pretensions and false claims, imperial power does not have the final word on God's good earth.

Verses 3-5 constitute the second scene. Jesus' death comes about because of the opposition of the Jerusalem elite, allies of Rome, and its governor Pilate (27:62-66). They were first introduced in chapter 2 as allies of Herod who seek to kill Jesus, king of the Jews. They have been "demonized" by the Gospel, which

Reflections
Jesus' Death (2)

Is Jesus' death the victory of his powerful opponents?

1. Jesus has predicted that the Jerusalem leaders, in alliance with the Gentiles (namely Rome), whose power and social vision he has challenged throughout (cf 12:14), will put him to death. See 16:21; 17:12, 22–23; 20:17-19.

2. Track the roles and actions of the Jerusalem and Roman leaders through chapters 26-27. How does Jesus interact with them?

3. Collisions between prophets and the powerful, those who challenge and those who defend unjust practices, are common in the biblical traditions. See 1 Kings 18–19; Jer 7:1-15; Amos 7:10-17.

4. Read Psalm 2 for God's perspective on the conflict between one anointed by God and the nations who resist God's purposes. Recall Matt 20:24-28 and 26:62-66.

5. Does Jesus' interaction with the powerful Jerusalem-Roman leadership offer any guidelines for Christians in disputes with powerful rulers?

Reflections
Jesus' Death (3)

Wherein is the good news?

1. How does the action of this anonymous woman (26:6-13) encapsulate the gospel and embody the good news so well that it should be told throughout the whole world?

(Continued on page 61)

regrettably presents them in the same terms as the devil (evil; tempting/testing; cf. 4:1-11, esp verse 8; also 16:1-4). Since 12:14 they have been committed to his death. After he challenged their Temple-based power in 21:12-17, tensions have increased along with their efforts to kill him (21:45-46).

The chapters outline the execution of their intentions. The alliance of Jerusalem and Roman power arrests Jesus (26:47-56), tries him (26:57-68), and hands him over to their ally, the Roman governor, for execution (27:1-2, 11-54). By their standards Jesus is very guilty. His blasphemy of claiming to participate in God's future rule as the Son of Man (see Daniel 7), ironically the means of their downfall, is an act of treason since they exercise all power (26:62-68). To Pilate, he is a kingly pretender (27:11-14), a charge Jesus does not dispute. He is as good as dead since only Rome decides who would be a client-king. Pretenders were routinely executed. Pilate spends the rest of the scene astutely assessing how much support this king has and gaining the Jerusalem crowd's support for his execution, ably assisted by the manipulative Jerusalem elite (27:15-26). Notions of a "weak Pilate" pressured into doing something he does not want to do simply make no sense in light of the fact that Roman governors represented and defended the interests of the empire. (For discussion of Pilate as a Roman Governor and of Matthew's scene, see Warren Carter, *Matthew and Empire*, pp. 145-68, and *Pontius Pilate: Portraits of a Roman Governor* (Collegeville: Liturgical Press, 2003).

But the narrative casts a theological perspective over the elites' activity. Their opposition to Jesus is opposition to God's anointed One, the Christ. True to Psalm 2, they resist God's saving presence revealed by Jesus, God's agent (1:21-23). They are still doing so in 27:62-66. But Psalm 2 also describes God's response; God laughs such opponents into oblivion (see 15:13). Jesus' crucifixion exhibits their powerful commitment to defend and maintain the current world against any critique or alternative vision, including God's. The cross also reveals their overreaching and overstepping

(Continued from page 60)

2. Check out the significance of anointing (or "christing") figures to enact God's purposes: Lev 4:3-5 (priests); 1 Kgs 19:16 (prophets); Ps 2:7 (kings); Isa 44:28-45:1 (Cyrus the Persian emperor). For what is Jesus commissioned? See Matt 1:21-23; 4:17; 11:2-6.

3. The good news of Jesus' death concerns, in part, a "ransom for many" (20:28). What does the image of "ransom" signify in the biblical tradition? Look at Exod 6:6; Deut 7:8; Isa 43:1. Jesus' death is a ransom from what? For what? For whom?

4. The good news of Jesus' death concerns, in part, "forgiveness of sins"(26:26-28). The same term "forgiveness" is used fourteen times in Leviticus 25 in references to the year of Jubilee, or forgiveness, in which *societal* injustices or sins are corrected or "forgiven." Of what does forgiveness consist in Leviticus 25 and Matt 9:1-8?

On Lev 25, see the notes in NISB, *182-85; on Matt 9:1-8, see the notes in* NISB, *1761-62.*

5. How does Leviticus 25 challenge or agree with the ways in which you have previously understood forgiveness of sins?

6. How does the use of "ransom" and "forgiveness" in the Biblical tradition inform our understanding of God's purposes, and of the mission and tasks entrusted to us as the church?

of all limits for human power in resisting God's purposes. Jesus' death is a moral confrontation with and rejection of power that lords over others, resulting in domination (20:25-28). Jesus' death reveals its brutal, self-interested, destructive, sinful nature that God will redeem. Jesus' resurrection and his return in judgment to enact God's reign (26:62-66) expose the limits of their power. They cannot keep him dead and they cannot resist God's purposes forever.

By contrast, the third scene offers a very different perspective (26:6-13). An unnamed woman anoints Jesus for burial. She is presented as a prophet and priest, and Jesus as an anointed king, serving God for the benefit of others. Not surprisingly, her actions will be proclaimed because they embody the gospel (26:13).

That Jesus' death is *for others*, for the benefit of and on behalf of others, has been established in 20:28. As a ransom for many (Isa 53:4, 10-11), it is a means of setting free. How does it do so? It exposes the sinful and destructive nature of the elites' rule as being contrary and resistant to God's purposes. It reveals the limits of their sinful power in not being able to prevent his resurrection (God's power), despite their best efforts. In 26:28 Jesus declares that the Passover cup is his blood "poured out for many for the forgiveness of sins." The notion of forgiveness is (as its use fourteen times in Leviticus 25 in references to the year of Jubilee makes clear; see Reflections #4, page 61) primarily about freedom and transformation. This setting free happens on both personal and systemic (socio-economic; slaves, debts, land) levels. Jesus' resurrection overcomes the sinful way of life that put him to death. It demonstrates that God's power for just life is stronger and will ultimately prevail.

The fourth scene offers a fourth perspective. Jesus dies because a disciple betrays him for money (26:14-16, 20-25, 47-56; 27:3-10). The narrative will portray subsequent acts of denial by disciples (26:56; Peter, 26:31-35, 69-75) in contrast to the woman's act of love (26:6-13), the women's loyalty (27:55-56), Joseph's courage (27:57-61), and Jesus' relentless faithfulness.

Reflections
Jesus' Death (4)

How does Jesus' death model aspects of faithful discipleship, in the context of numerous acts of faithlessness by disciples?

1. Follow through on Judas' role in 26:14-16, 20-25, 47-56; 27:3-10.

2. The Gospel warns about the effect of money and wealth on disciples. Look at 6:19-24; 10:8-10; 13:22; 19:16-22; 28:12. In our comparative affluence, what does our wealth do to our discipleship?

3, How do the rest of the (male) disciples fare? See 26:31-35, 56, 69-75.

4. By contrast, the women (26:6-13; 27:55-56) and Joseph (27:57-61)?

5. And Jesus? Note the contrasts in 26:36-46, 63-68.

6. What can we learn from these contrasts, and how do our conclusions impact our communal and individual practices?

The Risen Jesus

The sixth and concluding section of the Gospel comprises three sections. The risen Jesus appears to the two Marys and commissions them to preach the resurrection gospel (28:1-10). The elite meet to plan their spin that will counter claims of resurrection (28:11-15; cf 27:62-66). Jesus appears to the disciples in Galilee and commissions them to worldwide mission and assures them of his presence (28:16-20).

Why do Mary and Mary go to the tomb? There are no spices or mention of anointing a dead Jesus as in Mark 16:1. Instead they come to "see the tomb" (28:1). For Matthew, language of "seeing" often denotes understanding Jesus' teaching, a quality that at times divides disciples from nondisciples (9:27; 13:13-17). These women have "followed" (a discipleship verb) Jesus from Galilee (27:55). They have had opportunity to hear his teaching about resurrection (12:40; 16:21; 17:23; 20:19). The language of "seeing" appears four more times in this chapter to denote encountering the risen Jesus (28:6, 7, 10, and 17). The women, unlike the male disciples who have run away (26:56), come expecting to encounter the risen Jesus.

Amidst various signs of God's power and presence, the women meet an angel (28:2-3). This angel's authority is emphasized by the descriptions "of the Lord" (perhaps signifying the angel's origin and relationship to God) and "descending from heaven" (signifying origin from God's dwelling place, 5:34). The guards ironically become "like dead men" in this place of new life (28:4). They are not able to execute the

Lectionary Loop

Easter Sunday and Trinity Sunday, Year A

Reflections
He is Risen

What is the significance of Jesus' resurrection?

1. Why do the women come to "see the tomb"? The verb "see" is crucial. What does it signify? 9:27; 13:13-17; 28:6, 7, 10, 17. Note also 27:55 and 12:40; 16:21; 17:23; 20:19.

2. What is the significance of the Roman guards becoming as "dead men" in this place of new life? Look at Exod 14:21-31; Judg 7:1-8, 19-23; 1 Sam 17; Judith 11-16.

3. What does the choice of language of resurrection signify in verses 6-7? Examine Dan 12:1-3 and 2 Maccabees 7 for key passages in the origin of the notion of resurrection.

4. What is the link between Jesus' resurrection and that of believers suggested by the strange scene in 27:52-53? Check out Paul's use of the metaphor of first-fruits to show this link between Jesus' resurrection and the

(Continued on page 64)

elites' agenda to seal the tomb against God's resurrecting power (27:62-66). God's power renders these members of the empire's feared fighting machine lifeless, just as God destroyed the Egyptian army in the sea (Exod 14:21-31), as David routs the Philistines (1 Samuel 17), as Judith halts Holofernes the Assyrian general (Judith 11–16). God overpowers the empire.

The women, though appropriately afraid, hear the angel's divinely authorized message. Jesus is not there. The tomb is empty. Why? The rest of Matthew 28 offers two competing explanations. The elite will offer its spin in verses 11-15. But the angel "of the Lord," "from heaven," offers God's trustworthy perspective (28:6). The passive "has been raised" implies God's action. "As he said" connects the event with Jesus' reliable and trustworthy predictions.

The angel explains Jesus' absence by twice asserting "he has been raised from the dead" (28:6-7). This language, used also in 27:54, 63-64, is very important. The angel does not simply say, "He is alive," though that is implicit in the announcement. Rather, the language of being raised, the language of resurrection, places Jesus' being alive in a particular perspective and gives it a much larger significance.

For instance, it is one thing to say that a politician made a serious mistake or exhibited bad judgment. It would be a very different thing to claim that the action was "of Watergate proportions." The later image links the action with a serious constitutional context of crisis and resignation. Language of Watergate assumes a mistake was made, but by connecting it to a previous well-known event, the mistake's monumental significance is interpreted.

Likewise, the language of "being raised" attributes great significance to Jesus being alive. The language interprets Jesus' being alive by linking him to a cluster of ideas in some Jewish thinking about the end of the present world and age (called eschatology). The language of being raised is used in Daniel 12:2 to refer to the final judgment in which some are condemned and some are raised to everlasting life. This later group comprises those who died because they remained

(Continued from page 63)

general, yet-to-come future resurrection. Exod 23:16; Num 28:26; Deut 26:1-11, and 1 Cor 15:20, 23.

5. How does the knowledge that we live in between the time of Jesus' resurrection and the general, yet-future resurrection affect the ways in which we live individually and communally?

6. How does the fact that we are people of the resurrection distinguish us (commitments, values, practices, lifestyle) from those in the secular world?

7. How do we, in our ecclesial communities, support and sustain this distinctive resurrection perspective and lifestyle?

Study Bible

See the "*Excursus: The Influence of the Maccabean Martyrs*," *NISB*, 1611-12.

See the "*Excursus: No One Comes to the Father Except Through Me*," *NISB*, 1937.

Reflections

Jesus' Resurrection and the Mission of the Church

How does Jesus' resurrection shape the church's mission?

1. Identify the ways (28:11-15) in which the powerful seek to discredit and hinder the resurrection gospel? Why is it so threatening to them?

2. Jesus sends the disciples back to Galilee under the Gentiles to

(Continued on page 65)

faithful to God's purposes and refused to yield to the tyrant Antiochus Epiphanes in the 160s BCE. A similar scenario occurs in 2 Maccabees 7. It is not just that they live again, but that God enables them to participate in the post-judgment age in which God's life-giving purposes and reign are established.

To announce that Jesus is risen is to proclaim that God's new era is under way. Jesus' resurrection participates in the beginning of this era. His resurrection has significance not only for Jesus, but for God's purposes for all creation. Jesus' resurrection anticipates the general resurrection. The scene in Matthew 27:52-53 pictures the same reality. Paul uses the metaphor of the first-fruits (Exod 23:16; Num 28:26; Deut 26:1-11), the first part of the harvest that precedes and anticipates the rest of the harvest, to view Jesus' resurrection as anticipating the yet-future resurrection (1 Cor 15:20, 23).

The angel's words commission the women as the first preachers of the resurrection gospel. They are to proclaim it to the disciples and send them to Galilee. Why Galilee? Galilee was the location for much of Jesus' ministry (4:17-19:1). It is described in 4:12-16 as a place of danger (also 14:1-12), of death and darkness, because it is "Galilee under the Gentiles." It is not the Galilee that God intends. There is more redemptive work to be done there, but it is also not the extent of their mission as Jesus will explain in 28:16-20. As the women obey like good disciples, they meet the risen Jesus who renews the commission (28:8-10). The repetition in the narrative underlines the importance of the task.

While they go to carry out their task, the narrative changes focus (28:11-15). The Jerusalem leaders and Pilate's allies, the chief priests and elders, hear from the soldiers "everything that had happened." The phrase is very ironic. These soldiers were "like dead men" for most of 28:1-10 and "saw" nothing of God's resurrecting act! And the chief priests and elders, though having their mocking taunts and worst fears come true (27:41-42, 62-66), do not believe, but employ deception, spin, and bribery to maintain their

---

(Continued from page 64)

resume their mission (28:7, 10, 16-20). Galilee under Roman rule is described as a place of death and darkness (see 4:15-16). What are our Galilees? What mission do we need to be engaging?

3. Worship and fear accompany the disciples' final meeting with Jesus. What do they fear? In what ways does fear affect our willingness to take up the task of living and proclaiming the resurrection gospel?

4. How do verses 18-20 draw on Dan 7:13-14 and 2 Sam 7:13-14 to present Jesus' authority over heaven and earth? Why is this significant?

5. In an increasingly multi-religious world, what right do Christians have to proclaim the gospel? Are our particular claims necessarily exclusive claims?

6. What is the importance of the promises of God's presence that mark the beginning (1:23), middle (18:20), and end of the Gospel (28:20)? What difference does the Gospel show this presence making in the world by its presentation of Jesus' ministry?

7. How do we recognize and encounter God's presence in our lives and world? What impact does it have on our lives and church's mission?

power and deny and resist God's work. They develop an alternative story (28:13).

Meanwhile, back in Galilee, the risen Jesus meets with disciples. The scene has theological and christological significance in that Jesus participates in God's rule over all creation (28:18; rule that he has exhibited in his ministry over disease, hunger, demons, people, and creation), echoing the Son of Man vision of Daniel 7 and the promise to David of a reign that lasts forever (2 Sam 7:13-14). The scene also has ecclesiological significance in commissioning disciples, worshiping and doubting (28:17), to worldwide mission. Rome's Jupiter-given mission was, as various writers like Virgil and Seneca elaborate, to rule the world. The disciples' God-given mission contests that devil-inspired claim to sovereignty (cf. 4:8) by asserting God's life-giving, just, and eternal purposes (cf. 11:25) in the formation of a community of disciples that embodies Jesus' teaching. This mission lasts until "the end of the age," the time of the final establishment of God's reign. It is difficult and requires every disciple's effort in words and deeds, but it is guided and sustained by the saving presence of Jesus (28:18-20; cf. 1:21-23).

THE BOOK OF ISAIAH

A STUDY BY
MARY DONOVAN TURNER

*Mary Donovan Turner is the Carl Patton Associate Professor
of Homiletics of Preaching at the Pacific School of Religion in Berkeley, California*

THE GOSPEL OF ISAIAH
Outline

Introduction

The Pastor's Bible Study on First Isaiah

Who or what is a prophet? For many in our congregations the word conjures images of crazed men with glazed eyes standing in the wilderness preaching loud and uncompromising words about judgment, sin, death, and the life to come. To some a prophet is a person who has insight into the futures of individuals and nations; he or she is a fortune-teller. There is some truth here, but the picture is much more complicated.

In addition to the "Former Prophets," the prophetic books of the Old Testament include Isaiah, Jeremiah, Ezekiel and the twelve books from Hosea to Malachi. These twelve are sometimes called the Minor Prophets because of their shorter length.

The prophets were called forth to speak against religious and political establishments. The words they brought to the community often were introduced with the phrase, "Thus says the LORD." This messenger formula granted them divine and personal authority for the words that they brought. The covenantal formula —I am yours and you are mine—often undergirded their words of judgment and redemption. They tried to stir the moral imaginations of the community and invite a response in the lives of their hearers.

Prophets were called forth into a particular historical context to name the realities of life and interpret them from a theological perspective. They were, in a sense, the interpreters of the national story. They were the mediators between God and humanity. Many were not madmen running in the wilderness. They were, rather, consultants to kings. They were preachers to

Teaching Tip

The prophets of the Old Testament have been grouped under a variety of headings over the centuries.

Former Prophets (Josh, Judg, 1 & 2 Sam, 1 & 2 Kgs)

Latter Prophets (Isa, Jer, Ezek, and the twelve "Minor Prophets")

Major Prophets (Isa, Jer, Lam, Ezek, and Dan)

Minor Prophets (Hos, Joel, Amos, Obad, Jonah, Mic, Nah, Hab, Zeph, Hag, Zech, Mal)

Reflections
Thus Says the LORD

1. How would you react if someone were to enter a church meeting or stand up at a legislative session and end his or her address with the phrase, "Thus says the LORD"?

2. How is authority granted to leaders in communities of faith that are part of our Western culture? What about cultures in the present-day Middle East?

religious establishments. Their words could be heavy and ponderous, calling the community back into right relationship with God and back to life. There were also times when their words were filled with extraordinary hopefulness. They often spoke of what might happen in the future, not because they had uncanny gifts, but because they could see that the nation was on a self-destructive path and that disaster would surely result from misplaced priorities and misguided choices. The prophets addressed the perennial issues of faith. They tried to teach, and they often gave praise to the God who was a sustaining, judging, and redemptive presence among them.

We know little about the lives of the prophets. Our information about them and about the situations in which they spoke or wrote is quite fragmentary. The book of Jeremiah gives us glimpses into the excruciating life of a prophet who was called to bring an unpopular word to the communities around him. And in Jonah, we come to know the life experiences of one who chose, at least for a while, to run from the wicked city of Nineveh. Throughout the prophetic books we become aware of some of the temptations that those chosen to speak a word from God might face. One temptation was to whitewash the truth. It would be easy to close one's eyes and ears and say to the world that there is peace, when there is none. How tempting it would have been to bring a word that the king or priest wanted to hear, rather than one that was honest and uncompromising.

Because the life experiences and the historical circumstances for each prophet were different from the others, they often used unique metaphors and language to bring the message to their audiences. What prophetic texts linger in your mind and in the minds of those in your community? Some will know about the burning fire shut up in Jeremiah's bones (Jer 20:9). He could not stop speaking the word from God though he was chastised, alienated, and imprisoned for doing so. Some will know of the dry bones in Ezekiel and how God's spirit moved in the wilderness to bring them life (Ezek 37:7-14). Some perhaps will know about

Reflections
Who Were They?

The Bible does not uniformly or simply bring to a contemporary community the Word of God. We are called to study the texts and where they came from in order to gain a full appreciation and understanding of them. Therefore, there are a number of important questions that can be asked when we begin the study of a prophetic book.

1. Who wrote the prophetic book?

2. What was happening in the political, religious, and cultural worlds of which the prophet was a part?

3. How did this context shape and form the message of the prophet?

4. Did the prophet use particular words or images to talk about God and people?

5. Are there themes that the prophet used repeatedly?

6. How are the prophetic oracles like and not like contemporary preaching?

See Mary Donovan Turner's "Isaiah," in Chalice Introduction to the Old Testament *(ed. Marti J. Steussy; St. Louis: Chalice Press, 2003), 135-36.*

Hosea's unfaithful wife, Gomer. For the most part, however, much of the prophetic witness in the Old Testament remains out of the grasp and consciousness of our church members. Here is an amazing opportunity to explore and get a glimpse of the depth and the breadth of the world of biblical prophecy.

The books of the prophets are a loosely organized collection of narratives, visions, laments, prayers, oracles from God, songs, and other kinds of literature. As we will find in our study of Isaiah, it is often difficult to understand the pattern or the arrangement of the material. It is not easy to determine where one unit begins and ends, and this complicates the text's interpretation. The text bears evidence not only of an original hand, but also later ones as well. These editors, redactors, and interpreters received the words of a prophet and then modified or adapted them for new and changing contexts.

While many of the prophets of the Old Testament have been of particular interest to the Christian community (primarily because of the messianic prophecies thought to be fulfilled in the birth, life, and death of Jesus), not all of them have equally engaged our communities. Obadiah and Nahum, for instance, are not represented in the Revised Common Lectionary. Not all prophets are seen as equally authoritative for the church. Together, however, the prophets tell us something about God's love, about the mission and purpose of humanity, and about faithfulness.

Once in a "Preaching from the Prophets" class, the students and I read together the Old Testament lectionary text for the upcoming Sunday. In the text, God was railing against the community because they had not regarded the plight of the widow and the orphan. God was angry, and there were many words in the text that graphically illustrated the intense, hotly burning, smoking anger of God. One student asked, "Who could believe in this angry kind of God?" After a long period of silence another student answered, "Perhaps the widow and the orphan." We learned an important lesson that day about the interpretation of that particular text—how one interpreted the text depended on

Reflections
How We Read

Readers of the biblical text must ask questions of themselves.

1. What are the political, cultural, and religious worlds in which I am located?

2. How do my own experiences and understandings of God inform how I read?

3. What are the assumptions we hold regarding the biblical text? Does the biblical text represent "truth"?

4. Is the Bible an historical document? A literary one? A scientific one?

5. Why does one of us want to discount or discard a biblical text (or at least explain it away) while another holds fast to it?

6. Why is one text difficult for a particular reader and yet brings comfort to another? Share a personal story to illustrate your answer.

whether one was the oppressor or the oppressed! For one person, the text could be a wake-up call and a challenge to move toward compassion for the most vulnerable among us. For the most vulnerable, the widow and the orphan, it could be a reminder of God's unfailing care and concern for them.

The books of the prophets hold many challenges and adventures for us. We are called to study and examine the biblical witness. We are called to question it. Our faith is not lost in the process, but it can be redefined, enlightened, strengthened, and enhanced. Coming to this study with an open and inquiring mind and willingness to dialogue with other seekers/students will be invaluable. It is in community, where likeness and difference are accepted and where dialogue is encouraged, that truth and understanding often emerge.

Session 1

Isaiah: The Lord is Salvation

The Latter Prophets in the Old Testament include Isaiah, Jeremiah, Ezekiel, and the twelve shorter prophetic books from Hosea through Malachi. The prophetic material of the Old Testament makes up one-fourth of the canon, and Isaiah's sixty-six chapters make up one-quarter of this collection. That is one reason the study of Isaiah is significant, but there are other compelling reasons to study it as well. The book of Isaiah is quoted some twenty times in the New Testament. That is more than all other prophetic books combined! Words from the book of Isaiah are called forth at important moments as the Gospel writers tell their stories about Jesus. Matthew, for instance, quotes Isaiah when he explains to his reading audience the birth of Jesus. When Mary was found to be with child, the angel of the LORD came to Joseph and said, "Joseph, son of David, do not be afraid to take Mary as your wife, for the child conceived in her is from the Holy Spirit. She will bear a son, and you are to name him Jesus, for he will save his people from their sins" (Matt 1:20-21). Matthew goes on to explain that this fulfills what the Lord had spoken to the prophet Isaiah, "Look, a virgin shall conceive and bear a son, and they shall name him Emmanuel, which means, 'God with us'" (Matt 2:22-23).

Matthew also recalls words from Isaiah when telling the story about John the Baptist, who was preaching in the wilderness of Judea." "This is the one spoken of by the prophet Isaiah, he says, and quotes Isaiah 40:3. Directly and indirectly, Matthew pauses his storytelling to remind the listeners that what Jesus says and does fulfills what was spoken by Isaiah. (See, for instance, Matt 8:17.)

Reflections
Presuppositions

1. What are some passages of Scripture from the prophets that are familiar to you?

2. What knowledge about Isaiah do you bring to this study?

Reflections
The Old and the New

1. What are some of the challenges for Christians in reading the Old Testament and the Hebrew prophets in particular?

2. Can you think of situations where Christians are or were anti-Semitic? Through the centuries the prophecies of Isaiah have been quoted by Christians to show that God rejected the Jews in favor of Christians (e.g., Isa 1:9-17; 6:9-10; or 29:13).

See the "Excursus: Anti-Semitic Interpretations of Isaiah," NISB, 959.

3. Do you think it is possible for the Old Testament to be interpreted in its original settings, without reading it through the eyes of the New Testament?

4. What is the difference between the Old Testament and the Hebrew Bible?

Luke, in recounting the first act of Jesus' public ministry, tells us that, when Jesus was in the synagogue on the Sabbath, the scroll of Isaiah was given to him. He opened the book and read quotations from Isaiah 61 and 58. When he finished reading he said, "Today this scripture has been fulfilled in your hearing" (Luke 4:16-21). From just these few illustrations we can see that the New Testament is incomprehensible without understanding the Old Testament. To understand Matthew and Luke, it is helpful to understand something about Isaiah.

Coming to understand how the writers of the New Testament used the Hebrew prophecies in a new context teaches us some important lessons about meaning and interpretation. The words of Isaiah were read in a new context, and from that reading new meanings and understandings emerged. In much the same way, the words of Isaiah inspired the early church fathers and the Protestant reformers as well. Today we read the words of Isaiah in an altogether new context and we are invited to find understanding there.

The following six texts from Isaiah have found their way into the Revised Common Lectionary in Year A: Isaiah 2:1-5; 7:10-16; 9:1-4; 9:2-7; 11:1-10; and 35:1-10. These are read on the four Sundays of Advent, Christmas, and the Third Sunday after Epiphany. All of these readings are messianic prophecies or visions of a greater day to come. It is not surprising that they are clustered around the beginning of the church year when we celebrate the birth of Jesus.

The book of Isaiah gives us a long look at the history of the Judean people. Its narratives, oracles, and songs grew out of the experiences of the Judean people for approximately 250 years. We can, through the words of Isaiah, glimpse the religious, political, social, and cultural life of a small nation and its relationship to its God.

As early as the Middle Ages, the Jewish scholar Ibn Ezra began asking important questions about the book of Isaiah. Could the prophet of eighth-century Jerusalem really have written the latter chapters of the Isaiah scroll? Ibn Ezra was interested particularly in chapters 40–65. These seem to come from a different historical period and display different theological understandings and

Reflections
Three Isaiahs?

The name of Isaiah occurs sixteen times in chapters 1–39 but never in chapters 40–65. Why?

See the Introduction to Isaiah *in the* NISB, *955 for further explanation of why many scholars believe that the book of Isaiah is actually three books blended into one.*

Teaching Tip
Outline

In this study we will be looking only at First Isaiah, chapters 1–39 of the book of Isaiah in the Old Testament.

1–12 Introduction: Accusations against Israel and the Call of the Prophet

13–23 Oracles against other Nations

24–27 Isaiah's Apocalypse

28–33 Oracles Concerning Israel

34–35 The Final Vision

36–39 Conclusion: A narrative concerning Israel and Assyria, the Final Days

See the *NISB*, 957 for a more detailed outline of the book of Isaiah.

interests. The latter chapters speak of a different geography and had different moods, language, and themes.

From these beginnings came the understanding that Isaiah 1–39 (First Isaiah) was written before the exile, chapters 40–55 (Second Isaiah) were written during the exile shortly before Babylon fell to Cyrus of Persia, and chapters 56–65 (Third Isaiah) were written after the exiles returned home. This idea has enjoyed widespread, but not unanimous, support by the scholarly community. While there are crucial differences between these parts of Isaiah, one cannot draw tight and rigid boundaries between them. It seems logical that the words of First Isaiah were read and edited by later groups of prophets, including those who may have written chapters 40–65. And surely the words of First Isaiah gave impetus to the later prophets' words of redemption.

Isaiah was one of the earliest writing prophets; his ministry took place for about four decades in the eighth century in the southern kingdom of Judah. The name Isaiah means "The LORD saves," or, "The LORD is salvation," or even, "The LORD gives salvation."

We know from the introduction to the book that Isaiah is the son of Amoz. He experienced a call (Isa 6). He was married and may have had children who were given symbolic names. We know little more, perhaps because what was important was not the person of the prophet but the words that he spoke.

Isaiah brought prophetic words to Judah under the leadership of four kings: Uzziah, Jotham, Ahaz, and Hezekiah. As we will see in some of our textual studies, knowing the political climate in and around the small country of Judah is important. At the beginning of Isaiah's prophecy, the nation was prosperous and wealthy. These "better days" faded as a neighbor, the great Assyrian Empire, gained power. The small nation of Judah was caught in a crucible of conflict and crisis and overwhelmed with the surrounding nations. In our study of chapter seven we will see how important it is to understand these historical dimensions. The people hoped for a leader with wisdom who could save them. They hoped for a time of peace. In this arena of threat and hopefulness God's care and challenge was played out.

Reflections
Salvation

1. How does the idea that God brings salvation, or "saves" us, inform or challenge your own understandings?

2. In the Old Testament, salvation is usually a corporate or national deliverance of Judah or Israel. Do you think that God chooses sides today, favoring one nation over another? What qualifies a nation for salvation?

3. The prophets often were political spokespersons for the LORD. How do you see the relationship between religion and politics in your own tradition?

4. What is our own responsibility toward addressing foreign and domestic policy?

Untangling the varied layers of Isaiah 1–39 is as difficult as untangling the structure of Isaiah's sixty-six chapters. There is a theological and structural complexity about these chapters, a baffling internal movement that some believe is loosely chronological and some believe is thematic. Others think this is simply an anthology of prophetic utterances having no particular structure at all. Were some parts of these chapters written in the eighth century and other parts added later? Were changes made? What were they? What was the "core" of Isaiah's message? Why does the story of Isaiah start in chapter 1 and then again in chapter 2? Why is the call of the prophet not recounted until chapter 6? It is apparent that there were later additions and editorial comments added to Isaiah that became a part of our canon. If we could discern the original words of Isaiah, would these be more valuable to us than later additions?

Isaiah had to address several realities and perceptions. There was a pervasive external threat from the Assyrian Empire, which could easily overwhelm and destroy the small country of Judah.

♦ Would the king trust in God and be faithful as he ruled or would he, out of fear, put trust in military strategy and alliance?

♦ Would God protect Zion/Jerusalem from external threat, war, and destruction? Is Jerusalem, because it was a "chosen" city, invincible?

♦ What would be the future of the nation that was prone to idolatry, injustice, and unrighteous behavior? Would God punish such a people?

It is easy to see how these ideas come together to create a vision with thorny theological questions and challenges. For Isaiah, the sinfulness of the people would ultimately draw a response from the God who created them, who was bent not simply on delivering a message to Judah, but on her destruction. Assyria was chosen to be the nation to bring destruction to the people of Judah because of Judah's pride and lack of faithfulness. Through their punishment, the people would be refined, and a righteous remnant would remain. The community would then begin again, renewed to live in a creative and dynamic relationship with its creator.

Reflections
Chosen?

1. Does God hold expectations for us? Are there consequences for not recognizing or not meeting those expectations?

2. The present-day state of Israel and the Palestinian refugee camps suffer almost daily from horrible violence in their struggle to live with one another. What do you think the prophet Isaiah would say to the rulers of these nations if he were present, speaking for God?

Study Bible
Zion

See the "Excursus: Zion in Prophetic Literature and the Psalms," *NISB*, 960-61.

Session 2

"Justice" and "Righteousness"
The "Big Words" of First Isaiah

There are weighty theological words in Isaiah. If we were studying Second Isaiah (chapters 40–55) we would need to begin by taking a close look at the meaning of the word *redemption* and what we are claiming when we call God Redeemer. This is an understanding that is prevalent in Second Isaiah's sixteen chapters. In studying First Isaiah, however, we begin by examining two words that will be important in our discussions in weeks to come: *justice* and *righteousness*. These words are found together often in Isaiah, so that, while they are not identical in meaning, we suspect that they are related, perhaps intimately, with each other.

Note these few representative examples:

♦ In Isaiah 1 the complaint is that the city once filled with righteousness is now filled with murderers. As the prophecy continues we discover that when the city is one day restored it will receive a new name. It will be called the City of Righteousness, the faithful city.

♦ In Isaiah 5 we overhear the LORD singing a sad song. The LORD cared for and nurtured the people. The LORD expected justice from them, but sees bloodshed. The LORD waited for them to show righteousness, but heard cries of despair.

♦ In Isaiah 1, when hopes and dreams for a new ruler are named, the vision is that one day there will be a throne established with justice and righteousness (Isaiah 9), and that the

Reflections
Righteousness

The Hebrew word for righteousness is *tsedaqah*.

For more on the righteous one, see Mary Donovan Turner's *Old Testament Words: Reflections for Preaching* (St. Louis: Chalice Press, 2003), 85-86.

In emphasizing community, one of the early Jewish rabbis says, "It is well with the righteous and his neighbor."

H. N. Bialik and Y. H. Ravnitzky, *The Book of Legends* (New York: Schocken, 1992), 548.

1. What is the difference between being righteous and being self-righteous?

2. What is righteous indignation?

king will judge the poor with righteousness (Isaiah 11, 16).

♦ When the city of Jerusalem is restored, it will be filled with justice and righteousness (Isaiah 33). Justice and righteousness will be the signs of restoration that the realm of God has come. Righteousness is the hallmark of the coming age (32:1).

♦ What is this righteousness? In the Old Testament, righteousness was not only being right or living in accordance with a certain norm, law, or understanding. It was much more dynamic than that; it was living in covenant relationship with God and with others. A right relationship with God and a right relationship with other people were inseparable. The righteous one served God, and, at the same time, delivered the poor from their poverty and took care of the world's most vulnerable people. Often, in the prophetic world, these are the widow and the orphan; they are deprived of the protection and care of a male head of household.

There is a brief description of the righteous one in Psalm 37:21 and a more extended one in Job 29:12-16. Righteousness is an active living out of one's relationship to God in the world.

Justice is a more challenging word in our contemporary context. We often hear people cry out against criminals and terrorists by saying, "We want justice!" Sometimes what is meant by the cry is that we want revenge. We want those who have wronged us to experience the loss, the pain, and the suffering we have experienced. We cannot rest until this is so. But the biblical understanding of justice was different from this. It grew out of a legal context, so the word connotes judgment, as in a case before the court or the administration of law. The word could also mean verdict. In this sense, God was the judge who executed justice for the oppressed; who executed justice against those for whom justice is denied. The biblical com-

Reflections
Justice

The Hebrew word for justice, *mishpat*, may be related to the Egyptian word *ma'at*, which refers to balanced commercial scales that are used to weigh goods; thus we sometimes refer to a difficult decision as "hanging in the balance."

1. What are the meanings of the word "justice" as we use it in our world today?

2. Often there is cynicism about whether justice (or truth) is the aim or purpose of our legal system. Do you agree?

3. Some churches emphasize the mercy and grace of God in their preaching and their teaching. Others emphasize the judgment and unrelenting expectation of God for the entire community. How do you describe your own church's expectation about justice in the community?

4. Does your congregation understand God's expectation for it to be a righteous and justice-seeking force in the wider community? Does it also offer God's radical grace? How?

mand to do justice, then, was not considered a call to revenge. It was often connected with protecting the weak and the helpless. To those in biblical times, God's anger at the community had, at its root, a deep and abiding compassion for those who carry the burden of being "unworthy" in the world's eyes.

This intimate relationship between God's judgment on the oppressor and the call for the community to live justly is seen in Isaiah 3:13-15:

> "The LORD rises to argue his case; he stands to judge the peoples. The LORD enters into judgment with the elders and princes of his people: 'It is you who have devoured the vineyard, the spoil of the poor is in your houses. What do you mean by crushing my people, by grinding the face of the poor?' says the LORD God of hosts."

For these reasons, the word *justice* keeps close and comfortable company with the word *righteousness* (see also Isa 1:21, 27; 5:7,16; 9:7; 16:5; 28:17; 32:1; 33:5 for pairings of these two words) and also with the word for *love*. Many will be familiar with the oft quoted verse from Micah 6:8. What does the LORD require? That we do justice, love kindness, and walk humbly with God. It is this kind of prophetic call to keep our eyes, ears, and hearts sensitive to the needs of those on the margins that makes Isaiah comfortable company with liberation theologians and those who see the gospel calling us out to protect and minister to the most vulnerable among us.

Together, the words *justice* and *righteousness* bear witness to a God who holds expectations for how we live our lives together. The prophets bring a strong word of God's grace and mercy toward us. In their accounts, God was often pictured as the one who called the nation back to faithful living. God continues to call, seemingly never gives up, and never ceases to long for a relationship with the people. Then and now, there is a strong word of unrelenting expectation and anger when people fail to live according to the covenant. There are words of judgment.

Biblical scholars and theologians in both Jewish and Christian communities have wrestled for centuries

---

Reflection
Injustice

What memories do you have of injustice toward yourself and your family?

with this paradox or complexity in the nature of God. The early rabbis painted the picture this way: Thinking about the justice and mercy of God is like the king who had some empty goblets. He said, "If I put hot water in them, they will burst. If I put cold water in, they will crack." And so the king put hot and cold water into the goblets together so that the goblets were not harmed. It is like God saying, "If I create the world with mercy only, sin will multiply. And if I create the world with justice only, it will not survive. So I will create the world with both, so that it will endure."

Source

From William B. Silverman, *Rabbinic Stories for Christian Ministers and Teachers* (New York: Abingdon Press, 1958), 35.

Why?

The first chapter of Isaiah seems fragmented. It is a collection of pieced and patched together oracles that move us from foreboding words of accusation to a brief word of eventual restoration and hopefulness. Taken together, the varied pieces form a compelling picture of the realities of the Judean peoples and the challenge they faced from the God who created them. The chapter also gives a glimpse of a restored nation.

The book of Isaiah does not begin the way that we would expect. The book of Isaiah does not begin with the prophet's call by the LORD (which is what occurs in the books of Jeremiah and Ezekiel). Rather, it begins with a graphic description of the plight of God's people. Chapter 1 identifies the prophet Isaiah, son of Amoz, and it tells us when and where his prophetic career took place: it was in Judah and Jerusalem, during the days of the kings Uzziah, Jotham, Ahaz and Hezekiah. (This would be approximately the years 742–701 BCE.) Before we get a glimpse of the person of the prophet and his call in chapter 6, we are immersed in descriptions of the people of Judah and why it was so important that someone step forth to bring them a word from God.

The words in Isaiah 1 are graphic and chilling; they are urgent. The whole universe is called to hear the indictment, "Hear, O heavens, and listen, O earth; for the LORD has spoken." The LORD is bringing a legal charge against the community. The whole cosmos is being called to listen to the indictment that is then read. It has to do with the broken relationship between God

Teaching Tip

LORD is the name preferred by First Isaiah to name the deity. "LORD" is a translation of the Hebrew YHWH, or Yahweh. Very rarely does First Isaiah use the Hebrew word *elohim*, which is translated in the NRSV as "God."

Study Bible
Covenant

See *NISB* notes for Isa 1:2-20, 958 for description of covenant lawsuit.

Reflections
Who Are Prophets?

1. Who are the prophets in your community and world today?

2. Does our democratic process— where one party challenges or criticizes the other and the press challenges the major parties—effectively accomplish the same thing that the prophets did within a theocracy when they challenged the king? (A theocracy is a state ruled by God, who is represented through the clergy and sometimes the king.)

(Continued on page 82)

and the people. The people have rebelled. They have forsaken and despised their God, and are now estranged from the God who created them. Isaiah heaps descriptive word upon descriptive word to try to show the alienation, the great abyss, between divine and human. The words are strong and forceful. The people have not simply walked away; they have rebelled, forsaken, and despised. Is this an active, intentional, and purposeful moving away from God?

In Isaiah's account, his task is to reintroduce the people to their God, to remind them of the one who has nurtured them and cared for them, to help them remember the expectations God has for them. They have long forgotten, and perhaps they do not even know that they have walked away. But surely they have, and, like a parent who cares for her children and then is deserted by them, God is plagued with a single question: Why? (1:4-5). Even the ox and donkey know their masters, but not the people of Judah. They are identified as the nation and the people; they are also offspring and child. This is not a distant relationship that has been violated; this is a personal and intimate one. There is anger, hurt, and sadness.

Isaiah and the other prophets used many metaphors to describe God and the relationship God has with humanity. In First, Second, and Third Isaiah, God is described as a parent (father and mother) who cares for and nurtures his or her children. The parent imagery is especially helpful in that it describes a relationship that is intimate and life-long. It has dimensions of both freedom and dependency.

There are consequences for living the estranged life. The prophet vividly describes the plight of the people and the land. The people are like a bruised body that has not known healing. The cities of Judah are desolate, devoured and overthrown (1:6-8). These descriptions of person and nation are the backdrop for the charges and complaints that the LORD brings.

"What to me is the multitude of your sacrifices?" (1:11). The charges the LORD is bringing are related to the worship life of the people. They have brought their offerings, they have burned their incense, and they

(Continued from page 81)
3. Who is indicting the rulers over the harsh realities of our society today?

Study Bible
Covenant

On Isa 1:7-8, see *NISB* 958 for extended comparisons to "daughter Zion" as the ravaged female city. The female city is often described in disturbing images. See also 1:21-22 and 3:25-26.

have met in their solemn assemblies. The people have performed their rituals, and thought these were enough. They equated "right living" with "right ritual," or, worse, they understood "right ritual" as more important than "right living." But the rituals were not wholly satisfying to the LORD. They can no longer be endured; they are a burden. God will no longer listen to the prayers spoken there. God will not listen to the prayers that are uttered because the hands of the praying ones are full of blood—the blood of the dying, the poor, the oppressed, and the forgotten. God is hiding God's eyes from this shallow devotion and hypocritical posture. God cannot bear to see. The ones who have come to worship do not live life as the worshiped One demands.

Isaiah does not seem to be saying the worship or ritual life of the community is unimportant, but he is saying that it is not enough. Wonderful, glamorous, extravagant, or even relevant worship does not, in itself, impress the LORD. As clearly as can be spoken, Isaiah then outlines for the community what God desires from them (1:16-17): "Wash yourselves; make yourselves clean; remove the evil of your doings from before my eyes; cease to do evil, learn to do good; seek justice, rescue the oppressed; defend the orphan, plead for the widow."

The story does not end with God withdrawing and hiding from God's people. Like most of the Old Testament narratives, psalms, and prophecies, the final word is not fractured relationship and dismay. "Come let us reason together ..." says the LORD (1:18). Often this is translated, "Come let us argue it out." These sound very different from each other, but perhaps, in the end, they accomplish the same things. The request is for dialogue. Reason or argument is relationship continued, and they both hold the potential for restoration.

There is a lack of justice and righteousness in the city. The concern for the orphan and widow is demonstrated again. The words from the Sovereign, the Lord of hosts, the Mighty One of Israel in 1:24 begins with the sound, the cry of lament and mourning, "Ah!" God

Reflection
Violence

Isaiah describes a world that is growing more violent.

1. Is our world growing more violent and destructive? What signs do you see? Where is the hope?

2. What does it mean to correct oppression in our world? What is evil? Who is oppressed?

3. Who needs defending? Who is in need of a word of justice? Should we give our own lives or the lives of our children to correct oppression?

Study Bible

See *NISB*, 959. The LORD invites the rebellious children to litigate, "to argue it out."

is lamenting the way people are living life. Perhaps God is lamenting the devastation that will inevitably come upon them. After judgment and purification, the city will have a new name. It will again be called the city of righteousness, the faithful city. At the end of the accusations and indictments and judgments of chapter 1 there is this brief word of promise and of hope.

The initial question in the book of Isaiah—the LORD's question—"Why?"—never finds its resolution. It is the haunting question of Isaiah and other prophets as well. Why do the people wander off? Why do they continue to live in unproductive ways? Why do the people not choose life? Why do the people choose violence and estrangement from the One who created them and who loves them? Why?

Session 4   Isaiah 2:1-5, 6-22

Mountaintops, Plowshares, and the Cleft of a Rock

The book of Isaiah has two introductions. In chapter 1 we are given the name of the prophet and the context for the words that he spoke. In chapter 2 we begin again. "The word that Isaiah son of Amoz saw concerning Judah and Jerusalem" (2:1). As readers, we wonder if we will hear more of what we have already heard. Will chapter 2 be filled with the same indictments and complaints that the Lord has against the people that we read in chapter 1? No, these words are different. These are not about the people's past, and they do not describe how the people are living in the present. These are words about the future. "In days to come the mountain of the Lord's house shall be established as the highest of the mountains, and shall be raised above the hills" (2:2). We may be surprised, following the harsh realities described in chapter 1, that here is a word of hope, a vision for the way it will be someday. But such is the nature of the prophetic word; it can name the bitterness of the present and also the possibility of a better day. It is the prophet's job to do both.

The prophet describes a mountain. This is not just any mountain; this is the highest mountain. It is visible to all nations, and it is inviting. Drawn by its power and its majesty, the people are streaming toward it. But there is something more that entices them. It is a promise, a promise of peace.

"They shall beat their swords into plowshares, and their spears into pruning hooks; nation shall not lift up sword against nation, neither shall they learn war any more" (Isa 2:4). This saying is also found in Micah 4:1-3. It must have been, then, a common or shared hope

Lectionary Loop
First Sunday of Advent, Year A

Reflections
Hope

1. What is your definition of the word *hope*?

2. What is God-given hope?

3. The prophets appear to announce both judgment and hope at the same time. We seldom see this kind of behavior in human experience, expecting a personality to be either positive or negative. Can you think of examples in recent memory of a "prophetic leader" who could offer both judgment and hope? (e.g., Martin Luther King Jr's. "I Have a Dream" speech in 1963.)

among the peoples and particularly for those in Isaiah's time who knew of the constant lurking of enemy nations at their borders. It has found its place in our own society also. These words are found at the United Nations Building and are the watchwords for many peace activist groups.

At the time this study is being written, there are "hot spots" around the globe: Afghanistan, Korea, Iraq, Liberia, Israel, and others as well. There are always a host of places where people are living in danger, in fear of death, in fear of the destruction of their communities. We long for this kind of transformation from sword to plowshare and wish it would happen magically. We want it to be our miracle. But this does not happen without serious thought, effort, sacrifice, conversation, and compromise. Swords do not melt into plowshares; swords are beaten into plowshares. Isaiah knew that we must pray for it, long for it, and work for it.

The first verses of Isaiah 2 are about pilgrimage, and, while they describe a day sometime in the future, the verses can be instrumental in inspiring us now. Where are our pilgrimages taking us? Is our pilgrimage taking us toward the highest mountain? Can we lay down the swords of hatred that inflict wounds, that keep us at arm's length, and that protect us from one another? Dare we settle for anything less?

Following the vision of peace, there is a verse that might be construed as a reflection on what comes before the vision or perhaps a prelude to what comes after it. "O house of Jacob, come, let us walk in the light of the Lord!" (2:5). This single verse is interesting because a lone voice cries out to the nation to find a better way to live. Perhaps, by walking in the light, the people of the community will move toward the great vision and away from the realities of life as they now lead it. Those realities are named as the prophet envisions for the community the coming "Day of the Lord."

This will not be a day of glorious celebration, as one would expect. This is the day of judgment, and Isaiah gives us the reasons for it. The poem is exquisitely fashioned with a multitude of word repetitions that rhythmically function to bring an emphasized, "it cannot be said

Reflections
Swords and Plowshares

1. What does it mean to beat swords into plows? Symbolically, what does it mean to transform a metal weapon into a cultivation tool that brings sustenance and nurture?

2. What would the world be like if weapons of destruction weren't needed? What would it be like if weapons were transformed into opportunities for sharing, caring, and living well?

3. Is there such a thing as a "just" or holy war?

strongly enough," kind of message to the community.

Notice the first set of repetitions in 2:6-7. The house of Jacob is called to repent, and the description of their living is defined in three phrases that begin, "Their land is filled with ..."

- ♦ silver and gold; there is no end to their treasures
- ♦ horses; there is no end to their chariots and weapons of war
- ♦ idols to which they bow

These verses describe Israel's inhabitants as wealthy, well-defended people who are finding it difficult to be faithful to the LORD.

Notice another set of repetitions that occur throughout the remainder of the poem. The people are called to "enter into the rock." This is an interesting play on the metaphor of the rock, or the cleft of the rock. Often in the psalms, God is the rock or the cleft in the rock. This is a stronghold and the place where one can go to find solace, comfort in the storm, a resting place, a place that is secure. In this poem, one hides in the rock to get away from the terror and the glory of God (2:10, 19, 21). The people are bidden to enter the caves of the rocks and hide there. Perhaps in the interlude they will have an opportunity to think, meditate, reflect, and reorient their lives.

The word "against" is found ten times in 2:12-14. The LORD has a day against:

- ♦ all that is proud and lofty
- ♦ all that is lifted up and high
- ♦ all the cedars of Lebanon
- ♦ all the oaks of Bashan
- ♦ all high mountains
- ♦ all the lofty hills
- ♦ every high tower
- ♦ every fortified wall
- ♦ all the ships of Tarshish
- ♦ all the beautiful craft.

These are all big, proud, tall things. What is at stake here? Anything or anyone that is haughty, proud, high, and pulls us away from our relationship and dependence on God will be brought low. These verses describe the

Reflections
Paradise

Isa 2:1-4 describes a vision of a day yet to come.

1. What is your vision of the ideal world to come?

   What would the world look like if the realm of God were to be made fully present among us?

2. Based on severe persecution by the Roman Empire, many early Christians expected a day of terrible tribulation, when God's wrath would be poured out on sinful nations. How is this apocalyptic thinking in the New Testament similar to or different from the "Day of the Lord" that Isaiah announced to Judah?

Study Bible

On Isa 2:18-20, see *NISB*, 962 for examples in First and Second Isaiah of idolatry, which is anything that one might substitute for the worship of God.

"Day of the Lord." (See 2:11, 12, 17, 20.) It is a day when everything that keeps us from right living will be destroyed; a day of terror. The final appeal in chapter 2 is an interesting one. "Turn away from mortals, who have only breath in their nostrils, for of what account are they?" What does this mean? What is ultimately faithful, dependable and life giving? The answer is God.

Session 5

Isaiah 5:1-23

The Beloved

Isaiah 5 is an old-fashioned love song. Love songs often mourn relationships gone awry. The love song in Isaiah 5 is no exception. The prophet sings a song one would sing to a beloved. The lyrics tell of a farmer who went out into the field to sow and then harvest his crop. He anticipated a bountiful harvest, and his expectations were not unrealistic. The farmer's vineyard was on a very fertile hill. The vines would have all the nutrients they needed to produce the most luscious grapes. The farmer carefully tended the field, clearing it of stones, removing anything that would keep the young tender vines from growing (and these were the choicest vines). He watched over the crop to protect it and built a wine vat because he knew that he had done all he could to produce a magnificent harvest. Then the farmer waited.

It is here that the song changes to a minor key. There has been anticipation and expectation, but the farmer is disappointed. When the crops come in, the grapes that grow are wild grapes. They are not sweet; they are not suitable for the making of wine. The farmer has invested his time, his energy, and his resources for nothing.

The farmer then turns to the people of Judah and Jerusalem and asks them, "What more could I have done for my vineyard? Why was there not a good harvest?" His frustration and lack of understanding are poured out to the hearers.

Those hearing the song would pass judgment. They would say that there was nothing more the

Lectionary Loop
Proper 22, Year A

Study Bible

See *NISB*, 964. The lyrics in 5:2-6 from the ancient love song would sound very erotic to the prophet's audience.

Reflections

Us and Others

1. In what ways does our society encourage us to "look out for number one"?

2. How are we encouraged not to be aware of or sensitive to the needs of others in our communities?

3. What myths might be shared or exploited to squelch a compassionate response to the most vulnerable among us?

farmer could do. What should the farmer do now? The crop did not produce so it should be destroyed. The season is over; the crop is trampled. It cannot be used; it has not fulfilled its purpose. The audience hearing the song would agree with the farmer— abandoning the field is the logical and understandable thing to do!

Unknowingly, the audience has passed judgment on themselves. They were the choice vines. They were rich with promise. They were nurtured and protected by God. This is not just a love song about a farmer and his crop. This is a song about God and God's people. Emotions are raw and wounds are deep. The LORD made a commitment to the people and thought they would be committed in return. But the LORD's hopes were naive and his dreams misguided. The LORD has loved the people. The people have not loved in return.

What is the LORD's disappointment? How have the people been unfaithful? What did the LORD expect from the relationship that the LORD did not receive? We are not surprised when we discover that the LORD expected justice from the covenant people. But the LORD does not see justice-seeking among them, the LORD sees violence. The LORD expected righteousness, but hears people crying out in despair.

There are six (and possibly seven) cries of mourning that follow this love song. (See Isa 5:8, 11, 18, 20, 21, 22 and possibly 10:1.). These cries are translated "Woe" in the KJV and "Ah" in the NRSV. What is communicated in the first word in each of these verses is an expression of lament, an outcry, a sound of despair and mourning and grief. These are outcries of the desperation and pain of the world or in the world. Isaiah often uses this cry of lament and mourning to express his own sense of grief and loss.

Who is crying out?

♦ those who build around them houses and fields so that there is no room for others, who gather up all that is around them and keep others at a distance (see 5:8-10);

Study Bible

See *NISB*, 964. The parable of the wicked tenants, found in Matthew, Mark, and Luke, is based on the Song of the Vineyard in Isa 5:1-7.

Reflections

Wrestling With Isaiah 5

1. How do we see understandings of justice and righteousness reflected here in Isaiah 5?

2. What did the LORD hope for that the LORD did not receive?

3. Where do we see our own communities reflected in these cries? Are the LORD's standards too high or lofty for us? Can we attain them?

- those who celebrate with song and wine but do not regard the works of the LORD or see the work of the LORD's hands, their intoxicated state numbing them to the everyday glimpses of God at work in our world (see 5:11-17);

- those who draw iniquity with cords of falsehood, who are harnessed to sin, who sin and cannot let go (see 5:18-19);

- those who call evil good and good evil, who call light darkness and darkness light, who call what is bitter sweet and what is sweet bitter—those who are incapable of making moral distinctions (see 5:20);

- those who are wise in their own sight, the self-appointed wise ones (see 5:21);

- those who acquit the guilty for a bribe and deprive the innocent of their rights, who are concerned primarily about self, ease, and their own comfort (see 5:22);

- those who keep causing oppression, who turn aside the needy from justice and rob the poor of their rights, who make the widows and the fatherless their prey (see 10:1).

There is no explicit "good news" in Isaiah 5. There is no vision of the day to come where the people turn back to the LORD, repent, and begin acknowledging their responsibilities to God and to each other. There is no turning from their self-serving behavior. There are many other places in the Old Testament where the LORD begins to sing a love song about relationship restored, but not here. The people of the community are left to ponder the heavy and self-reflective words about their lives. They are invited to remember, again, how much God has invested in them in the past, how God has nurtured them and watched over them in hopes that they would be cultivated into a covenant-keeping, faithful people. Here we are left with the broken-hearted God, one whose anger may make us uncomfortable. But would we not want our God to be

---

Reflections
An Angry God

1. Do you accept or appreciate the understanding of an angry God?

2. Do we depend upon and expect God to hear, see, and then act against oppression?

offended by injustice? Perhaps the answer to that question, again, depends on whether we see ourselves as the oppressed or the oppressor and where we stand on matters of justice or injustice.

Woe is Me! (Woe is Us?)

Have you ever had an experience that you could not put into words? Maybe it was when you tried to explain how it feels to love a friend or a child. Perhaps it was when you were really afraid, or trying to describe a beautiful sunset. Or maybe you had an encounter with God that defied your own words.

Isaiah's encounter is described in chapter 6. Isaiah's vision is of seraphim, of God sitting on the throne, of shaking foundations and of smoke-filled air. These images help us understand and sense the magnitude of this experience. There is something big happening here. How does one find words to describe a God who is holy and mighty, scary and powerful?

The year was 742 BCE, the year King Uzziah died. By the standards of the editor of the book of Kings he had been quite successful. He had repaired the defenses of Jerusalem, reorganized the army, and secured the trade routes that ran through the little nation of Judah. In the year that he died, the nation was mourning and wondering what the future held for them. Once again the future of the tiny nation was unknown and unclear. What would happen to them?

According to the text, Isaiah is standing in the Temple when he sees the vision. The LORD is on a throne, high and lifted up. The seraphs are singing, "Holy, holy, holy is the LORD . . . " The understanding of God as "holy" is important in Isaiah. He frequently uses "Holy One" to name God.

Reflections
Holy, Holy, Holy

1. Was Isaiah in the Temple?
2. If he was in the Temple, was he there because he is a priest?
3. Was he awake or asleep? Had he ever experienced the presence of God in this way before?
4. Have you had a vision or a dramatic experience or encounter with God? How would you describe it?

In Isaiah 6, "holy" means separate from that which is common. It means wholly good, without evil. We sing about it this way in "Holy, Holy, Holy! Lord God Almighty": "Only thou art holy; there is none beside thee, perfect in power, in love, and purity." Holiness is perfection in power, love, and purity.

In Isaiah's vision, the building shakes, smoke rises, and Isaiah speaks. The first words of Isaiah are not in response to the LORD's words. The LORD has not yet spoken. The first words from Isaiah are in response to the remarkable vision before his eyes, but he does not describe the awesome and spectacular scene he has witnessed. He is not called to thanksgiving. He is called to confession: "Woe is me" (6:5). In contrast to the holiness and glory that he witnesses, Isaiah understands that he and the community in which he lives have "unclean lips" (5).

The seraph swoops down with a live coal, pressing it against his lips. Now he is purified and readied to respond to the calling of God. His guilt is gone. His sin is seared away. Forgiveness is a gift given to him. Then God asks, "Whom shall I send, and who will go for us?" And Isaiah answers with words popularized in contemporary litany and song, "Here I am; send me" (6:8).

It is God's words to Isaiah in 6:10 that bring the contemporary reader concern and confusion. Isaiah's given task seems to be making the people hardhearted, unseeing, and unhearing until they are, in the end, punished by God. These problematic words are quoted in all four New Testament Gospels to describe those who choose not to follow Jesus. These words, perhaps not expected by the one who has just volunteered to be sent out to the community, invite his final and understandable question: "How long?" (6:11). In response, the LORD describes a time when cities lay waste and are deserted. Even a world filled with the glory of God can become desolate through the sinfulness of humanity.

There is a recurring cluster of images and words in Isaiah 6 that lead us to understand more fully the significance of the call narrative and Isaiah as a whole.

Reflection
Holiness

1. In the hymn, "Take Time to Be Holy," what are the elements or qualities of a holy person?

2. Isaiah saw his vision and was led to confession. Is confession an important part of our worship?

3. Is confession an important part of our calling into ministry?

Study Bible

For more information on the "call" of Isaiah to be a prophet, see *NISB*, 966.

In the four New Testament Gospels, and specifically in Acts, the Jews are apparently described as the ones who have a hard heart and will not follow Jesus. See further in the "Excursus: Anti-Semitic Interpretations of Isaiah," *NISB*, 959-60.

The first image is that of the seraphim. The seraphim are thought to be fiery, serpent-like figures. The same word is used in the exodus narrative (Num 21:4-9) to describe the serpents running across the wilderness, biting the Israelites for their unfaithfulness.

Second, the temple is filled with smoke. It is filled with God's glory, a word that connotes a bright, illuminating, light-filled presence. In 10:16-17, glory is related to a burning, fiery presence: "Therefore the Sovereign, the LORD of hosts, will send wasting sickness among his stout warriors, and under his glory a burning will be kindled, like the burning of fire. The light of Israel will become a fire, and his Holy One a flame; and it will burn and devour his thorns and briers in one day." Glory is a burning presence.

And finally, there is the burning coal that the seraph brings down to touch the mouth of Isaiah. Through its touch he is forgiven and purified for the task of prophecy that lies ahead.

This picture of Isaiah's fiery cleansing and his mission foreshadows or works symbolically to depict the condition, fate, and mission of the Israelite community. In Isaiah's first response to the dramatic Temple vision, he indicates that his lips are unclean. So are the lips of those in his community. This vision is about Isaiah. It is also about the people of God. Through burning, he is made ready, and as we read through Isaiah we begin to understand that this is true for the nation as well. It is through a "burning" that the community will be cleansed of its sinfulness and salvation will be ushered in.

Note these references from Isaiah:

♦ 4:4 "once the Lord has washed away the filth of the daughters of Zion and cleansed the blood-stains of Jerusalem from its midst by a spirit of judgment and by a spirit of burning . . ."

♦ 6:13 "Even if a tenth part remain in it, it will be burned again, like a terebinth or an oak whose stump remains standing when it is felled."

Reflection
Sin

Does your congregation talk about sin? How?

Reflections
New Sprouts

Isaiah spoke to a particular situation, to a people on the verge of a massive regional war between Syria, Judah, Northern Israel, and Assyria (735-32 BCE). Does Isaiah's vision of a burning, purifying fire tell us about how new hope is often restored for God's people? What are other examples of (social) renewal "by fire"?

♦ 9:19 "Through the wrath of the LORD of hosts the land was burned, and the people became like fuel for the fire; no one spared another."

We sometimes idealize a pristine call to ministry, but there is a very difficult theological concept here: Hope lies on the far side of disaster! Isaiah's recognition of his own sinfulness came immediately, but not so with a community. Renewal does not come automatically or even easily. The sinfulness of the community will be seared away just as Isaiah's was in his Temple vision, but it will take something disastrous and monumental to change the course and fate of the nation.

There is a word of hopefulness here, perhaps. It is difficult to tell because translation of the last verses of chapter 6 is so difficult. "The holy seed is its stump" (6:13); these are the very last words of the call narrative. The stump can be a symbol of the former times and the possibility of new life. It is possible that out of the stump of the felled tree can come a sprout, new growth. A new tree can be born.

In cursory form, the message of Isaiah is that beyond disaster will come new life. A refined "remnant" will survive and begin life anew. The relationship between God and humanity will be restored again, and again.

A Child is Born

Immanuel. God is with us. We sing about it, and we pray for it. During Advent we light a candle as we read Matthew 1:23. We wish God to be born and reborn into our lives, into our world.

The story in Isaiah 7 helps us to understand the importance of this word Immanuel. It comes to us in the middle of a story about the king of Judah. These were difficult and trying times. Those much larger and more powerful surrounded the very small nation. How does one keep safe and secure in such a situation? With whom should one's allegiance be cast? Where is there hope?

Ahaz was the king at the time; he was only twenty years old when he took the throne. He ruled for sixteen years. The tasks of leadership were overwhelming. What kind of ruler was he? The book of Second Kings chronicles for us the life and times of each of the kings and their families. The writer evaluates the quality of leadership each king provided. Were their priorities "in line"? Did they keep their allegiances with the LORD? Not Ahaz; he did not do what was right in the LORD's sight (2 Kgs 16:2-4). We do not know why Ahaz became one of the most perverse and unacceptable rulers of Judah. We simply know that he made sacrifices to other gods and that his indiscretions caused confusion and chaos among the people he ruled.

It was during these times that the rulers of Aram (Syria) and Northern Israel mounted an attack on Judah. The thought that these two nations were allied against them caused great fearfulness in Judah. "The

Lectionary Loop
Fourth Sunday of Advent, Year A

Reflections
Integrity Gap

1. What kinds of leaders do we long for in our country? Our churches?

2. Sometimes we hear that a person's private or personal life should be separated (as in "none of our business") from his or her role as a public leader. Do you agree?

heart of Ahaz and the heart of his people shook as the trees of the forest shake before the wind" (Isa 7:2). There were two nations against one.

Ahaz was afraid, and he was part of a community in turmoil. It is often God's gift to calm the fearful soul. Throughout the Old and New Testaments alike we repeatedly read, "Do not fear. I will be with you."

God spoke these words to a fearful Moses as God called him to deliver the Israelites from their oppression in Egypt (Exod 3:12). Years later, God speaks through Second Isaiah to an exiled community, a community that fears it has no future. "Do not fear, for I am with you, do not be afraid, for I am your God; I will strengthen you. I will uphold you with my victorious right hand" (Isa 41:10). Later, the same message is given to the trembling shepherds keeping watch over their flocks (Luke 2:10) and to the women who stand at the entrance of the empty tomb (Mark 16:6).

God speaks to the nation's fear and sends a message of consolation. It is fourfold: "Take heed, be quiet, do not fear, and do not let your heart be faint" (7:4). Ahaz, of course, needed more. In order for Ahaz to be calm, he needed a sign from the LORD that all will be well. He cannot ask God for it, but Isaiah can. And the mysterious and ambiguous words of assurance are spoken, "Look, the young woman is with child and shall bear a son, and shall name him Immanuel . . ." (7:14). The Hebrew word here is rightly translated "young woman." There is a different Hebrew word for "virgin."

It is not the first time in the Old Testament that the birth of a child has been a sign of promise or hopefulness. Think about the births of Isaac, Moses, and Samuel.

Who is this child? There has been a lengthy historical debate. Was this a future king who would rule according to the expectations and desires of the LORD? Was it simply a child who would be born to a Judean woman, one who would someday, in the nation of Judah, experience peace? Perhaps we will never know the identity of the child, but we can know

Reflections
No Fear

1. Have you been a part of a struggling community, where there was fear about survival?
2. What were the signs of hope that enabled you to carry on?

Study Bible

Isaiah 7–8 includes two other symbolic children who are special signs: the prophet's own sons, Shear-jashub and Maher-Shalal-Hash-Baz. See further the "Excursus: Prophets and Sign-Acts" *NISB*, 968.

that, in a frightening and confusing world, there are reminders that God is present with us. Immanuel! When we hear these words of Isaiah during the Advent and Christmas seasons, it is good to remember that they were first uttered during dangerous and confusing times, times when the people's hearts were shaking as trees shake in the wind. These words were intended to bring comfort to Ahaz.

Ahaz, it seems, was not convinced of the surety of God's presence. He decided, the editor of Second Kings tells us, to put his trust instead in the mighty Assyrian army. While we are disappointed in his choice, it invites us to remember times when fear has prompted in us a desperate search for something or someone in whom we can put our hope. It invites us to think of times when we have closed our own eyes to the signs of God's comforting presence around us.

Isaiah presents faith as the believer's only adequate response to God. During the military crisis in chapters 7–9 (735 BCE) and the later one in chapters 36–39 (701 BCE), Isaiah proclaims faith in God as the only alternative to frustration and defeat. The prophet believed that feverish attempts of the king to strengthen his arsenals and defenses and the appeals to the other nations for military support were signs of unbelief. They were indications that the king was putting trust in humanity over God.

Reflections
Immanuel

1. Is God with us? Is God with our nation?

2. What in the world is God doing? What does it mean that Matthew's Gospel uses the words from Isaiah 7 to tell the story of the birth of Jesus? Could it mean that, to Matthew, Jesus was a sign of God's activity in the world? Could Matthew be saying that, through this child, the nation and the world would come to know salvation and peace?

3. Is Jesus the anchor when we are "our hearts are shaking like the branches and leaves of the tree shake in the wind"?

Session 8   Isaiah 9:1-7 and 11:1-9

A Shining Light and a Tree Stump

The messianic hope in the Old Testament was grounded in the belief that some day God would raise up a righteous king from the line of David to rule the people. The people longed for righteousness and peace, and the new king would implement justice. This hope was born out of experiences with kings who failed to live up to this ideal. Thus, in times when the nation was led by kings like Ahaz, there was the hope that a new child would be born, one who would grow and someday be a different kind of ruler, one who would truly live by and exemplify faith in God. In a world where Assyria was the large and constant threat, there came two messianic prophecies: Isaiah 9:2-7 and 11:1-9. Reading them provides us with some sense of what people longed for in a ruler.

The description of the idyllic ruler found in chapter 9 is prefaced by a description of the plight of the people. In 8:11-22 the LORD speaks to Isaiah and warns the prophet not to walk in the way of wayward people. Isaiah is called not to fear what others fear, but to fear only the LORD. Isaiah is called not to be in dread of what others dread, but to dread only the LORD's disapproval. Darkness becomes the formative metaphor that describes the plight of the wayward ones. They will experience no dawn (8:20). They will be distressed and hungry. They will be thrust into thick darkness (8:22).

Then, suddenly and miraculously, the mood changes and a new word of hope is offered. Those who walk in darkness will see a great light. With this

Lectionary Loop
Second Sunday of Advent, Year A

Reflections
Wayward People

1. Who are the wayward people in today's world?

2. How are we the wayward people in the global village?

For an understanding of what it means to "fear God" see Mary Donovan Turner's *Old Testament Words,* (St. Louis: Chalice Press, 2003), 63-65.

light, God's saving action begins and salvation will come. Words can barely express the joyful response of the multitudes. Finally, the light is named. The light is to come through a child. A child will be born, Isaiah tells the community—for us. The son is given—to us. The ruler will be called, "Wonderful Counselor, Mighty God, Everlasting Father, Prince of Peace" (9:6).

The Israelite king was considered sacred in Israel. Monarchy was rooted in the dynasty of David. This tradition was celebrated in worship (see the Royal Psalms 2, 18, 20, 21, 45, 72, 89, 101, 110, 132, 144). Isaiah 9:1-7 is, in all likelihood, a coronation liturgy for a king, perhaps the accession liturgy for Hezekiah or another. But here the liturgy serves another purpose. It is put here to offer a struggling community a word of hope.

There is another word of hope in Isaiah 11. As the chapter begins, the reader finds that Judah is now only a "stump." The stump appears to be dead, but it is not. Here is a new word, an intrusion of good news to the people of Judah who suffer under inept and unfaithful rulers. The character of this new king is described in great detail. Read carefully verses 2-5. The spirit of the LORD will rest upon this special one; three pairs of gifts will be his:

♦ the spirit of wisdom and understanding

♦ the spirit of counsel and might

♦ the spirit of knowledge and fear of the LORD

The text continues by describing what the new king will do. He will judge with righteousness and decide with equity. The text describes a ruler with a single-minded devotion to the community and to justice, a devotion that necessitates an abandonment of his own ambition. With this leadership, the order of the earth will be reestablished, and there will be a peace that affects all creation. What a dream!

The wolf shall live with the lamb, the leopard shall lie down with the kid, the calf and the lion and the fatling together, and a little child shall

Study Bible

See the "Excursus: Royal Psalms," *NISB*, 767.

Reflection
Lion and Lamb

Isaiah 9 and 11 are visions of reconciliation. Opposites are brought into a working whole, ancient antagonisms are resolved. The lion and lamb lie down together.

Where is this reconciliation being formed in church or society today?

lead them. The cow and the bear shall graze, their young shall lie down together, and the lion shall eat straw like the ox. The nursing child shall play over the hole of the asp, and the weaned child shall put its hand on the adder's den. They will not hurt or destroy on all my holy mountain (11:6-9*a*).

This is a vision where children are safe and where the most likely of enemies live side by side, where none will be hurt or destroyed because the whole earth is filled with the knowledge of the LORD.

The editor of First Isaiah places these visions of the ruler to come and of the hope this new kind of ruler will bring in the midst of a description of the stark realities of life. In a subtle but shocking way, Isaiah reminds us that, occasionally, we need to stop and allow ourselves the wonderful privilege of seeing life, not as it is, but as it can be. Ironically, in seeing how the world can be, we are sadly reminded of how it now is. We long for better thing, and Isaiah reminds us that better things come when we ground our lives in God and act faithfully.

These images of the child and the king who was to be born and eventually crowned are used in a new context in the New Testament, to describe some of the qualities of Jesus. New Testament writers, grounded in the Law, Prophets, and Writings of the Old Testament, knew the prophecies of Isaiah. New Testament writers brought forth the words of Isaiah to help the community reflect and understand the significance of the birth, life, and death of Jesus. The messianic prophecies found in Isaiah 9 and 11 were, in their minds, fulfilled.

Study Bible

See the "Excursus: Christian Interpretations of Isaiah's Hymns of the Ideal King," *NISB*, 974-75.

Session 9   Isaiah 12:1-6; Isaiah 25:1-10

Spacious and Wide
Abundant Living

S alvation. What does this word mean to you? To your church community? The word is likely to bring varied thoughts and emotions to the fore.

While Isaiah 12 has escaped the watchful attention and interest of many readers, its six short verses are important to the overall structure of First Isaiah. This psalm brings closure to the first unit of Isaiah. It is the exclamation point, we might say, to the eleven chapters that have gone before it. It offers an affirmative "yes" to the announcements of hopefulness and expectation found in chapters 7, 9, and 11. God, indeed, will offer salvation. We can be so certain of this that we can speak as if it has already happened.

What is this salvation? It is helpful to turn back to the story of Moses and the Exodus narrative. We can assume that First Isaiah is familiar with this story of deliverance. In it, the Israelites had left Egypt and begun their journey toward a land they had never seen. They set up camp between Migdol and the sea, just as the LORD told them to do. When Pharaoh found out that the Israelites had fled from slavery, he regretted giving them permission to go. He took the chariots and the officers and began to pursue the Israelites. The Israelites saw the Egyptians advancing. They were afraid, and they cried out to the LORD and to Moses. Moses said to them, "Do not be afraid, stand firm, and see the deliverance that the LORD will accomplish for you today" (Exod 14:13). The rest of the story, popularized by film and painting, depicts Moses stretching his hand out over the sea and the waves dividing to let the Israelites pass on into free-

---

Reflections
Salvation

1. What are your earliest associations with the word *salvation*?
2. How has your understanding of the word changed over time?

dom. At the end of the story, the narrator says to us, "Thus the LORD saved Israel that day" (Exod 14:30).

Salvation in the Old Testament often has to do with a community. It is the community that experiences it together. It is thought by some scholars that the word *salvation* is related to other words—those meaning spacious and wide. There is, in this understanding, hopefulness that God can deliver us from what restricts, constricts, or oppresses us. Thus, we are—in our salvation—given room, a liberating space within which we can live out our lives abundantly. Salvation is "of this world." It can happen to us over and over again as we are delivered from the difficulties that life brings to us.

Salvation is a poetic word in the Old Testament. It is found in the poetry of the prophets and the psalmists. They sing about the joy of salvation and the wells of salvation. Salvation gives them something to sing about. In Isaiah 12 we have two songs of thanksgiving. In the first (12:1-2), an individual gives thanks for salvation. In the second, a community gives thanks (12:4-6). We know this by the singular and plural verb forms that are used.

The first song clearly demonstrates the understanding that salvation is being delivered from a confining, restricting situation to a better place. The LORD has comforted and delivered. The LORD has become the refuge and defense for the one who is singing. This kind of holy presence is the antidote to fear and lack of confidence.

In the second song, the LORD has brought salvation to the community. The phrase, "wells of salvation" (12:3), leads us to understand a salvation that continually pours forth; it is living water.

This song calls the community to
♦ give thanks

♦ call upon God's name

♦ make known God's deeds among the nations

♦ exalt God's name, and

♦ sing praises.

Reflection
Room for Growth

God's deliverance brings us from a restricted place to a wider place, from restricted freedom to greater freedom.

What new or added responsibilities come with wider or greater freedom? Draw from your experience.

For more on the related meaning of the word salvation, *see Mary Donovan Turner's* Old Testament Words *(St. Louis: Chalice Press, 2003), 66-67.*

Reflections
Not I, but We

Salvation is often seen as individual, private, and personal. Isaiah gives us a different view; salvation is communal or corporate.

1. How does salvation come through the community?

2. Is there a corporate or national "soul" that is in need of salvation?

3. Think about songs, spirituals, and ballads of faithfulness that have been sung in the face of disaster and hopelessness. Think of a time when your own community has sung a rousing and heartfelt doxology of praise after a disaster. Is it important to sing God's praise when some are grieving?

The community is called to this kind of thanksgiving, even when there is little evidence around it that salvation and deliverance will come.

Isaiah 25 offers another important song of thanksgiving. This song is in the midst of Isaiah 24-27, which is often called the "Isaiah Apocalypse." These chapters speak of the end time, a time that will come some day. Much of these chapters is unfamiliar to us. Isaiah 25 plays an important role as a reading during Easter, Easter evening, Pentecost, and All Saints' Day. Perhaps it has made its way into the lectionary because it names some of the longings and yearnings we can have when the more painful realities of our lives overwhelm us. Will it ever be better? What do we have to hope for?

Notice that the first ten verses can be divided into two units. These distinct literary genres help us understand different elements in our worship.

The first unit (25:1-5) is a song of thanksgiving. It gives praise to a God who has done things that are "old, faithful, and sure" (25:1). This song speaks of a God who has been a refuge to the poor and to the needy in distress. This God is shelter and shade.

This song of thanksgiving for what God has already done is followed (in 25:6-10a) by a vision of what God will do. Like Isaiah 2, the vision takes place on a high mountain. Here, the LORD will make a great banquet for all people, complete with rich food and wine. There will be a wonderful world where the death that has swallowed men and women will now be swallowed. Tears will be wiped away; disgrace will be taken away. This wonderful confirmation of God's presence and care is not unanticipated. The people have waited for God to save them. Twice in the vision we are told that they have waited (25:9).

Waiting. It is not a very pleasing word. We can be a very impatient people, and the idea of waiting for something is not comfortable to us. We do not like to wait in line. When making a telephone call, we do not like to be put on hold because that makes us wait. Waiting can bring frustration and anger. It can make us anxious.

Reflection
Wait

Waiting is sometimes experienced as "wasting time" or "losing ground," but it can also be put to creative use.

How do you use waiting creatively?

Rarely do we think of waiting as a "theological" word, but it is. It is an important one, because waiting is related to preparation, expectancy, and hopefulness.

This relationship between waiting and hope makes sense. One waits only when there is hope. The idea of waiting on the LORD is important in the psalms.

♦ "Do not let those who wait for you be put to shame" (25:3a).

♦ "For you I wait all day long" (25:5).

♦ "But those who wait for the LORD shall inherit the land" (37:9).

In Isaiah 25, we read that the people wait for the LORD, and they will not be disappointed. The story in Isaiah 25 ends with confident assurance, a sense of comfort. But there is an ironic twist in Isaiah. In the love song of Isaiah 5, the LORD waits hopefully and expectantly for justice and righteousness, but the LORD waits in vain. The LORD is disappointed. The people who wait for the LORD, however, are never disappointed. Their confidence is not misplaced.

Maintaining the Status Quo

The women of Israel were the singers! They had the responsibility of singing at the festivals when the harvests came, when the wine was blessed. (See Session 5 on Isaiah 5:1-7.) They sang wonderful, joyful songs about the bounty of the crops and the ways they had been blessed by God. Women also sang the sad songs. They sang at funerals; they sang the laments over the dead. They were the professionals who sang about grief, loss, and despair. Isaiah brings a word to the women of Judah. They are singing their joyful songs, but they do not see the corrupt ways of the world around them. They do not notice that people are neglecting to walk with God. They are unaware that people are failing to live up to their covenant responsibilities with the holy God.

"Rise up, you women who are at ease, hear my voice; you complacent daughters, listen to my speech" (32:9). In the midst of the last chapters of First Isaiah as the calls to change and alarm intensify, and as Judah comes closer to her ruin, there is this stirring cry to the women of Judah. The call to them is compelling. "Rise up!" They are called to sing songs of lament and despair over the future of the nation. These are women who are at ease, who are complacent. These descriptive words are repeated for us over and again so that we clearly get a picture of them. Life is now good for them. There is a good harvest and fruitful vine. However, a time to be lamented is coming.

It is difficult for these women to imagine that life will not always be as they were then living it. They

> ## Reflection
> ### Change Agent
>
> What women of the past or present day clearly named the realities of the world around them and, either alone or with other women, brought about social change?

will not always have beautiful houses and food and drink aplenty. There will not always be joyous sounds from the city. And it is difficult for them to imagine that they are called to make changes in the world around them.

Isaiah calls out to them.
Tremble, you women who are at ease,
shudder, you complacent ones;
strip, and make yourselves bare,
and put sackcloth on your loins,
Beat your breasts for the pleasant fields,
for the fruitful vine (32:11-12)

Isaiah sees that the way the nation is living will eventually lead them to disaster. Isaiah knows that the prosperity some in the nation enjoy would be short-lived. There is no justice. There is no righteousness. Unless there is immediate change, disaster is imminent.

The Hebrew word translated as "complacent" in this passage is an interesting one. Sometimes the word is translated "careless." Sometimes "trusting." The women were trusting that their "at ease" way of living would never change and, in trusting that this would be their way of life forever, they became careless. They avoided thought about the plight of others in the community; they avoided thought about their community's priorities and needs.

There is urgency in Isaiah's message. It is the final wake-up call, so to speak. The time to act is now, Isaiah is saying to them. But the people are too short-sighted, too caught up in their own good fortune to notice the wider community around them.

A Conclusion to the Pastor's Bible Study on First Isaiah

There are visions of the final days in Isaiah that bring forth pictures of peace and bounty. One vision comes at the end of First Isaiah, chapter 35. In our complicated journey through First Isaiah we have heard oracles of judgment and astonishing words of hope. We have moved back and forth between God's wrath and

Reflection
Comfortable Living

How do we shake ourselves from insulated and myopic perspectives on life to see beyond our own comfort to the experience of others who are suffering from a lack of justice and righteousness in our neighborhood? In our world?

Teaching Tip
Last Prophecies

Isaiah 35 contains the last prophetic words before the historical narrative in chapters 36-39 that describe the last days of King Hezekiah and the announcement of impending exile. This historical appendix to the book of Isaiah is virtually duplicated and probably borrowed from 2 Kgs 18: 13-20:19. The last prophecies in First Isaiah, then, are found in chapter 35.

love, and we wonder where the story ends. What is the last word, the final image that the editor of First Isaiah wants to leave with us? Is it a harsh word of accusation, a word of impending doom, or a vision of something better? It is the latter. It is a vision akin to the many words of comfort and hope that are brought to the exiles in Isaiah 40–65.

Visions of the final days, when the nation and community are restored, often follow accounts of devastation and destruction. Such is the case here. Read Isaiah 34. It is filled with images of fury, corpses, flowing blood, and swords—a judgment of the nations. This devastation of the nations appears to be the prelude to chapter 35, a vision of the glorious return of the ones who were dispersed to Zion.

Isaiah 35 is filled with the unbelievable! It speaks of a time when the eyes of the blind will be opened, the ears of the deaf unstopped. The lame one will jump; the speechless will sing for joy. In the wilderness, there will be flowing water. Water will be abundant as desert lands turn into running springs. This is a picture of the grand homecoming, when those who have been exiled are brought home.

Verse 35:10 is found also in 51:11 and 52:8. Perhaps it is a stock phrase or song about the second exodus—the return of the exiles back to their homeland. It is filled with exuberant words about singing, joy, and gladness. All sorrow and sighing will flee away. This song is about the great, gathering God. Many of the biblical prophets bring hopeful words by describing this God who will gather the exiles in. (See Zech 10:8-10; Jer 32:37-38; Mic 2:12; Zeph 3:20; Ezek 11:17.)

The prophets also talked about the day when all nations will be gathered together by God, living a peaceful existence. "I am coming to gather all nations and tongues; and they shall come and shall see my glory" (Isa 66:18). That is the vision of Isaiah 35. Along with 2:1-5 and other words of comfort and hope, these texts give testimony to a spirit that, when challenged or oppressed or devastated, imagines a day when things will be better.

Reflections
Dangerous Words

1. How does Isaiah help you to face difficult questions of faith and live in hope?

2. How can Isaiah help us distinguish between facile hope and genuine hope?

3. What is the most troubling aspect of First Isaiah for you?

4. How can understanding the prophets, especially Isaiah, empower your congregation for its important ministries in the world?

According to legend, the evil son and successor to King Hezekiah, Manasseh, put Isaiah to death. This is recorded in a second-century work called The Martyrdom of Isaiah. *It reports that the prophet was sawn apart by the king's men after hiding in a hollow tree.*

Page H. Kelley, Interpreting Isaiah: A Study Guide *(Smyth and Helwys Publishing, Inc., 1991), 1.*

5. What makes prophecy such a dangerous profession?

6. What other prophets do you know who have met an early death?

The prophets had only words to use as their tools, but their words were threatening to the religious and political leaders alike. What makes words so powerful?

HEALING IN GRIEF

A STUDY BY

RICHARD WALLACE

Richard Wallace is author of ten Bible studies on grief. He earned the Th.D. from Luther Seminary in St. Paul, Minnesota where he is associate professor of pastoral care. As an ordained minister in the Evangelical Lutheran Church, he served congregations in Georgia, California, and Minnesota.
He speaks frequently on grief, violence, abuse, recovery, and African American culture.

Outline

Introduction

The Pastor's Bible Study on Healing in Grief

As a child, I often discovered, to my delight, the wonderful things my mother had packed in my lunch box. Though this memory dates me as a child of the late fifties and early sixties (when stay-at-home moms who fixed their children's school lunches were the norm), this image describes how we are similarly gifted and surprised by the church's ministry of response to grief and loss. During those times of grief and loss we discover the resources with which the church has endowed us, unaware of what we are carrying until we need it and can gain access to it. Cyprian of Carthage (ca. 251–256 CE), on the unity of the "catholic" church, wrote, "He cannot have God as a father who does not have the Church as a mother." Cyprian lifts up the image of the church as a nurturer.

As a parish pastor who walked with persons during their times of loss and grief, I was myself comforted by the biblical and liturgical resources of my Lutheran heritage—first, because these ensured that I was not delving into the dark abyss with others, using only my own meager resources to illumine the path; and second, because I was comforted, knowing that those with whom I walked were often also familiar with the same tradition. I could generally be confident when I read, "In my Father's house there are many rooms," that they and I were in a familiar place together. I was convinced that the words of our funeral liturgy could speak to the depths of their experiences of grief and loss better than any words I could manufacture on my own. I have often wondered about what people who were not formed and shaped by a religious tradition or grounded in a sacred text and rit-

Sources

Granger E. Westburg, *Good Grief: A Constructive Approach to the Problem of Loss* (Minneapolis: Fortress, 1979)

Barbara Bartocci, *From Hurting to Happy: Transforming Your Life After Loss* (Notre Dame, Ind. Sorin Books, 2002)

James W. Moore, *When Grief Breaks Your Heart* (Nashville: Abingdon, 1995)

Ronald H. Sunderland, *Getting Through Grief: Caregiving by Congregations* (Nashville: Abingdon, 1993)

Blair Gilmer Meeks, *Standing in the Circle of Grief: Prayers and Liturgies for Death and Dying* (Nashville: Abingdon, 2002)

Andrew J. Weaver, Laura T. Flannelly, and John D. Preston, *Counseling Survivors of Traumatic Events: A Handbook for Pastors and Other Helping Professionals* (Nashville: Abingdon, 2003)

ual, do emotionally and spiritually when confronted by loss and grief.

But it has also been my experience that I can no longer assume a familiarity with these resources, especially across generations. As I have sat in nursing homes and convalescent hospitals and have seen the power of a biblical text come forth as my stuttering tongue spoke it, I have seen in those settings scriptural passages evoke hope because the listeners have been formed and shaped by them. I have seen people who did not need a hymnal or prayer book because they knew the liturgy by heart. There were Alzheimer's patients who, while they could not remember their names, could recall the liturgy. I have wondered to what degree this will be the case for my generation and subsequent generations since, as moderns and postmoderns living in times when tradition and master narratives have been set aside; the forming and shaping that emerges from these texts is at risk.

Faced with this reality, the pastoral task is twofold. First, there is the obvious need to inculcate a familiarity with those biblical texts that can speak to the depths of our experiences of grief and loss. The second task is to expose people to the depths of those texts—in the words of the psalmist, "Deep calls to deep" (42:7). In these Bible studies, we will explore and expose some of these texts with the intent of making them reflexively assessable during times of grief and loss. At the same time, we will attempt to foster what Howard Stone and James Duke describe as "deliberative theology."

In fact, the discussion thus far reflects their description of the dynamics between embedded and deliberative theologies. Of embedded theology they write:

> It is rooted (embedded) in the preaching and practices of the church and its members. It is the implicit theology that Christians live out in their daily lives . . . . The theological messages intrinsic in and communicated by praying, preaching, hymn singing, personal conduct, liturgy, social action or inaction, and virtually everything else people say and do in the name of their Christian faith, fall into this category.

> # Reflection
> ## Biblical Memory and Loss
> When you, as a pastor or lay church worker, visit someone who is sick, do you find that the sick person is able to draw on memory with biblical stories or family narratives? Why?

The way in which these texts functioned for earlier generations is what Stone and Duke mean by embedded theology. What is important in Stone and Duke's discussion is that the words *embedded* and *deliberative* are not judgments against any approach to theology, but, rather, descriptive of how we develop our thoughts about God. For instance, think of the way that we pray, the words that we use, and the way we organize those words that form the prayer. When we are praying, both privately and publicly, embedded theology is forming and shaping us. Similarly, those biblical texts that speak to the depths of our experiences of grief and loss convey the embedded theology that informs the way that we grieve. So, in one sense, these Bible studies will seek to convey the embedded theologies of grief and loss. These theologies, say Stone and Duke, "began in us before we could speak" and have been reinforced by church activities as well as "the life example of our parents, friends, and ministers" (p. 14).

We will be looking at some of the biblical texts that earlier generations knew by heart.

Following a recent worship service, I overheard two of the seniors from the community of faith of which I am a part speaking about their activities for the upcoming week and the arrangements they would have to make. Included in their conversation were arrangements for attending the funeral that had been announced during the service and noted in the bulletin. What struck me was the matter-of-fact way they spoke of attending. As I reflected on this, it seemed that there was something more than just attending involved for them; as retired persons they had the time, and taking time for funerals was part of their living. Further, I thought about reports of those from my generation and later who, perhaps, did not attend any funerals until later in life. I did not attend my first funeral until I was sixteen, but I have heard from my cohorts that they did not attend their first funeral until they were twenty-something or thirty-something. Imagine the difference between the embedded theology of grief and loss for those who attend funerals regularly compared to those who have not been to a funeral until late in life. The comparison is not unlike the difference

Source

Howard W. Stone and James O. Duke, *How to Think Theologically* (Minneapolis: Augsburg Fortress Press, 1996), 13.

117

that exists between generations of African Americans when it comes to singing "Lift Every Voice," also known as the Negro National Anthem. My generation still has to read the words, but those of earlier generations know the words by heart. The words and the images have become part of them. Imagine how the theology of grief and loss in the words, "Where, O death, is your sting?" (1 Cor 15:55), becomes embedded in those for whom attendance at funerals is a part of living.

As we are looking at the texts that convey the embedded theologies of grief and loss, we will also engage in what Stone and Duke describe as "deliberative theology." "Deliberative theology," they write, "is the understanding of faith that emerges from a process of carefully reflecting upon the embedded convictions (p.16)." They give the example of a child who falls into a swimming pool and drowns. The anguished family asks why God let their child die. To Stone and Duke, this "Why?" represents a "question of faith for which their embedded theology had not prepared them." Embedded theology provides comfort, but deliberative theology seeks understanding.

Instead of utilizing these texts as bandages to cover up the open wounds of grief and loss, they will be utilized to expose the wounds to the light that can heal.

Given the themes that have been discussed in this introduction, the first Bible study is on 1 Thessolonians 4:13-18: "But we do not want you to be uninformed, brothers and sisters, about those who have died, so that you may not grieve as others do who have no hope" (v. 13). This text has an embedded theology that appears to speak against excessive grief. Next, we will look at several psalms, designated by Walter Brueggemann as "lament psalms" in his article "Formfulness for Grief." Following the lament psalms, we will look at several texts that speak to grief and loss in broad terms guided, for example, by Mitchell and Anderson's *All Our Losses, All Our Griefs: Resources for Pastoral Care*; Pauline Boss's *Ambiguous Loss: Learning to Live With Unresolved Grief*; and the grief and loss experienced by what Andrew Sung Park described as the "sinned against." The concluding Bible studies will look at some of the classical biblical texts for funerals.

> ## Teaching Tip
> ### Embedded and Deliberative Theologies
> Discuss examples of the embedded theology of comfort and the deliberative theology of faith seeking understanding. Show how both are important in the life of faith. Do people tend to fluctuate between the two depending on their needs and circumstances?

Session 1   1 Thessalonians 4:13-18

Grieving With Hope

In his introduction to First Thessalonians in the *New Interpreter's Study Bible*, Raymond Collins writes that Timothy, Paul's faithful companion, returned from his visit with the Christians in Thessalonica with a generally positive report on their situation, but seems to have hinted at a deficiency in the Thessalonians' life of faith: "Night and day we pray most earnestly that we may see you face to face and restore whatever is lacking in your faith" (3:10).

Furthermore, according to Collins (see Study Bible), this report prompts Paul to write the letter, which is the most ancient of Christian writings, even predating Mark's Gospel.

Perhaps the hope that is forseen in 4:13 is lacking in the faith of the Christians in Thessalonica. These Christians lived in the city of Thessalonica approximately twenty years after the death and the resurrection of Jesus. Their city was home to a multitude of religious cults in addition to a strong Jewish presence. During this time, there was the anticipation of the immediate return of Jesus and the end of history. Imagine the anxiety generated between the anticipation of Jesus' return and the reality of the suffering that the Christians in Thessalonica were experiencing (see 2:13-16). Added to this anxiety was the question of what would happen to their loved ones who died before Jesus' return.

It is with this question that the passage seems to speak most directly to our contemporary situation. We, like the Christians of Thessalonica, live in a context of competing faith claims, caught between the "now" and the "not yet." Dan Browning writes that modern individuals live on "bits and pieces, yes, scraps of meaning."

Lectionary Loop
Year A, Proper 27

Study Bible

Raymond F. Collins's "Introduction to First Thessalonians," *NISB*, 2115-21; see also the "Excursus: Day of the Lord," *NISB*, 2126.

Reflections
Return

1. What do you think happens to your loved ones when they die?

2. Do you think that Jesus will return? In what manner?

119

Perhaps we encounter this lack of unity when we sit down with family members to prepare a funeral and find ourselves dealing with the various scraps of meaning that the family members want to bring to the funeral. In such settings, we may find ourselves struggling to ensure that the Christian meaning is more than one scrap of meaning among many. For example,

What is distinctive about the ways that Christians grieve? In Thessalonica two thousand years ago, as it will be the case today, grief becomes an "evangelistic" act. Instead of taking it for granted that the "Apostles' Creed" will be included in the funeral, we may have to explain the significance of its inclusion.

Paul's letter to the Christians in Thessalonica—explains to them what is distinctively Christian about the way they grieve, so that they may not grieve like those who have no hope. Then and now, Christians sustain hope that their dearly departed will be included in the resurrection. Christians of the first century lived in a culture in which many persons believed either in the natural immortality of the soul or in immortality conferred by rites of initiation into the many cults. Paul's letter is intended for those of us who are attempting to live in the sure and certain hope of the resurrection, while existing in a cultural context that is defined by the denial of death.

Contrary to belief in the natural immortality of the soul, immortality conferred by initiation into a cult, or denial of death, Christian hope resides in the resurrection of Jesus Christ: "For since we believe that Jesus died and rose again, even so, through Jesus, God will bring with him those who have died" (1 Thess 4:14). Christian hope is always countercultural. Flannery O'Connor, who wrote with a disturbing realism, said to a friend that she wrote the way she did precisely because she was a Christian and that there is "nothing harder or less sentimental than Christian realism." In other words, Christian hope is not based on denying the reality of death. In fact, because of the hope that is grounded in the resurrection of Jesus Christ, Christians can confront death in the sure and certain hope of their own resurrection. Therefore, Christian funerals need not be occasions

Reflections
Christian Grief

1. How do Christians grieve differently than those who are not followers of Jesus?

2. How is the life of a Christian a witness to those who survive?

3. What are the "usual" components of funerals in your religious tradition?

4. Which of these prayers, practices, or lessons do you find meaningful and which, in your estimation, have lost their effectiveness?

Reflection
Counterculture

How do we hold onto our faith in the midst of cultural contexts that are contrary to what we believe to be true?

Source

Leander E. Keck, "The First Letter of Paul to the Thessalonians," *in The Interpreter's One-Volume Commentary on the Bible: Including the Apocrypha with General Articles* (Nashville: Abingdon, 1971), 871.

where hope is sustained through suppressing the full range of emotions that are associated with grief. Crying and feelings of sadness are not in themselves signs of the lack of hope. Grieving with hope means giving vent to the full range of our emotions.

By extension, Paul's description of those who had died, whom he referred to as "those who had fallen asleep" (NRSV variant in 4:13), was not an attempt to lessen the blow of the reality of death by calling it something less offensive. Instead, it conveyed the belief in the temporary status of death, a status that had been achieved by the resurrection of Jesus Christ. "For this we declare to you by the word of the Lord, that we who are alive, who are left until the coming of the Lord, will by no means precede those who have died" (4:15).

To our contemporary ears, a statement such as "Grandmother has fallen asleep in the Lord," may sound like language intended to lessen the blow of the reality of death, or may sound like something you say to children as a way to make death analogous to their experience of rest. However, as we explore this passage and Paul's intent we see that it is a pure form of the gospel. Because of Paul, one gains a renewed appreciation for the words, "Rest In Peace" (RIP). These words can be much more than a pious saying to put on someone's tombstone; the words can be an affirmation of faith.

First Thessalonians 4:15-18 is apocalyptic literature because we recognize the symbols and expectations that are present in the book of Revelation. The late Harry Mumm, professor of New Testament at Pacific Lutheran Theological Seminary, called the book of Revelation a theological shot in the arm for Christians during a time of persecution. Current historical research indicates that there probably was no official persecution of churches by the Roman government. However, apocalyptic thinking, and Scripture in general, still provides Christians with an inoculation against hopelessness during times of grief.

The anxieties of the Christians in Thessalonica are generated by the deaths of their loved ones before the

Source

Peter S. Hawkins, "Flannery O'Connor," *in Listening for God: Contemporary Literature and the Life of Faith,* eds., Paula J. Carlson and Peter S. Hawkins (Minneapolis: Augsburg Fortress, 1994), 15.

Reflection
Epitaphs

Have you ever come across or thought about meaningful epitaphs?

Study Bible
Parousia

See special note on *parousia* and discussion of 4:13-18 in *NISB,* 2119-20.

Parousia. In the end, the question is how these images innoculate us against hopelessness, so that we may not grieve as others do, as others who have no hope. "Therefore, encourage one another with these words" (4:18).

Is God Big Enough to Handle Our Grief?

How many times have we have heard someone express her or his true emotions about a recent loss and then immediately follow with an apology for saying out loud what was actually felt inside? They may say something like, "This is how I am feeling, but I know that what I am feeling is wrong, that I should not be feeling this way," or, "I should not be angry with God for allowing this to happen. I should not be wondering about why God did not hear or listen to my prayers." How many times have we ourselves felt what the psalmist dared to utter aloud?

> Will the Lord spurn forever, and never again
>   be favorable?
> Has his steadfast love ceased forever? Are his
>   promises at an end for all time?
> Has God forgotten to be gracious? Has he in
>   anger shut up his compassion?
>   *Selah* (77:7-9).

Two of the dominant emotions related to loss are a sense of isolation and the feeling of loneliness. What tends to intensify these senses of isolation and loneliness are the supposedly unacceptable reactions. Walter Brueggemann suggests that grief takes on form in the lament psalms of the Bible. He writes that, "by the use of the form, the grief experience is made bearable and, it is hoped, meaningful. The form makes the experience formful just when it appeared to be formless and therefore deathly and destructive."

However, in order for this kind of form to make sense in modern faith communities, the lament psalms must become part of our public worship.

Reflections
Anger

1. What are the dynamics and the implications of anger toward God?
2. Can you envision regular use of lament psalms in your worship services?

What would be the advantages? The disadvantages?

Study Bible

See the "Excursus: Enemies and Imprecations," *NISB*, 857.

In the opening words to his article, Brueggemann states the problem quite clearly: The lament psalms offer important resources for Christian faith and ministry, even though they have been largely purged from the life of the church and its liturgical use. Such purging attests to the alienation between the Bible and the church.

Lester Meyer (see other Resources, this page) surveys the Lutheran *Book of Worship*, the Episcopalian *Book of Common Prayer*, and the *Lectionary for Mass: The Roman Missal* and observes that the lament psalms are conspicuously absent in all three. He quotes Brueggemann's commentary on the psalms, saying, "It is no wonder that the church has intuitively avoided these psalms. They lead us into dangerous acknowledgments of how life really is."

Picture the results if these psalms were to become part of our public worship. Besides being disruptive and jarring, the results would be similar to what happens when addiction or abuse get talked about from the pulpit; the feelings and experiences that isolate and separate individuals from the community are legitimized, and strugglers gain their voice. A modest goal is to begin this process by proposing the lament psalms as texts for Bible study. The goal is to initiate a familiarity with the lament psalms that might, in some small measure, approximate the familiarity of Psalm 23:38-39.

While driving, I heard a radio commercial for scientology that directed listeners to consider scientology if they found that their "God-concept" was problematic. My rejoinder to the frequent commercial, often spoken in the privacy of my car: "I do not have a God-concept, but a relationship." I mention this because in the lament psalms we see the importance of a relationship between God and God's people. It is a relationship that is big enough to contain the fullness of the emotions associated with grief. We see that the psalmists dared to speak what it was they were feeling, both the praises and the complaints, and the ground did not open and swallow them up, nor did God strike them with lightening.

The lament psalms are intensely personal and inti-

Sources

Walter Brueggemann, "Formfulness of Grief," *Interpretation* 31 (3), (1977): 263-265.

Other Resources

Lester Meyer, "A Lack of Laments in the Church's Use of the Psalter," *Lutheran Quarterly* 7 (1), (1993): 70f.

Artur Weiser, *The Psalms: A Commentary* (Philadelphia: Westminster Press, 1962), 66.

Walter Brueggemann, *The Message of the Psalms: A Theological Commentary,* Augsburg Old Testament Studies (Minneapolis: Augsburg, 1984), 53.

Study Bible

See Toni Craven and Walter Harrelson, "The Psalms," *NISB,* 750.

mate. This is why they can speak so powerfully to our own experiences of grief and loss.

Some Lament Psalms to Consider

- In 77:11-20, we see a pattern that is frequently repeated: lament followed by praise. Psalm 13:1 is classic in this sense. "How long, O LORD? Will you forget me forever? How long will you hide your face from me?" is then followed by petition in verses 3-4, and concluded in verses 5-6 with the affirmation of God's steadfast love.

- Psalm 88 is an excellent psalm to probe the depths of emotions associated with grief, particularly the feelings of isolation and abandonment. Often, whenever there has been a loss as a result of death, tremendous support immediately follows the loss, but in the months following the bereaved find themselves increasingly alone.

- Psalm 22 contains infamous words: "My God, my God, why have you forsaken me? Why are you so far from helping me, from the words of my groaning?" (22:1). This verse offers yet another opportunity to probe feelings of having been alienated.

- Words from Psalm 6:6-7 seem more than adequately to capture the experience of grief.

- Because enemies and foes were often left unspecified, they may be broadly identified. Since many believed that illness was a punishment for sin and, therefore, an attack, the enemies and foes could very well be the illnesses themselves. Psalm 35 is a good example of this belief.

- In spite of holding God responsible for all that is happening to him, the psalmist maintains a relationship to God that results in praying for healing.

Teaching Tip
Psalms of Lament and Today's Context

Approximately forty percent of the psalms are petitions and laments. Based upon the list compiled by Lester Meyer and another one compiled by Artur Weiser, the psalms of individual lament are the following: 3–5; 7; 13; 17; 22; 25–27; 31; 35; 42; 51; 52; 55–57; 59; 64; 77; 88; 94; 102; 109; 120; 123; 140–41; and 143. The psalms of community lament are the following: 11; 58; 60; 74; 79–80; 83; 90; 108; 123; 129; 137.

Ask three or four persons to read a psalm of lament. Ask the group if they can think of a situation or person that would find it meaningful

Reflection
Blame

When confronted with overwhelming pain and suffering, some persons blame God, while others seem to become more pious. What appears to make a difference in these reactions?

Grief and the Korean Concept of Han

A host of persons have expanded the definition of "grief" so that now it is understood as the response to any kind of loss. Kenneth R. Mitchell and Herbert Anderson, have constructed a typology in *All Our Losses, All Our Griefs*. They identify six major types of losses:

♦ *Material Loss:* the loss of a physical object or of familiar surroundings to which one has an important attachment.

♦ *Relationship Loss*: the ending of opportunities to relate oneself to, talk with, share experiences with, make love to, touch, settle issues with, fight with, and otherwise be in the emotional and/or physical presence of a particular other human being.

♦ *Intrapsychic Loss*: the experience of losing an emotionally important image of oneself, losing the possibilities for "what might have been," abandonment of plans for a particular future, the dying of a dream. Although related to external experiences, it is itself an entirely inward experience.

♦ *Functional Loss:* powerful grief evoked when we lose some of the muscular or neurological functions of the body.

♦ *Role Loss:* being stripped of a specific social role or of one's accustomed place in a social network.

♦ *Systemic Loss:* when the interactional system, in which patterns of behavior develop over time, is disrupted or destroyed.

This typology helps us understand how someone's reaction to a current loss may be related to the accumulated losses she or he has experienced within a given time frame.

Source

Kenneth R. Mitchell and Herbert Anderson, *All Our Losses, All Our Griefs: Resources for Pastoral Care* (Philadelphia: Westminster Press, 1983), 36-45, *passim*.

Identifying other losses someone has recently experienced helps us understand how that person may respond to the loss she or he is currently facing. The empty nest or a recent retirement may, in the face of some other loss, block the usual movement through the grief process. One loss is standing in the way of the "other mourning" that needs to take place.

Individual and community laments in the book of Psalms provide a language and a forum for people who are experiencing accumulated losses. If we consider the accumulated losses experienced by the people Israel as a result of the Babylonian exile, we may gain a deeper appreciation for Psalm 137 and its ability to speak to the multiple losses that people whom we encounter in our current ministries have experienced. Perhaps there is nothing we can say; our words would be inadequate. The inadequacy of words to address someone's accumulated losses is a universal theme; one often found in the Bible (think of Job's friends when they first arrive! Job 2:11-13).

The power of Psalm 137, which is one of the community laments, is that it can speak for us when our own words will be inadequate. Imagine the impact upon public worship if this psalm was read from the perspective of people who could not muster the strength to sing their own songs in a strange land because they were so overwhelmed by their accumulated losses. Verse 9 ("Happy shall they be who take your little ones and dash them against the rock!") could be heard as the bitterness and resentment that fester when people are overwhelmed by their accumulated losses. Renita Weems, in her book *Battered Love* invites us to think about such an impact when she imagines a worship service where an African American child recites this psalm in the midst of the congregation. The congregation's reaction to this recitation of the notorious verse is telling. Perhaps we ought to regard all those imprecatory psalms (Psalms 7; 35; 58; 59; 69; 83; 109; 137; 140) as the overwhelmed speaking the unspeakable and uttering the unutterable to a God with whom they have an intimate relationship.

Reflection
Loss and Losses

When an older person loses a spouse through death, what are some of the other typical losses she or he has experienced or is experiencing at the time of the partner's death?

Source

David K. Switzer, "Grief and Loss," *Dictionary of Pastoral Care and Counseling,* Gen. Ed., Rodney Hunter (Nashville: Abingdon Press, 1990), 472.

Reflections
What to Say?

1. How do we speak and what do we say to those who are overwhelmed by their accumulated losses?
2. What are the inappropriate things to say?

If grief and loss abound and accumulate across cultures as part of the human condition, one type of grief is indeed caused by others. Racism, sexism, and classism are grief experiences for their victims. To explain the weighty effect of this grief, theologian Andrew Sung Park develops this concept of *"han"* in *The Wounded Heart of God: The Asian Concept of Han and the Christian Doctrine of Sin.* "Han is the abysmal experience of pain . . . . Han produces sadness, resentment, aggression, and helplessness. It is the hardened heart that is grieved by oppression and injustice."

The words and images of Psalm 58:6-9 appear to capture the experience of the Korean concept of *han*:

> O God, break the teeth in their mouths; tear
>   out the fangs of the young lions, O LORD!
> Let them vanish like water that runs away;
>   like grass let them be trodden down and
>   wither.
> Let them be like the snail that dissolves into
>   slime; like the untimely birth that never
>   sees the sun.
> Sooner than your pots can feel the heat of
>   thorns, whether green or ablaze, may he
>   sweep them away!

Hopelessness as the result of oppression is not sin, but *han*.

Not being able to sing the Lord's song in a strange land (Ps 137:4) is han.

The enemies in Psalm 58 are unspecified. Could it not be that the enemies might represent anything that threatens hope? Therefore, we might understand that one can become so oppressed by losses that she or he becomes hopeless. Instead of regarding it as sin it should be regarded as han.

In the African American and Jewish cultures, Andrew Sung Park observes that the psalms of lament are expressed with melancholy music:

The blues and Negro spirituals of African Americans epitomize this passive sad collective han. The frequent minor intervals and the repetition

Sources

Renita Weems, *Battered Love: Marriage, Sex, and Violence in the Hebrew Scriptures* (Minneapolis: Fortress Press, 1995), 107-109, *passim.*

See also the "Excursus: Enemies and Imprecations," *NISB,* 857.

Sources

Richard Wallace, "Racism, Grief, Chemical Abuse and Dependency, and African-American Males: Towards A Conceptual Model of Pastoral Care" (Ph.D. diss., Luther Seminary, 1996), 1.

Andrew Sung Park, *The Wounded Heart of God: The Asian Concept of Han and the Christian Doctrine of Sin* (Nashville: Abingdon Press, 1993), 15, 16, 40.

Reflections
To Despair is Han

1. What are some of the social/cultural processes of rejection of persons that leave the victims feeling loss as grief?

2. Why do some Christians think that chronic despair is self-indulgent?

3. How do you distinguish between despair and chronic depression?

of the first line in the usual three-line stanza evoke the deep melancholy of their collective soul.

The songs of the Jewish people are quite melancholic as well. Many songs end in minor keys, communicating their mournful spirit. The underlying ethos of the Jewish people is han.

Our own expressions of grief, no matter what form or fashion they take, can be patterned after the form of the lament psalms, where complaint and praise are usually present together. Therefore, before we move to praise and thanksgiving, we can be honest about our feelings. God can handle it.

Reflections

Is Despair a Form of Sin?

Some Christians think that depression can be self-indulgent, which would be a form of sin. Mental health professionals claim that one in four persons will, at some point, suffer from a serious case of depression.

1. How do doctors treat despair? When is medication the answer? When does a person need to change behaviors?
2. How can a friend recognize if despair is chronic depression?
3. Is there a spiritual difference between depression and despair?

For more information on depression and its symptoms, see the National Institute of Mental Health's website, **www.nimh.nih.gov**.

A Grieving Parent

The death of a child is an assault to our senses and pushes us to ask, "Why does God allow this to happen?" That is why this passage is particularly troublesome. Why does God spare the life of David, who has committed the sin, but causes the child to die on the seventh day? Was not this child innocent? On some level, parents whose children precede them in death are themselves struggling with why God took the child and spared them. Rather than avoiding the difficulties that passages like this one create, they ought to be confronted, for its messiness and ambiguity reflect the messiness and ambiguity of the lives that we live.

Whenever we experience any kind of suffering, the feeling that we have done something to deserve it creeps in, despite our redemption bought by Jesus' blood and righteousness. We wonder, "Is this punishment for some deed out of my past? Is God punishing me because of some unrequited sin? What have I done to deserve this?" It seems to me that, quite contrary to Harold S. Kushner, who wrote the book *When Bad Things Happen to Good People*, there are many of us who function at a deeply hidden level with the notion that "Bad Things Happen To Me Because I am a Bad Person." David commits the sin, and his child dies. The child's death is retribution for David's sin, pure and simple.

The doctor tells a parent that his or her child has an inoperable, terminal disease and that death is imminent. In spite of the prognosis, the grieving parent still holds out hope for a miracle, a reversal of the immediately inevitable, while at the same time waiting for death.

> **Source**
>
> See Session 2, "Is God Big Enough to Handle Our Grief?"

> **Source**
>
> Harold S. Kushner, *When Bad Things Happen to Good People* (New York: Schocken Books, 1981).

Verse 16, "David therefore pleaded with God for the child," drips with the pathos of an already grieving parent. How many parents have pleded with God to heal a child suffering from leukemia or some other disease whose process is named in the words of Psalm 38:3? "There is no soundness in my flesh because of your indignation; there is no health in my bones." How many parents have occupied the chapels in hospitals and enlisted their families and friends in pleading with God for the child? How many parents have come to God, hoping that God had just one more miracle for their child?

An implicit assumption is that this child's disease and death were the will of God. However, if this were the case, why is David pleading with God? Does David's pleading anticipate the pleading of Jesus in the garden? "Father, if you are willing, remove this cup from me; yet, not my will but yours be done" (Luke 22:42).

If it is God's will for a child to suffer and die, I take the view of Dr. Rieux, a character from the novel *The Plague* by Albert Camus, the French existentialist. During the height of a plague in the Algerian city of Oran, Dr. Rieux, Father Paneloux, and others witness the prolonged agony of a dying child.

A moment after the child dies, Rieux rushes from the room, a bewildered look on his face. When Paneloux tries to stop him, Rieux turns to him fiercely: "Ah, that child, anyhow, was innocent, and you know it as well as I do!" Overcome by the child's death, Rieux goes outside and sits on a bench. Paneloux joins him, urging him to love even that which passes human understanding. Rieux shakes his head. "No, Father, I have a very different idea of love. And until my dying day I shall refuse to love a scheme of things in which small children are put to torture."

While we tend to think of a grieving parent from the North American context—where the scene might be one of parents and immediate family gathered around the bed of their dying child in the latest-equipped ICU—let us not forget the grieving parents of children who die from malnutrition, the collateral damage of

---

Reflection
Grief and Guilt

Do you know of people who have added guilt to grief because they believe the death of a dear one was caused by their hidden sin?

Reflection
Grief and Loss of Faith

Do you know of someone who has turned against God because he or she believes God has taken a loved one through death?

Source

James Cone, *Black Theology and Black Power* (New York: Seabury Press, 1969) 123f, citing Albert Camus, *The Plague*, trans. by Stuart Gilbert (New York: Modern Library, 1948), 196f.

war, the "Columbine effect," or a hail of bullets from a drive-by shooting.

Marjorie Hewitt Suchocki may offer some insights about David and the pleading of other parents facing the death of a child. She writes that "prayers, even when specific, are offered with an openness toward well-being for the one for whom we pray, and then the prayers are released."

She seems to be saying, pray for the miracle and then (if I might borrow a phrase from recovery people), "Let go and let God." She calls prayer a partnership with God, not a manipulation of God. This is interesting in light of the stories we have all heard where someone promised service to God if God would grant a request. What Suchocki is challenging is the notion that David's pleading, and that of other parents confronting the imminent death of a child, is an attempt to bargain with God. Although bargaining with God may be part of our grief process, David's fasting and prayers were sincere actions that were not intended to manipulate God into doing what he wanted.

A recent saying often heard in public worship is, "When praises go up, blessings come down," Such sentiment treats God as a slot machine, with praises going in and blessings coming out. The problem is that the blessings pay out with the same level of probability that is experienced from actual Las Vegas slot machines. So if we can just get the correct praises, the blessings will surely follow, right? Perhaps David did not plead or fast enough, or Jesus, who prayed so earnestly that his sweat became like great drops of blood falling down on the ground (Luke 22:44), did not pray hard enough.

Finally, what are we to make of David's behavior following the death of the child whom he had asked God to spare? His servants are surprised that, after the child's death, David readily breaks his fast. He responds:

> "While the child was still alive, I fasted and wept; for I said, 'Who knows? The LORD may be gracious to me, and the child may live.' But now he is dead; why should I fast? Can I bring him

Reflections
Presuppositions
1. What are some examples of prayer used to manipulate God?
2. How would you distinguish the sincere prayers of grieving parents for their sick child from manipulative prayers?

Source

Majorie Hewitt Suchocki, *In God's Presence: Theological Reflections on Prayer* (St. Louis: Chalice Press, 1996), 36, 65.

Teaching Tips
Difficult Scriptures
Discuss the following questions:

1. Many difficult and troubling texts, like the lament psalms, are omitted from public worship. What are your feelings about such omissions?
2. Failure to address difficult issues in the church may contribute to bigger problems later. Could this principle also be applied to the Bible?
3. How would you handle difficult biblical texts in a church setting?

Source

Walter Brueggemann, "The Formfulness of Grief," *Interpretation* 31(3) (1977).

back again? I shall go to him, but he will not return to me" (2 Sam 12:21-23).

Is this simply what the healthy resolution of grief looks like? In his commentary on 2 Samuel 12:15*b*-23, Walter Brueggemann says that David "moves quickly from the feeble realm of death to the vitality of life. He dresses, he worships, and he eats. He resumes life."

Clearly, this is easier said than done but is, nevertheless, necessary. We know that someone's grief work is progressing in a healthy manner when she or he can become interested once again in the things of life. As those who walk with grieving parents, we may able to contribute to the healing process in a modest way by affirming God's presence in their lives in spite of the absence of the miraculous.

Source

Walter Brueggemann, *First and Second Samuel, Interpretation: A Bible Commentary for Teaching and Preaching* (Louisville: John Knox Press, 1990), 283.

Session 5   Psalm 113:1-9

The Grief of the Childless

In addition to the wonderful image of a God who gives the barren woman a home, Psalm 113:9 gives us some indication of the status and fate of childless women in ancient Hebrew society. Andrew Sung Park demonstrates how this status was looked upon in Asian societies, and he lists the seven eligible grounds for divorce according to Confucian principles (see Reflections).

Married women in China, Korea, and Japan have suffered under such unfair rules. In contrast, their husbands could have extramarital sexual relations, keep concubines, commit theft, and be talkative. In a case of failure to give birth to a son, a husband's parents usually pressured him to divorce the wife. Since a divorced woman was rejected by her own family, her husband's family, as well as by society, most women were willing to accept anything to keep their marriage intact, including concubinage. While we might agree that the status and fate of childless women has considerably improved since Hebrew society of the Old Testament and the Ch'ing dynasty, we would also have to agree that, in some places, a stigma remains for those who either have no children at all or are not able to produce any sons.

(Another passage to consider on the grief of the childless is Isaiah's prophecy regarding God's blessing to the eunuchs; Isa 56:3*b*-5).

Thus far, we have talked about how familiarity with biblical texts that are utilized in public worship form and shape us. We also made note of the lost possibilities for forming and shaping as a result of the intentional

> ## Reflections
> ### Cultural Bias on Childbearing
> The Confucian principles for divorce are called *Chi-chu-chih-e* in China, *Chil-Guh-Chi-Ach* in Korea, and *Shichiyo no sei* in Japan. Beginning under the Ch'ing dynasty (1644-1912) in China, there have been seven grounds under which a man could arbitrarily divorce his wife:
> - If she behaves disobediently to her parents-in-law.
> - If she fails to give birth to a son.
> - If she is talkative.
> - If she commits adultery.
> - If she is jealous of her husband's concubine.
> - If she carries a malignant disease.
> - If she commits theft.
> 1. How does the Bible deal with the issue of women who cannot bear children?
> 2. Is there such a stigma in your part of the world?

omission of certain texts. Now I want us to reflect on what forming and shaping occurs with the inclusion of texts like Psalm 127:3-5 in public worship:

> Sons are indeed a heritage from the LORD,
>> the fruit of the womb a reward.
> Like arrows in the hand of a warrior are the
>> sons of one's youth. Happy is
> the man who has his quiver full of them.
>> He shall not be put to shame
> when he speaks with his enemies in the gate.

What are the childless ones in our congregations hearing when such a text is read?

I am going to speculate that there is more familiarity with Psalm 127:3-5 than there is with Psalm 113:9 or Isaiah 56:3*b*-5—no doubt due in some part to the positive and happy messages in this psalm as opposed to the uncomfortable images of barren women and eunuchs.

I wonder if we ever stop and consider how the childless might hear this Psalm? What is the embedded theology that is being conveyed? I will never forget the time my wife, also a pastor, called my attention to the disjointedness of a song the youth choir was singing one morning; it included repeated lyrics of how blessed they were because they had their feet and their hands, while there was a quadriplegic child sitting in her wheelchair as they sang in that sanctuary.

As you may recall from the introduction, deliberative theology is the result of reflecting on embedded theology. When we are pushed to consider what it means for the childless when we read such texts, we then, in the words of Stone and Duke, move into the realm of deliberative theology. Moving into the realm of deliberative theology may assist the childless with the kind of grieving related to what Mitchell and Anderson described as intrapsychic loss (see Session 3).

The deliberative theology that facilitates the grieving from intrapsychic losses is an understanding that our relationship with God does not mean things are supposed to turn out the way we want them to or think they should. Faith in God does not guarantee a certain

Source

See sidebar on sources in Session 2 for titles by Walter Brueggemann and Lester Meyer on how texts in public worship that form and shape us.

Study Bible

See the "Excursus: Honor and Shame," *NISB*, 1456-57.

Source

Howard W. Stone and James O. Duke, *How to Think Theologically* (Minneapolis: Augsburg Fortress Press, 1996).

future. In fact, it seems to me that faith in God assures adventures that consist of passing through interesting nooks and crannies and unexpected turns in the road. Often times the question is, "Do I give up my notion of the way things are supposed to be, or do I follow where God might be leading me?" For the childless and those longing for a son, it means additionally letting go of the society's definitions of value and worth. Psalm 113 is subtle but radical, for it praises God for acting contrary to the society's definitions of value and worth.

Without casting judgment on those who feel compelled to pursue even artificial means for conception through the current science and technology of fertility, let us reflect on how much of that may be driven by the embedded theology that might lead them to believe that their self-worth is determined by their ability to give birth to their own children. Let us also reflect on how the embedded theology ("Sons are indeed a heritage from the LORD") is related to the advances in the science and technology of fertility that now create the possibility of predetermining the gender of one's child and the consequences of such developments. And, of course, we cannot overlook the ancient patriarchal preferences for male children as we hear such a text.

One obvious place that our reflections will take us is adoption as a true blessing from God rather than a consolation prize.

The God who gives the barren woman a home, making her the joyous mother of children, suggests an image of how God abundantly provides. When God blesses us with something that at first does not appear to be of great value, there is usually an overabundance. With all of the children who are waiting to be adopted and often end up in foster care, there are many would-be parents who are missing out on God's abundant blessings. In making this claim about adoption, I am not underestimating the emotional challenges that adopting parents may find themselves facing. While the *home* in Psalm 113:9 might be regarded as the heavenly home, I regard the congregation as a home for both the barren woman and the eunuch, who become a joyous mother and an "un-dry

---

Reflection
Adoption

What is the attitude in church toward the issue of adoption? Is it truly seen as a blessing from God or just a consolation prize for a barren couple? What might be some ways of changing this view if it persists?

137

tree" (Isa 56:3) to the children in the congregation Many of us have been formed and shaped by those who were called "the mothers and fathers of the church."

Finally, we must regard the birth of all children as a blessing from God. Not only does this mean that daughters are as valued as sons, but also that the term "illegitimate child" is no longer a valid term, and that the quadriplegic and the differently-abled are indeed gifts in the heritage from the Lord.

Session 6   Romans 8:26-39

Unsanctioned Grief

How does the family grieve when there has been a suicide in its ranks, and how can the community of faith offer support and comfort? I recall officiating at the funeral of a child who had committed suicide. Because of the circumstances, the funeral could not be held in the sanctuary of the deceased child's church. I therefore agreed to conduct a graveside service for the family.

What I carried from that experience was the pallor that hung over the grave, the family's sense that their loss and grief were unsanctioned and illegitimate. They were grieving the loss of a child who would not bless them with grandchildren; the future that they had hoped for with all its promise was dashed upon the rock of their child's act of desperation, desperation they would forever grieve because they could not touch it with their own capacity to love. They were grieving this loss with very little support and care from their faith community, while being further ostracized by a society that regards their grief as outside of the norms of respectability.

There are six suicide episodes recorded in the Bible: Judges 9:54; Judges 16:28-31; 1 Samuel 31:1-6; 2 Samuel 17:23; 1 Kings 16:18-19, and Matthew 27:3-5. What is interesting about all of the biblical suicides is that, despite their tragic nature , there is not an inherent judgment against the acts themselves. In fact, the view that suicide is an unpardonable sin did not come about until the fourth century. Suicide was a "fairly common occurrence" in the early church, notes Paul W. Pretzel, and was not condemned since the church

Lectionary Loop
Year A, Proper 12

Reflection
Suicide
What are the most prevalent attitudes toward suicide in your faith community?

Study Bible
See the "Excursus: Suicide," *NISB*, 436-7.

Source
Paul W. Pretzel, "Suicide (Ethical Issues)," *Dictionary of Pastoral Care and Counseling* (Nashville: Abingdon Press 1990), 1234

approved of "self-sacrifice and martyrdom." It was the writings of St. Augustine and, later, St. Thomas Aquinas that first convinced the Christian community that suicide was a sin. Later writers—among them Sir Thomas More, Donne, Hume, and Kant—encouraged society to treat suicide more tolerantly.

Taking a tolerant position does not imply that suicide should become acceptable or be regarded as a reasonable act. Suicide, however, does not place the victim outside the realm of God's grace. Nothing, including suicide, will separate us from the love of God in Christ Jesus (Rom 8:38-39).

What this observation means for the church is that we should not add to the anguish being experienced by the family and friends of a suicide by ostracizing them and forcing them to suppress their grief.

I believe the experience of officiating at such a funeral made me sensitive to other losses that could result from unsanctioned grief. For instance, with the stigma still attached to AIDS, someone who is grieving the death of a loved one or friend from AIDS-related complications may not be in a situation where she or he can openly talk about grief. One need only think of the many funerals attended in the last twenty years where hazy and obscure details were whispered about surrounding the death of the deceased.

What about the family and friends of someone who dies as a result of a state execution? How do they grieve and how are they supported by their faith community?

These questions are particularly important to Christians because of the manner in which Jesus, our Lord and Savior died: He was executed by the state as a threat to state security and as a criminal. It seems to me that, in order to recapture the scandal of the cross, we should be wearing miniature gas chambers, electric chairs, and lethal injection syringes around our necks. If I may take the liberty of contextualizing 1 Corinthians 1:23: ". . . but we proclaim Christ crucified [executed by the state], a stumbling block to Jews and foolishness to Gentiles." These statements may seem offensive, but so was death by crucifixion in the first century.

Reflections
Unacceptable Death
What are the most "unacceptable" ways of death and dying in the thinking of the people to whom your congregation ministers? What about someone who dies of AIDS? Someone who is executed by the state?

Teaching Tip
Plan the funeral of a person executed for crimes against the state. The deceased person was raised in the church and the parents are still active. Discuss ways to make the funeral service meaningful for the friends and family. Should the guilt or innocence of the deceased person be an issue? What if innocent victims were involved? Discuss also the biblical texts and theme of the funeral sermon. Finally, decide where the funeral service will be held.

Imagine the grief and shame of Jesus' mother and aunt standing near the cross of Jesus (John 19:25b) as they watched their son and nephew being crucified on the emblem of suffering and shame, "condemned as a threat to the state by Roman law and cursed by God according to Deuteronomic law" (Deut 21:23). Or, imagine the grief and shame of Joseph of Arimathea, who was a secret disciple of Jesus because of his fear of the religious authorities (see the notes on 9:22, 12:42-43 and the comments at 2:18 in the *NISB*.) Even so, Joseph asked Pilate to let him take away the body of Jesus. Pilate gave him permission, so he came and removed the body (John 19:38). A secret follower of Jesus was faced with the prospect of also grieving in secret because of the fear that the religious authorities would do to him what they had done to Jesus. When it was not safe for a disciple to acknowledge that he even knew Jesus, how was he going to grieve Jesus' shameful way of dying in public?

One of my parishioners is related to a person who was executed with the abolitionist John Brown (1859). For years, it was a deeply buried family secret. In this instance, it was generations of unsanctioned grief. One can only guess about the persons in our congregations who are experiencing unsanctioned grief. These are people whose grief is on the periphery of our memorial rituals of remembrance. The task for the community of faith is to draw these people and their grief from the periphery to the center. Again, it is when the unmentionable is mentioned and the unnameable is named in public worship space that those who grieve in silence can be empowered to share their grief with the gathered community.

Another group that we should add to those whose grief is regarded as unsanctioned are those who suffer pregnancy loss, which includes miscarriage, stillbirth, and newborn death. In his book *Pastoral Care in Pregnancy Loss: A Ministry Long Needed*, Thomas Moe cites the following from Therese Rando, who writes in her book, *A Parental Loss of a Child*, that those who had miscarried were often viewed as "illegitimate mourners" by society. "We now realize that

Sources

Jouette M. Bassler, "Cross," in *The Harper Collins Bible Dictionary, Revised Edition,* Paul J. Achtemeir, General Ed. (San Francisco: Harper, 1995) 212.

Martin Hengel, *Crucifixion* (Philadelphia: Fortress, 1977).

Sources

Thomas Moe, *Pastoral Care in Pregnancy Loss: A Ministry Long Needed* (Binghamton, New York: Haworth Press, 1997), 64, citing Therese A. Rando, *Parental Loss of a Child* (Champaign, Ill: Research Press Company, 1986), 131.

parents begin to bond with their child long before the actual birth."

For those of us who, from liturgical traditions, observe All Saints Sunday, remembering those who have entered eternal rest during the last year gives us an opportunity to acknowledge the loss publicly. I think it ministers to the families and friends of suicide victims to include them in public prayers while, at the same time, ensuring that the family members enjoy the privacy they might need and maintaining confidentiality.

Finally, as we reflect upon the grief and shame of Jesus' family and disciples, we do so proclaiming that their unsanctioned grief gave way to joy. For those whose deaths were scandalous and those left to grieve them, we point to the thief on the cross to whom Luke's Gospel has Jesus saying, "Truly I tell you, today you will be with me in paradise" (Luke 23:43).

Session 7

The Grief of the Poor

In December of 1996, I had the opportunity to travel with a group of colleagues to South Africa and Zimbabwe. It was a transformative experience for the entire group. In South Africa, we traveled to Johannesburg where we spent a sobering afternoon in Soweto Township. First, we were struck by the ominous towers of a nuclear power plant that appeared to loom over that township filled with poverty and squalor, twin significations that, in the minds of former powers, the human beings there did not count. Second, there was a portable memorial to the Soweto Uprising, where hundreds of Soweto residents, including many children, were wounded and killed. We toured the memorial in silence because we could not find any words to express accurately what we were feeling. We returned to the van we were traveling in, numbed by the uncertainty of how to respond to what we had seen as secondhand witnesses. We remained in silence, each of us lost in our own private thoughts. Our next stop took us to the Lutheran diocesan house. As we were wondering how these human beings could endure their past and present miseries, we encountered a wedding celebration in all of its vibrancy. There was our answer: Life exists in the midst of the poverty and squalor, *in spite of* the continuing aftereffects of apartheid.

It was during our trip to Bulawayo in Zimbabwe that I had another transformative experience; it took on the quality of conversion. It caught me by surprise in a church, when I heard a sermon on Luke 16:19-31. I suddenly realized that as an African American I was the "rich man who was dressed in purple and fine linen

Lectionary Loop
Year B, Proper 27; Year C, Proper 5

Sources

Kate Tuttle, "Soweto, South Africa, South African township near Johannesburg," *Africana: The Encyclopedia of the African and African American Experience,* Kwame Anthony Appiah and Henry Louis Gates, Jr., eds. (New York: Basic Books, 1999), 1767.

Reflections
Human Suffering

Where have you seen human suffering that left you speechless? Did you do anything about it?

who feasted sumptuously every day" (Luke 19:19). It was a sobering realization, made in the midst of the ongoing hospitality of which we were recipients. What I experienced was the richness of those who had so little in terms of material wealth. However, let me say very directly that I am not appealing to the nobility of poverty, but rather to what Mahatma Gandhi referred to as vitality. And this vitality stems from something that the poor receive despite the absence of material wealth. Gandhi's notion of vitality is related through a conversation with Howard Thurman that Thurman records in his autobiography:

> The result is that when we first began our movement, it failed, and it will continue to fail until it is embraced by the masses of the people. I felt that they could not sustain the ethical ideal long enough for it to be effective because they did not have enough vitality . . ." He continued, "The masses lacked vitality for two reasons. First, they were hungry . . . . The second reason for the lack of vitality was the loss of self-respect.

It seems to me that the widow of Zarephath (1 Kgs 17:8-24), who is ready to die after she prepares a final meal for herself and her orphan son, is grieving the loss of vitality. The loss of vitality occurs when poverty becomes more than an external situation affecting the body and creeps into the soul. Here is a woman who has lost the will to live. While the widow and orphan son's physical situation was problematic in its own right, her plight was made all the worse by a social situation where compassion was lacking. The story of this widow and her orphan son grieving the loss of vitality occurs as part of the larger story of Elijah's contest against the prophets of Baal and his subsequent confrontation with Jezebel. The grief of this widow and her orphan son was a sign of how bad things were as a result of Jezebel's missionary zeal in promoting the worship of Baal while suppressing the worship of YHWH.

As a result of this apostasy, God's concern for wid-

Source
Howard Thurman, *With Head and Heart: The Autobiography of Howard Thurman* (San Diego: A Harvest Book, Harcourt Brace & Company, 1979), 133.

Reflection
Failed Ethics
What important ethical ideal has Christianity failed to embrace? Why?

ows and orphans as revealed in the Law and the Prophets was being neglected by the community of faith. Whenever there was a wholesale turning away from God of Israel, the widows and the orphans were the victims; not God's victims, but the victims of the larger community that was turning away from God. While their vulnerability to poverty was itself problematic, what was more destructive was the loss of hope. The psalmists were particularly vengeful against those who would cause such discouragement among the most vulnerable (see Pss 73 and 94). Similar oppressors were condemned by the prophet Amos (Amos 8:4-14).

The harshness of God's judgment is pronounced on those who create hopelessness among the needy and the poor, a condition that Cornel West describes as "nihilism": "the lived experience of coping with a life of horrifying meaninglessness, hopelessness, and (most importantly) lovelessness."

God sends Elijah to bring hope to this widow and her orphan son, a hope that has an ongoing concrete reality—a jar of meal that was never empty and a jug of oil that did not fail.

We must acknowledge the incarnational nature of God's grace, which is finally and ultimately revealed in Jesus the Christ who appropriates the Isaiah text (Isa 61:1-4) for his earthly ministry (Luke 4:18). It is good news that is a restitution tenfold of the hope that was robbed from the poor.

This is not a divine ordination of the poor, as if Jesus says, "You always have the poor with you" (John: 12:8*a*), he is revealing God's plan for human relationships. But it is incarnational hope that sustains the most vulnerable in a world where, due to human sinfulness, the rich get richer and the poor get poorer. God provides the poor—not with a general hope that in the "by-and-by" things will get better, but hope in the day-to-day when the worst that can happen does indeed happen. It is a practical hope because even when the poor have been abandoned by everybody else, they have not been abandoned by God, who can make a way out of no way.

> ## Reflection
> ### God of the Oppressed
> Why is God portrayed in the Bible as partial to the needs of the oppressed and dispossessed? *Read and discuss* Exod 3:7-9; Pss 12:5; 113:7-8.

145

Let Us Indeed Go There

At a church where I served as an interim pastor, I had an unforgettable encounter with a parishioner. As I drove into the church parking lot on a Sunday morning, he literally ran out to meet me. He was holding a copy of either *Newsweek* or *Time* that had on its cover a picture of the universe with a question in captions concerning God's place in the scheme of things. This person was overjoyed as he said to me, "Finally it's okay to ask the questions I've been asking!" You see, this person was still grieving the loss of his only son, and this father was part of a congregation where his questions about the goodness of God were not encouraged. Whenever he wanted to ask probing questions, he was dissuaded from going there. He wanted to reflect on embedded theology in a community of faith that, in subtle ways, discouraged this kind of reflection. Probing these deep questions was his grief work. However, this congregation, given its developmental stage, was unable to support him where his grief work was leading him.

The intended task for these three final Bible studies is to reflect upon biblical texts (embedded theology) that are preached at funerals. In preparation for these studies, I surveyed the hymnals and worship books of several denominations. In my surveys, I discovered Job 14:1-2, 5-10, as one of the suggested texts for funerals in the 1966 *Book of Common Prayer* from the Episcopal Church. As I compared this suggested text with those included in the hymnals and worships books from other denominations, I noted that the Job text most often suggested for funerals is Job 19:23-

27*a*, containing the words, "I know that my Redeemer (vindicator) lives" (19:25). I was intrigued by the inclusion of the Job 14 text and wondered about the reasons for its selection.

I wondered if its selection as a funeral text was a reflection of the spirit of the times. By 1966, the bombing of the Birmingham church that killed four girls had already occurred (September 15, 1963). So the question poised in this text would have been in the spirit of those times: "But mortals die, and are laid low; humans expire, and where are they?" (14:10).

As you read these Bible studies, you probably detect my cynical side, critical of simple solutions to solve complex human conditions. It is the inclusion of the wisdom literature with all of its ambiguity, however, that assures me that God was clearly involved in the creation of the biblical canon.

Imagine how jarring Job 14:10 would be when read at a funeral or memorial service, not to mention the unnerving prospects of preaching from such a text amid flowers and hushed tones, with the organist softly playing "My Hope Is Built On Nothing Less Than Jesus' Blood and Righteousness." Before moving to praise, however, some of us need to reflect on the embedded theology contained in hymns like this one.

The parishioner who ran out to greet me was one of many who needed to give serious second thoughts to his initial understanding of the faith, to engage in Anselm's definition of theology: faith seeking understanding.

R. Scott Sullender, who has written quite extensively on grief, identifies *lamentation* and *consolation* as two different biblical traditions for "grief." It seems to me that the lamentation tradition is dominant in the wisdom literature, with the book of Job being a strong representative of the genre. In fact, reading the impassioned debates and complaints on the suffering of the just, one can see the form and sense the atmosphere of lament in the book. Sullener places the lament tradition closer to modern psychology because they both emphasize the value of freely and completely expressing one's feelings.

Reflection
Funeral Sermons
Read Job 14:1-2, 5-10, 14 and 19:23-27 and discuss how they could be used as texts for a funeral sermon.
See the "Excursus: Life After Death in the Old Testament," NISB*, 434-35.*

Reflection
Faith Alone
A person whose spiritual walk is characterized by "faith seeking understanding" seems to be on a God-empowered quest to know more about faith and life. How might a person who applies "faith alone" in all matters of Christian living be in conflict with the "faith seeking understanding" Christian?

Sources
R. Scott Sullender, "St. Paul's Approach to Grief: Clarifying the Ambiguity," *The Journal of Religion and Health* 20 (Spring 1981).

Another way to think of the similarities between the lament tradition and modern psychologies is in regard to their common commitment to probe the deeper questions, to go beneath the tip of the iceberg. In Job 14, the question is preceded by the assertion that a tree can continue to exist after being cut down (14:7-9), but that humans die and disappear (Job 14:10). What is interesting about this passage and others like it from the book of Job is how severely it challenges the notion of "the patience of Job." There is nothing patient in this question. Not only is Job impatient with the answers from the embedded theology, which is being expressed through the well-intended piety of his friends, but Job is also impatient with God, with whom he wants a hearing. He wants God to show up with some answers to his deep ponderings.

Job's questions are upsetting to his friends because they may lead them to engage in reflection about their own embedded theology. This point highlights the need for an effective ministry of presence to those who grieve. Can we be a non-anxious presence to those whose probing questions lead us, and may even drive us, to engage in uncomfortable reflection upon our own embedded theologies? Or do we become like Job's friends, who could not handle their own anxieties raised by Job's questions?

There is a mutual benefit for the entire community of faith in walking with someone probing the deeper questions as they are trying to understand and come to terms with their loss. They encounter the graciousness of God through the body of Christ that is the community of faith gathered around them while our reflections are deepened whether we are ready or not. Such is the nature of living in community; your questions may upset me, but they lead me to ever-deepening reflections upon our common faith.

A few years ago I heard one of my faculty colleagues, Mance Jackson, from the Interdenominational Theological Center in Atlanta, preach a sermon from Luke 5:4-6.

He was suggesting that, just as the disciples had to go out in the deep water in order to catch fish, we as the church were similarly going to have to address deep things to catch people. As the church that walks with people in the midst of their grief, we must not run when they need to probe deep questions as a vital part of their healing grief work.

As I reflect upon the needs of this searching parishioner and the ways that we could have walked with him in his grief, I wonder how he could have been assisted if this passage and others like it had been placed in his lunch box by the nurturing church (metaphorically speaking). I wonder how he could have been formed and shaped by these texts with their probing questions?

Before we can use these passages as sermon texts, we have got to build an exposure and familiarity to them, similar to the already familiar texts like Psalm 23. My hope is that this Bible study, in a modest way, will begin this process.

R. Scott Sullender warns against the abuse of either the lament tradition or the consolation tradition. In the remaining Bible studies I hope to heed Sullender's warnings by emphasizing the consolation tradition. However, in both remaining studies I will be operating with the assumption that although the consolation tradition is generally reflected in texts with which many of us are familiar, they may not be as familiar to younger generations.

Sources

R. Scott Sullender, "St. Paul's Approach to Grief: Clarifying the Ambiguity," *The Journal of Religion and Health 20* (Spring, 1981), 71-72.

Session 9   John 14:1-6

Plenty Good Room
in My Father's Kingdom

The hospice social worker had just come back into the room where we gathered after talking with my mother, who was dying. When she shared with us that they had talked about my mother's fear, I was immediately drawn to this text. In the days following, as she was slipping into that place where she was being separated from cares and concerns of the living, I would sit by her bed and read passages of consolation from the Bible, such as John 14:1-6. These texts offered mutual comfort to both the dying and those getting ready to grieve their deaths. They had formed and shaped both of us—through the funerals she attended during seventy-seven years of living and the sermons that I had the privilege of preaching across a quarter of a century.

It was as if we both knew where to go to find the words that neither of us was capable of manufacturing on our own, words to speak to her fear of dying and my fear of losing the one whose womb brought me into the world.

For me, it was another opportunity to discover what the church had placed in my lunch box and what my mother had also placed there. If I could design a bumper sticker it would read, "If you know where to find the words of consolation in the Bible, thank that person in the community of faith who took seriously the vows made at your baptism." The embedded theology of songs like "Plenty Good Room in My Father's Kingdom," a song from the African American spiritual tradition, offers consolation and comfort.

Lectionary Loop
Year A, Fifth Sunday of Easter

Reflections
Comfort
How were you most comforted as you sat or stood at the bedside of a dying loved one? If your loved one was conscious, how was she or he comforted by the experience?

According to Sullender, first-century Christians, and Paul in particular, appropriated the consolation tradition from the Hellenistic cultural context that surrounded the early church and imbued it with a distinctively Christian hopefulness.

Concerning the genre, Sullender writes that consolation letters were sent for a variety of reasons, such as death, exile, and loss of property, but that the basic theme was always that mourning is futile or grieving must be done with moderation and brevity. Sullender believes that the consolation tradition assumed that healing occurs when a bereaved person can temper grief with reason, moderation, and self-control.

Sullender summarizes the consolation tradition as the assumption that healing occurs to the extent that a bereaved person can temper grief with reason, logic, and philosophy. For Sullender, Paul formed a blend between the traditions of lament and consolation. "Out of this blending," he writes, "Paul developed a pastoral approach to grief that is colored by the tension between these two traditional approaches and by his personal eschatological understanding of loss."

Sullender's analysis of Paul's blending of these traditions from a variety of perspectives suggests that what we moderns are facing may not be new. In fact, it seems to me that what we are facing is an exciting time similar to the excitement that faced Christians in the early years of the church. So we might conclude that there was an inherent missional component to Paul's pastoral approach as there should be to ours as well.

So, it is no surprise that the trite phrase, "In my Father's house are many mansions" (John 14:2 KJV), continues to speak to us moderns and postmoderns. In the rush to get to my mother's side in time, I did not bring my NRSV; all I could find in the house was a King James Version with the sayings of Jesus in red. As I read these words of comfort from Jesus to his followers, stumbling through the language of King James, the content of the words comforted me. I recalled a conversation earlier with other educated

Sources

"Plenty Good Room," 99 in *Songs of Zion,* J. Jefferson Cleveland, ed. (Nashville: Abingdon Press, 1981).

For examples of Greco-Roman consolation literature, cited by Sullender, see Seneca, "On Consolation to the Bereaved," in his *Ad Lucilium Epistulae Morales,* (Cambridge, Harvard University Press, 1962) vol. 3, p. 129, and his "Moral Essays," (Cambridge, Harvard University Press, 1965) vol. 2, p. vii.

R. Scott Sullender, "St. Paul's Approach to Grief: Clarifying the Ambiguity," *The Journal of Religion and Health* 20 (Spring, 1981), 65, 71-72.

Sources

Pauline Boss, *Ambiguous Loss: Learning to Live With Unresolved Grief* (Cambridge: Harvard University Press, 1999), 16f.

Howard Thurman, *Jesus and the Disinherited* (Richmond, Ind.: Friend United Press, 1981), 13.

Richard Wallace, "The Theological View of Aging that Permeates the African American Experience," in *Aging, Spirituality, and Religion: A Handbook, Volume 2,* Melvin A. Kimble and Susan H. McFadden, eds. (Minneapolis: Fortress Press, 2003), 337.

colleagues who, even though they valued our intellectual liberation from the abuses of the King James English, had to admit its remaining power to speak poetically to our deep hurts and especially those of our parents and grandparents.

The embedded theology of these words of comfort spoken by Jesus, the Good Shepherd, to his flock promises inclusion in God's kingdom to those who have been excluded in this life. This last point is substantiated by the prevailing theme of John's Gospel regarding who is an insider and who is an outsider. Unlike the places in the world where there is limited room, in the kingdom of God there is unlimited room. Again, there is the theme of God's overabundance.

The relevance of the consolation traditions is also observed by Pauline Boss in her book *Ambiguous Loss: Learning to Live with Unresolved Grief*: Boss began meeting with several Anishinabe women in Northern Minnesota, who all had family members with dementia. Their "spiritual acceptance" of their relatives' conditions and "harmony with nature rather than a mastery over it" encouraged her that "ambiguous loss does not have to devastate."

> The insights from *Ambiguous Loss* lead me to think of the consolation tradition as applicable to those times when we are, as Howard Thurman said, "the masses of humanity with our backs up against the wall." During those crisis times, all we can do is be comforted by embedded theology. It is the theology that has been embedded in us because the community of faith across generations has comforted one another with these words.

We have so interiorized the images contained in John 14:1-6, that it evokes comfort in us by the mere hearing of the words. It is not my intent to suggest that thinking is secondary, but that the comfort certain words evoke in us occurs without the necessity to engage the intellect.

When Jesus says, "Do not let your hearts be troubled. Believe in God, believe also in me (14:1)," it is not an appeal to analyze ourselves or our beliefs. It is an appeal to believe. The effect of what Jesus says about comfort in our hearts has little to do with our intellectual assent to certain facts about Jesus. We simply acknowledge the fact that we are comforted by what Jesus says. Yes, "There's Plenty Good Room in My Father's Kingdom."

Session 10   John 11:17-27

Living Between "Lord, Have Mercy" and "Thank You, Jesus"

The title for this session, from Dr. Toinette Eugene, has become part of my consciousness. Most recently, I used it when I preached a sermon from John 11:11-27. As I was making a point during the sermon about Mary and Martha's complaint, I realized that in the last year I also had been living between "Lord, have mercy" and "Thank you, Jesus"; that is, between complaint and confidence.

When my mother's condition worsened and her hospice team told the family that her death was imminent, my sister called me and said that I needed to return as soon as I could book a flight. While she was picking me up from the airport, my sister collapsed in my arms. The EMT's who arrived at the scene could not revive her. She died soon after being taken to the hospital. My sister preceded my mother in death by thirteen days. So when I was preaching from this text and saying to the congregation, "Have not we all been where Mary and Martha were and also said, 'Yes, I believe in the resurrection, but, Lord, if you had been here, my brother would not have died,'" I realized that I could have easily said, ". . . but, Lord, if you had been here, my sister would not have died."

The losses that I have shared in these last two Bible studies occurred less than one year from the time that I write them. At this point, I have my good days and bad days. On the bad days, I am living closer to "Lord, have mercy"; then, there are other days when I am closer to "Thank you, Jesus." Such is the nature of grief.

In her notes on verses 21-22 from John 11:17-37 in the *New Interpreter's Study Bible*, Gail R. O'Day writes "Martha's words contain both complaint (v. 21) and

Lectionary Loop
Fifth Sunday in Lent A

Study Bible
Gail R. O'Day's notes on John 11:21-22, *NISB*, 1931.

confidence (v. 22, even now)." Martha's complaint was based on the miracle she was hoping for that would have prevented her brother's death.

In his commentary on the Gospel of John, Francis J. Moloney writes, "She then confesses her faith in him as a miracle worker, accepting that Jesus' earlier presence would have cured her brother (v. 21)." However, as a miracle worker, Jesus had reached the limits of his power according to the way persons in that day thought of possibilities for resuscitation. Everyone there thought there was nothing that could be done, now that Lazarus was dead and had been in the tomb for four days. Yet, Martha's faith in Jesus' ability as a miracle worker is strong: "But even now I know that God will give you whatever you ask of him" (11:22).

I really appreciate the title that Moloney has given to the raising of Lazarus narrative in his commentary: "a resurrection that will lead to death." It is an ironic framing of our status as "tweeners"; that is, we live "between the now and the not yet." Martha's "now" was that if Jesus had come to Bethany in time her brother would not have died. Her "not yet" was the general resurrection that was to occur in some undetermined time in the future. (see the note about Daniel 12:2, *NISB,* 1931.) She was grieving the death of her brother in the "now" because that was what was most real to her. This was her "Lord, have mercy" complaint. The resurrection that she believed in was "not yet" a reality. It was something that was far on her horizon and had not yet become accessible to her daily living. All she could hope for was the miracle that would still lead to death. The difference between the two realities was so vast that it defied time itself.

Only the theological term, "prolepsis," can adequately capture the meaning in this text.

Prolepsis (Greek, "anticipation"): the principle of real anticipation, which comes from the way in which Christ's resurrection represents in advance what will happen at the end of history.

One might ask, could the word "preview" not sufficiently capture the meaning of Lazarus's resurrection?

Source

Francis J. Moloney, *Sacra Pagina Series, Volume 4, The Gospel of John,* Daniel Harrington, rd. (Collegeville, Minn.: The Liturgical Press, 1998), 327.

Reflection
Healing
When, in the face of a loved one's dying, do we stop asking for or hoping for miraculous healing? Share your stories.

Study Bible
See the note about Daniel 12:2, *NISB,* 1931.

Source
Gerald O'Collins and Edward G. Farrugia, *A Concise Dictionary of Theology* (New York: Paulist Press, 1991), 194.

We should, therefore, understand the story of the raising of Lazarus from the grave as a preview of Jesus' resurrection, which, in turn, is a preview of our own resurrection. However, the problem with "preview" is that it only provides us with a view of what is yet to come. No, the raising of Lazarus from the grave is more than a preview of coming attractions featuring the resurrection of Jesus. When Jesus told her that her brother would rise again, Martha understood him to be talking about coming attractions, and she responded appropriate to that understanding: "I know that he will rise again in the resurrection on the last day" (11:24). But right now, today, she said, my brother is dead, and if you had been here he would not have died.

Right now, today, my sister is dead, which is my "Lord, have mercy" moment, especially when I am in touch with how her death is affecting me and the rest of her family. My sister, who was eleven months and twenty-three days younger than me, died when she was fifty years old. As a result of her death, there are the grandchildren that she will not get a chance to hold, the husband with whom she will not have a chance to grow old, the mother she will not follow in death the way it is supposed to be. What we are grieving are the relationship losses. Like Martha, when the death of my sister in the now becomes most real to me is when I am closer to "Lord, have mercy." Of course, I believe that she will rise again in the resurrection on the last day. But right now, today, my sister is dead, and that is the reality that is most real to me.

As contemporary Christians, especially postmoderns, who gather at funerals and gravesides, it seems to me that our understanding of the resurrection is probably closer to Martha's understanding. This is precisely why our situation is so similar to the Christians at Thessalonica that Timothy describes to Paul as lacking in faith. We have become vulnerable to grieving as others with no hope because our understanding of the resurrection has become too future-oriented.

The power of the resurrection is no longer accessible as an everyday reality for us. However, it is precisely as contemporary Christians who gather at funerals and

Reflection
Loss
At a time of loss, how can a balance be reached between separation/sadness and hope/celebration?

gravesides that we have the opportunity to be comforted with these words that Jesus said to her, "I am the resurrection and the life. Those who believe in me, even though they die, will live, and everyone who lives and believes in me will never die" (11:25-26). The raising of Lazarus does not just point to the future, the not-yet; it also brings the future of Jesus' resurrection to the present, everyday reality of Martha, Mary and all of those mourning the death of Lazarus. It is the foretaste of the feast to come—not a smell, not a picture, but a taste. The resurrection touches us in the depths of our being. It is when the "not yet" becomes the "already." The resurrection is now our reality, for we live in the sure and certain hope of our resurrection. Jesus came, not to just tell us about the resurrection in general, but that he is the resurrection and the life. This is the classic funeral text; Jesus' words are the ones we read when the body is led out of the church and to the graveside. Sometimes, we need to go to funerals to hear what it is that we believe. When we hear it continually in our life and ministry together, it becomes our implicit/embedded theology. It makes what we believe an accessible resource in our grieving. The distances between "Lord, have mercy" and "Thank you, Jesus" have been considerably narrowed. It is the sure and certain hope of the resurrection in our everyday reality that enables us to make it from "Lord, have mercy" to "Thank you, Jesus," because the resurrection now appears upon the horizon and the Son touches us.

These days, as I do my grief work and process the significant losses that I have recently experienced, I realize that precious memories are not all that I possess, and for this I say, "Thank you, Jesus." These texts are our final will and testament, what was bequeathed to us from past generations and what we bequeath to generations after us. These days, there is an interest in people drawing up ethical wills where they can outline the values and ethical principles that they wish to pass on to their progeny. When we gather at funerals and hear these texts, it is a reading of the will. Here we discover the resources for grieving that have been passed on to us from former generations, the great cloud of witnesses to the faith.

UNSELFISH PRAYER

A STUDY BY
DAVID ALBERT FARMER

David Albert Farmer is Pastor at Silverside Church in Wilmington, Delaware.
He also serves as adjunct professor of humanities at Wilmington College.
For eighteen years, he edited Pulpit Digest.

Introduction

The Pastor's Bible Study on Unselfish Prayer

Formal research is not required to prove that most prayers offered by most Christians, Protestant and Roman Catholic, are requests for favors from God. Many favors are utterances that amount to directives toward God—telling God what to do, in other words. Prayer of this kind is usually out of line. At the very least, our prayers should be more balanced, and when we do feel the need to ask God for some particular help or guidance it must be done in an unselfish manner. That is the purpose of this set of Bible studies.

The Pastoral Example

To get us right to the heart of this vital practice, we will examine several key biblical passages to guide our thoughts and hopefully, beyond our thoughts our practice of prayer. Before we get to these exciting and inspirational Bible passages, however, we must spend some time reflecting on the meaning and modeling of prayer itself.

As ordained leaders, our own ways of praying privately and certainly in public worship are the main lessons on prayer that our congregants hear. They hear us praying not only in worship but also as they step into relationships of marriage and commitment, when their babies are born, beside their hospital beds, at the graves of their loved ones, and during or after a pastoral counseling session. These moments of prayer will have a much greater impact on their understanding and practice of prayer than any book they will ever read, however widely read that book might be.

During these studies, many pastors will invite fellow seekers into times of prayer, by asking them to "try out"

Sources
Five Great Books on Prayer

1. *In God's Presence: Theological Reflections on Prayer,* Marjorie Hewitt Suchocki (St. Louis: Chalice Press, 1996)
2. *Dimensions of Prayer,* Douglas V. Steere (Upper Room, 1962)
3. *Prayer: Finding the Heart's True Home,* Richard J. Foster (San Francisco: Harper San Francisco, 10th ed. 1992)
4. *Praying the Psalms,* Thomas Merton (Collegeville, Minn.: Liturgical Press, 1956).
5. *Guide to Prayer for All God's People* (Upper Room, 1994)

Reflections
Public prayer

1. When is public prayer appropriate?
2. What form does public prayer take in your congregation?
3. How are prayer requests filtered through the worship and small group life of your congregation?
4. As a pastor, do you meet with a prayer group each week?

the kind of unselfish prayer that is suggested by each of the Bible studies. Simply talking about prayer, no matter how insightful the discussion, will not make much of a difference to anyone. After all, prayers are for praying, not for posting in public.

Now that you are reminded to pray often with the people of your congregation, enabling members to learn by your own habits, we are ready for a list of general principles about the nature of prayer. Distilling a subject into a list can be risky. Lists are especially mundane in sermons. I once heard a thirty-minute sermon with fourteen points! Each point was a part of that single long list. The sermon was not very good to my way of hearing, because it was essentially a laundry list of the preacher's random thoughts. However, lists in teaching, lectures, and seminar settings are often very effective. I say that as a rationale for the following lists.

What Prayer Is Not

◆ First and foremost, prayer is not the human-divine communion designed for a self-induced alternate reality, in which the local deity is busy trying to help those who have homes, plenty to eat, and more than all the basics. Prayer is not for helping you win the lottery or otherwise come to wealth while most of the people in the world—especially children—have barely enough or not enough to eat. The Creator God, the God who loves all human beings in all parts of the world, does *not* affirm the modern-day materialism and greed of the "first world." The jump from "Give us this day our daily bread ..." to "Whatever wealth you *claim* in Jesus' name is yours," is illogical, absurd, and out of touch with the God who, from ancient days, is said to have brought down the haughty and powerful while raising up the poor, the struggling, and the marginalized. Material advantages are *not* signs of God's special favors for the divinely preferred. God is not more pleased with a person of wealth than with one of the nameless homeless and hungry Indians whom Mother Teresa gave her life to serve.

◆ Prayer is neither a clever way to produce some magic words that will press, challenge, or obligate

> **Reflection**
> **Global Topics**
>
> Think about the prayers that you utter or think during the course of a week. How often do your prayers focus on personal and on global topics?

God to do what is against God's grain to do, nor an excuse for our not taking the time to notice that God is already doing what we are asking God to do (even though it might not be quite up to our standard).

◆ Prayer is not an ongoing list of imperatives, telling God what to do. (And putting "please" in front of the request does not make it any less of an imperative that is directed toward God.) Instead of thanking God for what God is already amazingly at work doing, instead of asking, instead of considering God's great love and full knowledge of every situation about which we might pray, we still are most inclined to give God "to-do" lists in our prayers:

• Be with Aunt Suddie.
• Heal Brother Joe!
• Make my tax refund be fat.
• Get me through this exam!
• Don't let that policewoman see me run this stoplight!
• Make this sermon end.

◆ Prayer is not an attempt at any form of one-way communication. Prayer, of necessity, requires us to listen to God, and, unlike us, God is not in a rush. God does not feel obligated to "get back to us" in any time frame we might impose.

◆ Prayer is not predominantly focused on an individual's perceived needs and preferences, such as a nice little visit to Santa's lap at Christmas time. Prayer is divine-human interaction that takes into account one's place within the whole human family, within a world setting. "Give us this day our daily bread" (which is not prayed as an imperative) was never intended to be anyone's way of securing a daily, divinely arranged dining deal. In that prayer, one of many that Jesus prayed, the *us* does not refer to "me and mama." That *us* is a global "us." That *us* is a for-God-so-loved-the-world "us." (By the way, there is plenty of food to feed all of the people in the world today. The problem is not with provision. God

---

Reflections
Blab It and Grab It

Many genuine yet uninformed Christians learn about prayer by watching how TV preachers pray as a "tactic," sometimes for miracles and at other times for fundraising.

1. How is prayer represented on the TV cable channels?

2. Some TV preachers (and their counterparts in local churches) present prayer, based on a study of Scripture passages, as a matter of claiming God's blessings in faith. Does God want you to prosper? Does God expect you to suffer?

3. Some TV programs feature hunger ministries that ask for prayer and money. What has been your experience with this form of missionary prayer when substituted for hands-on ministry?

4. When is it appropriate to ask for prayer and money?

and the fine agriculturalists and the devoted scientists have seen to the food supply. The problem is with those of us who haven't listened long enough to God in prayer to hear God's call to get involved in the stewardship of distribution.)

What Prayer Is

In the following studies, based on five vital passages of Scripture, we will see that prayer is communion and conversation with God that includes plenty of time for listening and is:

- ◆ Respectful of God and how God works
- ◆ Reflective of God's love for all people
- ◆ Individually and communally focused
- ◆ Expressed by one who is fully honest with self and with God
- ◆ As concerned with what God wants us to do as with what we want God to do for us
- ◆ Cognizant of the fact that God is pulling all human beings and societies toward wholeness
- ◆ Filled with expressions of adoration, gratitude, and celebration for what God has *already* done and is doing. God, after all, is the force "who by the power at work within us is able to accomplish abundantly far more than all we can ask or imagine" (Eph 3:20).

Session 1   Psalm 32

Moments of Truth

Ascribing human emotional attributes to God is as anthropomorphic as giving God, who is S/spirit, hands and eyes and even, as in Moses' story, a backside. We talk about divine attributes in human physical terms because it is a shorthand way of trying to describe some aspect of the indescribable.

Many people realize that a reference to the voice of God, for example, is not an audible voice like the voice of human beings. God's *voice,* except as it may be spoken through those persons closely enough attuned to divine realities to be able to speak them, is inaudible. Nonetheless, we may often use the word *voice* to describe the powerful pulling and leading of God's Spirit (God's unseen presence). Frankly, we may not always *hear* God's voice any more clearly than we hear a friend or loved one when she or he attempts to say something to us while we're engrossed in a television show or a good book.

Similarly, when we give God human emotional attributes, we must realize that God is not of limited human capacity and that God does not *feel* as humans feel. When we say that God loves or that God is angry, we are drawing parallels to human experience. God's *love,* of course, is infinitely more than the greatest acts of human love. God's *anger* is based on perceptions of God that make God act and react like human beings as well as a way of trying to account for life's difficulties with a providentialist perspective.

We should understand that God is not subject to the limitations of human emotional experience in any way. When we have said something like, "God is offended," or

Reflections
Voice of God

1. Many Christians say that they have heard God speak audibly in prayer or contemplation. Has this happened to you?

In discussion be very open and affirming of those who have a literal understanding of biblical metaphors, such as God's voice, or other divine attributes that we describe as human characteristics.

2. Genesis 1:27 asserts that we were created in God's image. Does this include our emotions and needs?

Study Bible

See "Excursus: In God's Image," *NISB*, 7.

"God regrets having done this or that," we are clearly projecting our limitations onto God who has no limitations.

The sacrificial system in ancient Israelite religious practice (as well as in the other ancient religions that taught the requirement of animal or food sacrifice) was based on a concept of God as a potentially jealous and/or furious deity who must be appeased. Christians believe that the God revealed in Jesus to the world, however, was clearly not a God who wanted or needed to be appeased in order to extend love and favor upon humankind. Judaism, which does not seek a reinstitution of temple sacrifice to appease God's fury over sin, likewise understands the limits of defining God's attributes through human emotions or features.

These foundational facts must be remembered when we come to the issue of confession. We do not "confess" our failures to God because God missed the latest CNN report or because God is going to be even angrier with us if we don't. *Confession* is really nothing more (or less) than honest communication with God about our inability to be all that God desires for us to be; it's an exercise in "getting real," a way of being authentic.

No honest communication ever takes place between two people when one is pretending to be something other than what she or he really is. Most of us can be very skilled at not letting others know who we really are by hiding behind barriers that others may not even notice we have built. Some of those to whom we speak may think for a while that we are the most open and honest people they have ever run across, but that impression will not last.

As we are careful not to try to make God one of us, we come to the practice of confession free from any pressure to list every single deed we have done that was less than selfless and respectful of our Creator, of fellow human beings, and of ourselves. Rather, we consciously open ourselves to God just as we are, without pretense, with no façade, no false piety. In that state of mind we can get to the point of true communion with God. Without such honesty, no true interaction/exchange will take place—not because God turns away from us, but because we have not taken down the

Reflections
Limits

We often say that God has no limitations.

1. Do you think that God's power is limited by human evil? Can God directly protect you from evil?

2. How does prayer help God overcome evil in this world?

Study Bible

See the "Excursus: Penitential Psalms," *NISB*, 797. Penitential Psalms include Pss 6; 32; 38; 51;102; 130; and 143.

Reflections
Honesty

1. Other than not wanting to take the time for consistent communion with God, what are some of the reasons we resist being honest with God?

2. Are there ultimately destructive results that come from our failure to be honest with God?

3. Are there times when being honest with God can lead to destructive consequences? (See below on "moments of truth" experiences.)

By Example

1. Who taught you the most about how to pray?

2. Why are we not inclined to teach others how to pray?

barriers we have built around ourselves. Fig leaves are not the only things human beings have tried to hide behind when honesty in God's presence was too uncomfortable or just too much trouble. God will be known to us in the depths, or not at all.

Walter Harrelson points out in the *NISB* study notes on Psalm 32 that this psalm is designated by its heading, *maskil,* as a didactic song and/or a prayer that shows good skill. The community had decided that the teaching of this worship song was good stuff, and while no communal worship statement may ever voice precisely the experience or the need of every individual involved, it is broad enough to be generally true for most of the people who worship at any given time. Thus, it is of value, and those who sing and pray accordingly demonstrated good prayer skills. There is much to be learned about prayer from one another!

Psalm 32 is a communal hymn extolling the virtue/necessity of confession, which is much more about simply being honest with God as to who and where we are than it is about apologizing or, worse, groveling. Simply coming openly and authentically into God's presence brings *forgiveness* of transgressions (32:1*a*) and the *covering* or *hiding* of sin (32:1*b*). No formulaic verbal expression must be offered.

Though it may be painful for us, emotional intimacy with our Creator eventually brings us happiness. There is no joy for us in life or in contact with God as long as we live as the great pretenders. Happiness finds its way to us when we get rid of the deceit (Ps 32:2*b*).

Verse 5 is pivotal in the theological thought of this didactic song. The psalmists do not "ask" God for forgiveness; they simply *acknowledge* their sin. I take sin to be any and all types of individual and societal self-centeredness leading to disregard of God and of the well-being of others. I cannot hear in that word anything like "low-life" or "depraved." Confession is a decision not to try to hide our selfish choices from God (as if verbalizing them surprises God!). Confession is acknowledgment, and forgiveness is God's predictable reaffirmation of us.

Verse 5 is all about a "moment of truth," those pow-

Study Bible

Even though the pronouns suggest an individual is praying, she or he might very well be leading the congregation in a prayer that has the gathered community thinking of itself as a singular entity. "The psalms stem directly from the actual worship of the community." See the Introduction to Psalms, *NISB*, 749.

erful times when we have risked total honesty in order to be fully present with the God who created us and who draws us into the fullness of life if we follow God's lead. As a result, we may find profound joy. In addition, the psalmists sing of at least two other ways in which such intimacy with God benefits us.

Such a bond with God brings us strength for facing life's unending challenges (Ps 32:6-7). God's presence —discovered in intimacy that grows out of honesty— does not keep all trouble away, but the effects of distress cannot defeat us when such a vital closeness to God has been established and sustained.

God's presence with us also serves to lead us, guide us, and counsel us as long as we are willing and as long as we remain honest (32:8-9). This is easier said than done, since we have more experience trying to hide ourselves from God than with being genuine in communion with God. However, until we learn to trust God and God's goodness more than we trust ourselves and all the temporal ways we have leaned on to help us get by, we will never take the risk of being honest with God.

The ancient worshipers were not taught in this psalm to ask God for a single thing, not even forgiveness. A prayer of confession/acknowledgment is one expression of purely unselfish prayer even though the possible positive results can be overwhelming: "Steadfast love surrounds those who trust in the LORD" (Ps 32:10b).

Reflections

Sin

1. What is your view of sin?
2. How do you define sin?
3. How is sin understood in your congregation?
4. Is there something distinctive about how your denomination views sin and confession? Can you recall a dispute about sin in your congregation or denomination?

Theodicy

1. Does a right relationship with God guarantee more blessing than suffering?
2. Does a healthy prayer discipline guarantee that distress cannot defeat us?

Study Bible

For more on profound joy (blessing), see the "Excursus:) Ashre," *NISB*, 754.

Session 2 Daniel 4:28-37

On the Other Side of Despair

We live in a culture and a time when more and more people hold God responsible for everything that happens—from a gambling win to a murder, from a professional promotion to a war. Whether we intend it or not, this attitude demonstrates the fact that we blame God for our misfortunes. Some of us, in an attempt to honor God's sovereignty, claim in the midst of a tragedy that "God is teaching me a lesson in this catastrophe," or that "God doesn't put on us more than we can bear."

Though brought up in a church and a community that comforted themselves with such a view of God's providence, my pastoral experiences with parishioners in tough times caused me to despair about what I could actually offer those who struggle with the problem of pain.

We know that some measure of suffering is a predictable part of life. No one has ever been able to explain to the satisfaction of all the source of evil or its prevalence. I find it counter-productive for us to think that God either "causes" or "permits" our tragedies. Some in the congregation might say that my faith is lacking and/or that I, a mere human being, have no right to question any aspect of what they call "divine ways." To the first criticism, I would answer, "Faith has nothing to do with how well my beliefs measure up to yours; faith is a way of describing my confidence in God." To the second, I would say, "I have never been convinced that God has anything to do with random tragedies occurring in a broken world."

Perhaps we can help our students get away from the

Reflections
Prayer and Pain

1. What is the best way for us to relate to God in the midst of our suffering?
2. How might our circumstances of suffering deepen our prayer lives?
3. What do you think of someone who can praise God in the midst of his or her suffering? Naive? Grateful? Defiant?

Study Bible

See also the "Excursus: The Portrayal of God in Job," *NISB*, 748.

need to hold God accountable for the evil and the awful, and thereby relieve them of the contradiction in attempting to affirm God's love, on the one hand, and God's cruelty, on the other. I cannot explain, with a cogent philosophical or systematic theological explanation, why debilitating disease and terminal illness are inherent to human experience, but I certainly do not think that they come to us and to those we love because of God.

What I can say with great confidence, however, is that God goes with us through the darkest of hours and that, at the end of our earthly days, we persons of faith will be able to look back and say, "At no moment in time did I face any challenge or difficulty without God's uplifting presence as near as I would allow it." Now, would it not be wonderful to be able to get rid of the baggage that has us angry with God as we struggle in the midst of our difficulties? Most of us are a long way from that point, regardless of how theologically progressive we might be. Still, if we saw God as compassionate, as the source of our strength rather than as active or passive pain-giver, our lives and our experiences of the seemingly inevitable would be positively transformed.

God pulls persons of faith through, not into, what is destructive and debilitating. Retrospective moments of prayerful affirmation of God's indescribable power and loving presence will strengthen us and undergird our confidence in God. Thus, prayer can lead us to that new place where we will not blame God for our troubles. These moments are what we have in Nebuchadnezzar's prayer on the other side of his despair.

Daniel 4:28-37 is an underestimated passage of Scripture. Perhaps it is avoided because there is an awkward correlation between God's unusual connection to the Babylonian King and the severe mental illness that Nebuchadnezzar endured.

The weight of the world came to rest on the king's shoulders. He became aware of just how many people throughout the great Babylonian Empire depended on him to meet their basic needs. That responsibility became overwhelming to him. His well-attested arro-

Reflections
Dark Night

Many Christians go through periods where God's absence seems unavoidable and overbearing, especially after tragedy. St. John of the Cross wrote a book about it, *The Dark Night of the Soul*.

Have you experienced a time where God's presence seemed hidden or elusive, so far out of reach and distant that you sensed despair? What did you do about it?

Study Bible

For alternate ways of understanding the story of Nebuchadnezzar's "metamorphosis," see Matthias Henze's comments on Daniel 4:28-33, *NISB*, 1239.

gance aside, he was obviously concerned for the well-being of his subjects.

Further, as is not uncommon for people in power, the strong and influential king became preoccupied with the possibility that his power would be lost or taken from him. Daniel respectfully challenged the king to claim his mortality and stop trying to live as if he were a god. Daniel took his ruler's refusal to let God be the one and only G/god as immoral. Nebuchadnezzar did not want to give up power, even if it meant untold worries and loss of health. Power meant pressure, but power also meant prestige. Finally, the pressures won, and Nebuchadnezzar lost.

Nebuchadnezzar first felt his anxiety subconsciously. He initially realized that something was wrong with his ability to enjoy inner peace because of trouble sleeping, then because of a disturbing dream.

Of the dream-interpreters to whom the king had access, only one was able to help Nebuchadnezzar understand the meaning of the dream and, thus, the foundation of his increased inability to function healthily and to govern effectively. That interpreter was Daniel, and the dream was a warning to the king that he would lose his grip on power. As it happened, he not only lost his grip on his power, but also on his sanity.

Understanding exactly what happened to Nebuchadnezzar is difficult. Some scholars have suggested that he was stricken with a disorder called *lycanthropy*. Lycanthropy is a rare condition (a theme discussed mostly in science fiction and apparent in fantasy literature, such as the Harry Potter novels) in which a person believes that she or he is a wild animal, such as a wolf. Hair is reported to grow all over the body in these depictions. The biblical text says that Nebuchadnezzar grew hair and noticeable claws. He suffered in this state for an unspecified period, but probably at least for several months. When he finally recovered from the illness, and had the time to think rationally about what he had endured, he might very well have scoffed at Daniel's God for playing such cruel games with people's lives. But this budding monotheist did not attribute the cause of his suffering to God. Instead,

---

Reflections
Mental Illness

One in four families will encounter a loved one with mental illness during their lifetime.

1. If you have experience with a person who is mentally ill, have there been occasions where you or someone in your family held God accountable for this illness, either in causing it or not removing it? How do you feel about it now?

2. How has your congregation understood and ministered to persons experiencing mental illness?

For more information see the website of The National Institute of Mental Health, http://www.nimh.nih.gov.

Reflections
Abdication of Power

Which powerful leaders in history have been willing to give up or set aside their power?

Dreams

1. Does God communicate with people through dreams in the present day?

2. Do you sometimes try to interpret your own dreams to others?

he prayed a beautiful prayer, an unselfish prayer, of profound insight, which honored God as the true God.

> When that period was over, I, Nebuchadnezzar, lifted my eyes to heaven, and my reason returned to me, I blessed the Most High, and praised and honored the one who lives forever. For his sovereignty is an everlasting sovereignty, and his kingdom endures from generation to generation. All the inhabitants of the earth are accounted as nothing, and he does what he wills with the host of heaven and the inhabitants of the earth. There is no one who can stay his hand or say to him, "What are you doing?" (Dan 4:34-35 NRSV)

The king claimed to have learned in his struggle that a prideful attempt to set God aside and take God's place has obvious negative consequences. The great Babylonian king could return to routine and responsibility without any illusions about who the real power in the world actually was, and he could do so with an honoring prayer on his lips.

Reflections
Thanksgiving

Walter Brueggemann in his book *The Message of the Psalms* (Minneapolis: Augsburg, 1984) describes the thanksgiving psalms of the Bible (e.g. Pss 30; 34; 40; 138) as psalms that celebrate the transition from problem to resolution, from disorientation to new orientation. How is the experience of Nebuchadnezzar one of thanksgiving? How about the experience of Jonah in Jonah 2? How might you compose your own thanksgiving psalm to God with similar experiences in your lives?

172

Preoccupation with Praise

Rather than pleading with God, asking favors of God, or making demands on God—which are prayer staples for most people—prayers of celebration should be the dominant prayers in our lives. The two primary types of celebratory prayers are prayers of praise and prayers of thanksgiving. This session deals with praise, the following session will deal with thanksgiving.

Praise is any expression of admiration and awe for who God is. Thus, a prayer of praise is any and every expression of admiration and awe for who God is. Praise is preoccupation with God's essence and wonderment that God would have anything at all to do with us. Praise is standing, sitting, kneeling, or lifting one's face and arms out of reverence in the presence of the one true and living God. Praise is a silent or public proclamation of God's great power and glory, continually and consistently conveyed through divine expressions of loving, creating, and liberating all life in the universe.

Verbal prayers of praise can just barely be prayed because of the limits of language. That's why we sometimes use our bodies to express things that words cannot convey. Even the other words we use to try to define the praise of God carry us to some of the few words in the vocabularies of all human speech that try to combine a sense of utter excellence and mystery with the best or the highest that we can know or imagine: adoration, adulation, eminence, eternality, exaltation, glory, grandeur, greatness, honor, jubilation, magnificence, majesty, resplendence. The foundation of all prayer is not a list of our needs and wants; the core of all true prayer is praise of God.

Reflections
Celebration

Worship styles are changing rapidly in our culture. To manage the change, most churches establish multiple worship services, with more recent forms of music.

1. Why does the language of praise seem to change with the times and the culture?
2. Why do some worshipers want the language of praise always to remain dependable?
3. What differences do you notice between private prayer and corporate ways of praising God?

In public worship, we have relied heavily on our hymns (and now our Scripture choruses) to express our praise. In the same way that music conveys the emotion of a motion picture, perhaps it is the poetry set to melodies that stirs us, touches us, inspires us, and helps us more readily express our praise than can our prosaic efforts alone.

> Holy, holy, holy, Lord God Almighty,
> Early in the morning, our song shall rise to thee.

or

> Joyful, joyful we adore thee,
>   God of glory, Lord of love;
> hearts unfold like flowers before thee,
>   opening to the sun above.

Some of the great words of praise that can help our hearts soar with joy and affirmation of God's greatness come from poetry that was never set to music. Do you know the following words from Coleridge's "Hymn Before Sun-rise"? (This could very well be set to music, but I have never heard it sung.)

> Ye Ice-falls! ye that from the mountain's brow
> Adown enormous ravines slope amain—
> Torrents, methinks, that heard a mighty voice,
> And stopped at once amid their maddest plunge!
> Motionless torrents! silent cataracts!
> Who made you glorious as the Gates of Heaven
> Beneath the keen full moon? Who bade the sun
> Clothe you with rainbows? Who, with living flowers
> Of loveliest blue, spread garlands at your feet?—
> God! let the torrents, like a shout of nations,
> Answer! and let the ice-plains echo, God!
> God! sing ye meadow-streams with gladsome voice!
> Ye pine-groves, with your soft and soul-like sounds!
> And they too have a voice, yon piles of snow,
> And in their perilous fall shall thunder, God!
> Ye living flowers that skirt the eternal frost!
> Ye wild goats sporting round the eagle's nest!
> Yet eagles, play-mates of the mountain-storm!
> Ye lightnings, the dread arrows of the clouds!

Source

Geoffrey Wainwright wrote an entire systematic theology under the rubric of liturgy: *Doxology: The Praise of God in Worship, Doctrine, and Life* (Oxford University Press, 1984).

Source

Samuel Taylor Coleridge, "Hymn Before Sun-Rise, In the Vale of Chamouni" lines 49-69 in *Selected Poetry and Prose of Coleridge*, ed. D. A. Stauffer, The Modern Library (New York: Random House, 1951), 104-5.

Ye signs and wonders of the element!
Utter forth God, and fill the hills with praise!

We have a word that is used to describe all hymns and all formulae to praise God: doxology. Praise of God is absolutely foundational, not only to prayer per se, but also to worship in general and to other aspects of the church's life.

The liturgical portions of Scripture are certainly filled with praise. One thinks immediately of the psalms, for most of them originally functioned as hymns that were sung in the corporate worship of ancient Israel. Many persons, especially the youth in our congregations, are moved by one of the migratory Scripture songs, such as the phrase from Psalm 18, that have been set to stirring contemporary beats and now are sung with praise bands while the words are projected on a screen:

I call upon the LORD, who is worthy to be praised,
so I shall be saved from my enemies (Ps 18:3).

Because there is so much misunderstanding about the book of Revelation and its proper interpretation, few of us will notice that praise literally fills the last book of the Christian Bible. Praise figures prominently in the message of the Apocalypse.

The first glimpse into heaven that the Seer gets is a view of heavenly worship. God's throne is surrounded by twenty-four elders wearing white robes and golden crowns, enthroned on lesser thrones than God's. God, though unseen, is more personally attended by four beings with composite traits of all the creatures originally created by God to live and serve God upon the earth. While serving God, these beings periodically break out into a song of praise, "Holy, holy, holy, the Lord God Almighty, who was and is and is to come" (Rev 4:8c). When this chorus is sung, the twenty-four heavenly elders fall down on their knees in awe and reverence and sing their own song: "You are worthy, our Lord and God, to receive glory and honor and power, for you created all things, and by your will they existed and were created" (Rev 4:11).

A particularly stirring prayer of praise is found in

> ## Reflection
> ### Psalm 150
>
> Psalm 150, the final psalm, captures the best of everything that has preceded it in the collection of psalms as we now have them. Read it, and discuss its perspective on praise. Invite participants to re-write it in their own words.

> ## Reflection
> ### The End of Days
>
> See *NISB*, 2220, for more of Eugene Boring's explanation of heavenly worship at the end of time.
>
> How can or does the entire creation praise God?

the book of Ezra. The Babylonians destroyed the first great Jewish Temple in Jerusalem. The Jewish people were simultaneously forced into a long Babylonian exile during which power actually passed from the Babylonians to the Persians. It was under the rule of the Persian King Cyrus that some of the Jews began to return to their once beautiful Jerusalem. It had been sacked and burned in the Babylonian conquest, but there evolved a dream to rebuild the Temple.

During the time of Ezra, the dream became a practical endeavor. A story of praise is set against the massive task of laying the foundation for the great new Temple. When that task had been done, and before anything else was built upon the foundation, a celebration was arranged. The priests showed up in their vividly colored vestments and brought their trumpets. The Levites played their cymbals. Evidently, between the priestly blasts of the trumpets and the clashing of the cymbals, the priests and the Levites sang responsively, perhaps antiphonally, a hymn of praise:

> God is good, for God's steadfast love endures forever toward Israel (Ezra 3:11*b*, author's adaptation).

The gathered congregation responded with a great shout of praise. Praise can be loud sometimes because we become excited about who God is!

Not everyone present was entirely happy. Some people wept at the praise ceremony for the newly laid foundation of the Temple-to-be-restored. They remembered the beauty and grandeur of the first Temple and how the Babylonians had burned it to the ground as the Jews were rushed away into exile. They wept loudly. At a distance, people could hear all these loud sounds but could not distinguish the cries of pain from the shouts of joy (see Ezra 3:13*a*). This bittersweet experience may mean that even tragedy cannot silence praise; or perhaps it observes that, in the praise of a worshiping community, there are always cries of pain raised with the sounds of praise. Neither can silence the other.

Study Bible

See the possible reasons for the tears in Ralph W. Klein's notes on Ezra 3:12-13, *NISB*, 659.

Session 4   Psalm 92 and 1 Thessalonians 5

Good to Give Thanks

"It is good to give thanks to the Lord, to sing praises to your name, O Most High," (Ps 92:1-5*a*). The psalmist confirmed a reality that has not changed: giving thanks to God is a good thing. It may also be an unavoidable practice for those who can discern God's handiwork.

In this particular prayer, I see two types of divine action that are the bases for expressing prayerful gratitude: indications of God's steadfast love and instances of God's faithfulness. Remembering these works makes the people of God joyful in worship. How could they not be happy as they allow recollections of God's love and faithfulness to flood their thoughts and memories?

We affirm with the psalmist the importance of giving thanks, of being people who understand the source of all good gifts and who actively and openly express appreciation for these gifts. But be sure that prayers of celebration—either praise or thanksgiving—are not intended as ends in themselves. There is always a movement, a process, in God's scheme of activity.

When God graces us with any kind of gift, the proper response is to be thankful. Beyond being thankful (or perhaps as a part of being thankful) we must pass on at least part of what we have received. If there is nothing tangible to pass on, then at the very least we must point to the source of the gifts and blessings in our lives. A financial gift to one's church, for example, is passing on a portion of what one has received; giving food to a food pantry is ministering to the destitute, as is adopting a needy family for the sharing of Christmas gifts; so is preparing and serving a nutritious meal to people who are homeless and have no place or

Reflections
Pass It On

1. Is it possible to discern God's grace in your life if others do not sense that grace is coming from you?
2. Is it possible to sense forgiveness from others if you are not forgiving those who offend you?
3. Is it possible for someone's actions against you to be unforgivable?

means to get a meal together for themselves.

A church exists to be a conduit of God's blessings to its community and to the world beyond. God gives us nothing to stockpile selfishly. Pretending to be thankful without sharing the blessing or the gifts we have received from God is as empty as pretending to receive God's forgiveness when we fail to forgive those who wrong us. It just does not work.

God initiates the whole process by giving to us. We receive the gift with gratitude, and then we share what we can. If the gift is tangible, we share a part of it for the good of someone else. If the gift is emotional, we share from our hearts with someone who needs some of what has come to us. And if there is nothing to share in these ways, we at least point to the giver of all good gifts—our gracious God.

Prayers of thanksgiving come in at the point of our receiving a gift as well as later when we remember having received some kind of blessing from God. These gifts from God are not the kinds of presents for which a single thank-you upon receipt will do—even though books of etiquette may be satisfied if a solitary expression of gratitude are sent out. Prayers of thanksgiving offered in the present, once gifts are received, might even be compared to good manners. Fortunately, God is not like us and is not sitting around in heaven sulking because we failed to say thank you every time we should have said it.

We make ourselves thankful people because it is the right thing to do and because we cannot be our best selves if we are so demanding and greedy and self-centered that we cannot be bothered with voicing a simple thank-you. I say it specifically that way because, in our modern world, there is such a push to be hoggish and self-absorbed that we have to work aggressively against those influences.

Furthermore, tastes and preferences in our society of plenty have driven us never to be satisfied with anything other than exactly what we want. Some of us annually sweat the task of buying a gift for at least one such *discriminating* person in our families or circle of friends. This is the person who gives such a detailed

Reflections
Define the Gift

1. What kinds of tangible gifts have you received from God?
2. What counts as an emotional gift from God?
3. How did you know that God was the giver of these gifts?

Reflections
Winners

Often during a sporting event a player will make a score and then pause with a gesture of thanksgiving toward God.

1. Does God favor the winning player who made a score?
2. Is the player thanking God for making him a winner?

Or is the player instinctively a thankful person?

list that shopping for her or for him is little more than painting by the numbers. More fun still are the persons who set up registries, having picked out their own gifts ahead of time. There can be no thankfulness on the part of these people unless they get exactly the gift and the brand they have pre-specified. Any minor variant makes the entire gift unacceptable.

Culturally, we have lost sight of the meaning behind the phrase "it's the thought that counts." For many people, it is not only the thought that counts; it is the expectation to be given exactly and only what is expected. Gift-giving becomes drudgery.

We can catch ourselves doing the same thing with God's gifts, and maybe to a greater degree. If God does not give us squarely what we demand, and on a schedule determined by us, then we turn up our noses to any gift God offers us. If it is not precisely what we want, we treat God like the uninformed relative who did not have the good sense to give us a suitable gift. We attempt to give God the cold shoulder.

On this matter of being thankful for all that God gives us, whether or not we get exactly what we want, consider a Pauline passage that takes some people off the deep end in the other direction. You are aware that the Apostle Paul had significant adversity in his life. To be sure, he brought some of it on himself, but it was adversity nonetheless.

Pauline scholars take his two letters to the Thessalonians to be his first letters, and thus the oldest written material that we have in our New Testament. In 1 Thessalonians the very early Paul enthusiastically admonished his sisters and brothers in Christ to: "rejoice always, pray without ceasing, give thanks in all circumstances" (1 Thess 5:16-18a).

Paul is not suggesting that we be thankful *for* all circumstances, *for* everything that comes our way. Enjoyment of suffering or adversity can be a bizarre mental disorder. What Paul presses other Christians to practice with him, though, is a thankfulness in all circumstances; not, for example, for a tragedy as it is taking place, but for God's presence that is with us in and through whatever difficulty we must endure. Many

Study Bible

See the Introduction to The First Letter of Paul to the Thessalonians, *NISB*, 2115.

Reflections
Eschatology

Paul urges thanksgiving (and right living) no matter what happens during the destruction that will come at the end of time (1 Thess 5:1-11).

Can you think of anyone who endured apocalyptic suffering (e.g. during the Holocaust, or during other catastrophic events) and yet still testified to God's comforting presence?

difficulties in life are apparent for nearly all of us. We can get through them, yet absolutely nothing can come our way without God standing with us. In the darkest night of any soul, when the wind has been knocked out of us and time has stood still because the thought of any future is unbearable, God comforts us. God holds us in God's arms. Is there a more priceless gift? And, honestly, is there anything we need more than that?

So, it is good to give thanks to the Lord. Giving thanks in all circumstances is in order for people of faith. To underscore the importance of ongoing thanksgiving to a great and giving God, in ancient Israel, the priests and Temple assistants had assigned duties around the clock. Some of them read passages from holy writ. Some of them sang or played instruments. Some of them kept the fires going in the altar of sacrifice. And some were assigned the task of expressing gratitude to God without ceasing for God's historic and present gifts to the people of Israel: "Heman and Jeduthan and the rest of those chosen and expressly named to render thanks to the Lord, for his steadfast love endures forever" (1 Chron 16:41). Giving corporate thanks was so important to the people of Israel that they believed prayers of thanksgiving should literally be offered at all times.

Study Bible

The whole experience of public worship in ancient Israel was founded on the need for thankfulness. "The conclusion to the Chronicler's ark narrative [1 Chr 16:4-43] institutes public worship," *NISB*, 594.

Praying Unselfishly for Myself and Those about Whom I Care

Having avoided selfishness and self-centeredness in prayer, this question must now be answered: Is all prayer regarding me and my needs selfish? Absolutely not. Each of us knows most of the time whether or not our desires are real needs or pure wants. Within want and need is the distinction between unselfish and selfish prayers. Are we praying for what we really need to "get by" (our daily bread)? Or are we trying to use prayer as a means of achieving the American dream, asking God to give us luxury automobiles, big bonuses at work, and citizenship in a country with absolute military might?

Desiring health for our loved ones and ourselves is not selfish in the least, and we should certainly pray without ceasing in thanking God for pulling us (individually and communally) consistently toward health. This is what God does whether or not we ask! When we are unhealthy and needing to seek various means for having our health restored, then we can thank God for God's willingness to direct us as we listen anew.

Using Jesus as our guide, we notice two very telling interactions that he had with persons who were ill.

First, Jesus affirmed those who sought out a means to be made whole. He spent most of his time helping people find physical, emotional, and mental wholeness. Recall the unnamed woman with the "issue of blood," as the ancient storytellers put it. "She had endured much under many physicians, and had spent all that she had; and she was no better, but rather grew worse" (Mark 5:26).

Health practitioners and waiting rooms had obvious-

Reflections
Felt Needs

The science of marketing is based on the study of "felt needs."
1. Is there a difference between needing something and wanting something?
2. Is it okay to want something as long as you don't expect God to give it to you?

Teaching Tips
Healing

Mark 5:26 summarizes the last few years in the life of someone you know. Use this statement and your reflections to give some consideration to the widespread need for healing in our world.

Encourage the group to share a few stories on this subject.

ly exhausted this woman! She had an image of Jesus that led her to believe that if she could make minimal physical contact with him, healing would flow into her weary body. She would not have to bother Jesus with an appointment or a health history. If she could just squeeze through the crowd (which was difficult given her physical weakness from persistent blood loss), and as much as brush up against the faith healer, she was convinced that the bleeding would stop.

The only thing that surprised the woman who turned out to be more persistent than her bleeding was that Jesus did realize that his powers had been tapped. "Who touched me?" he asked (Mark 5:32).

The woman, who now felt physically well for the first time in years, suddenly became paralyzed with fear. She managed to tell Jesus her story and, much to her surprise, Jesus was delighted. "Daughter," he said with jubilation, "your faith has made you well; go in peace, and be healed of your disease" (Mark 5:34).

Second, Jesus actually asked someone before pointing him toward health if he, in fact, wanted to be well. If congregations and pastors assume that everyone who is ill wants to be well, they are mistaken.

There is a powerful turn in the story that opens John 5. Jesus encounters a man who, from all indications, wants to be well more than anybody in the world wanted to be well. He had thirty-eight years of effort to prove it. And yet amazingly, before offering some healing options, Jesus asks him a question that makes Jesus seem a little unfocussed at best: "Do you want to be made well?" (John 5:6*b*). There is no healing, even if all the right prayers are uttered, if the person who is ill lacks the desire to be well. Wellness is not a condition that God forces upon any of us.

A very much sought after clinical psychologist left her lucrative private practice a few years ago and became a public school psychologist. I was acquainted with her when she became part of the instructional team for one of my sons, who was struggling with learning differences. She became his heroine. As I knew her better, I asked her why she had made the move from a higher to lower income. Her answer made me thankful:

Reflections
Twice Healed?

Why did Jesus say what he said at the end of 5:34 when, according to verse 29, the woman was already cured?

See Mary Ann Tolbert's thoughts on the matter in her commentary on the two verses, *NISB*, 1817.

Study Bible

According to Gail R. O'Day, the length of the man's illness, thirty-eight years, indicated its "seeming permanence," *NISB*, 1916.

Reflections
Checkup

1. Are we prayerfully concerned about our own health most of the time, or only when we are ill?

2. Have we trained ourselves not to care—and, therefore, not to pray—about the plight of the millions who are dying from starvation and disease?

"Because I wanted to work with people who really wanted to make productive changes in their lives."

Again, there is nothing selfish about wanting to be well, and wanting health and wholeness for our loved ones and for persons anonymous to us whom we know. It is the Christian's desire, even obligation, to pray for those who suffer, such as the huge percentage of persons on the African continent infected with the HIV virus.

One of the clearest of all signs that our prayers are unselfish is that they focus on others who have needs, not just ourselves or those close to us. A desire for our personal health is the most natural thing in the world; no one could conceive of such a concern as an indication of self-centeredness. As a matter of fact, in this particular area, it is often a selfish thing not to be concerned about optimum health.

Conclusion: A Pastor's Response

One's theology of providence becomes very critical at the juncture of healing and wholeness. This is true whether you are the patient, the person offering the prayer, or both. Personally, I cannot accept the idea that God wills or allows anyone's illness or suffering. Thus, I am careful to avoid the impression that a prayer addressing the matter of restored health is a prayer that asks God to undo what God has readily willed.

As a pastor, I have radically changed my prayer utterances with a parishioner who is in some kind of a health crisis—from surgery that is about to be performed to news of a potentially irreversible illness. I have moved away entirely from prayers that say such things as:

◆ "God, I pray that you would heal Sister Laura."
◆ "God, if it be your will, let Brother Sam be whole again."

What are the theological presuppositions of these two prayers? I note three: a) God is powerful and can heal the sick; b) If I ask properly and effectively, God might do some healing; and c) God might as easily, however (and for unknowable reasons), will the continuation of the disease and ultimately death. Any pastor should have problems with "b" and "c" because either I (b) or God (c) would bear the blame for a significant part of human suffering.

Instead, I pray as I hold the hand of someone who is anxious or suffering, saying:

◆ "Gracious God, in a world where so many forces work against our health and well-being, we are grateful beyond words that you, without fail, work for our wholeness."

◆ "God of strength and encouragement, we rest in the reality that you go with our loved one into this surgery and that your desire is for full restoration."

◆ "God of love and compassion, we know that you want for all of your children the abundant life and lives lived to their fullest temporal extent. Therefore, if there are pathways for healing about which our friend does not know, we seek your leadership in finding those sources."

CHRISTIAN FAITH AND POWER

A STUDY BY

THORWALD LORENZEN

Thorwald Lorenzen, a native of Germany, is pastor of the Canberra Baptist Church in Canberra, Australia, following many years as a professor of systematic theology and theological ethics at the International Baptist Seminary in Rueschlikon, Switzerland.

CHRISTIAN FAITH AND POWER
Outline

Introduction

The Power of Weakness and the Weakness of Power

P ower is part of human life. We speak of military, police, and economic power. We speak of power in relationships between husbands and wives, and between parents and children. Religious people may speak of being overcome by a spiritual power. The use of the word *power* is quite fluid. It is related to varied social interactions such as force, influence, authority, control, domination, and even violence.

When we speak of power as it relates to the Christian faith, we seek to interrelate our experience and our use of power with that which concerns us ultimately, our faith in Jesus Christ. We seek to gain an understanding of power that is in harmony with the Christian message. This study will lead us to discover that the Christian faith transfigures our understanding, as well as our use, of power. Aspects of the Jesus story invite us to understand power as the power of love, and these aspects help us to distinguish between the power of weakness and the weakness of power.

A good illustration of the connection between faith and life is the text of Paul in 2 Corinthians 5:17-21. Faith in Christ introduces the believer to ". . . a new creation: everything old has passed away; see, everything has become new!" (2 Cor 5:17). This newness is their reconciliation with God through Christ (2 Cor 5:18). Believers are introduced to a new reality. They have become ambassadors for Christ. They have the privilege of God making God's appeal through them (2 Cor 5:20).

Now the question of power arises. Any appeal uses some sort of power. How does the apostle speak of power in the context of the Christian gospel? Paul says,

"…we entreat you on behalf of Christ" (2 Cor 5:20). The word that Paul uses for "entreat," *deomai*, means "begging." Therefore, the form of power in a Christian context cannot be imposing or coercive. It must be an expression of the reconciliation that God has brought about through Christ.

The Dalai Lama has said, "It is my belief that whereas the 20th century has been a century of war and untold suffering, the 21st century world should be one of peace and dialogue. As the cultural advances in information technology make our world a truly global village, I believe there will come a time when war and conflict will be considered an outdated and obsolete method of settling difference among nations and communities."

I once read an account of a talk given by the Dalai Lama. At the end of the talk, someone from the audience asked, "Why didn't you fight back against the Chinese?" The Dalai Lama looked down, swung his feet just a bit, looked back up and said with a gentle smile, "Well, war is obsolete, you know." Then, after a few moments, his face grave, he said, "Of course, the mind can rationalize fighting back, but the heart would never understand. Then you would be divided in yourself; the heart and the mind, and the war would be inside you."

Power—Its Promise and Problem

A few distinctions will help us to prepare the way for discussing some biblical texts that deal with various aspects of power.

♦ *Power and force.* A judge and a police officer have power. Laws, rules, and customs of societies grant such power to them. At their best, they exercise their power for the common good. At their worst, they misuse their power. A police officer may have to use force to restrain a criminal from doing harm to others. At the same time, the use of verbal and physical force can indicate a misuse of power. Force becomes illegitimate when it is used to threaten, to air one's own anger, to manipulate justice, or to arbitrarily force another human being into subjection.

♦ *Power and violence.* Violence is an intensified use of force. There is violence in the home, and there are structural forms of violence such as torture and war.

Source

His Holiness the Dalai Lama: In My Own Words, compiled and edited by Mary Craig (London: Hodder & Stoughton, 2001), 115.

Teaching Tip
Jesus and God's Way

God's ways are revealed in Jesus' Sermon on the Mount (Matt 5:3-7:27) and the Sermon on the Plain (Luke 6:20b-48). Refer to a more detailed look of this subject in my article: "Just War," accessible at **www.canbap.org** in the sermon archive.

Jesus intentionally rejected the violence of the Zealots who sought to usher in the kingdom of God through the use of force. Instead, Jesus fleshed out his conviction that the ways of God have to do with love, trust, forgiveness, and reconciliation. Both the United Nations and the World Council of Churches have espoused this approach by calling upon the global community to seek ways of overcoming the use of violence.

♦ *Power and hierarchy.* Power is often associated with hierarchy. There are hierarchies in the family (parents and children), in the military (army generals, other officers, soldiers), and in governments that empower various institutions to facilitate the regulation of effective social functioning. At the same time, history teaches us that power can easily become corrupt. Patriarchy denies equality to women. Some clergy and even some parents have misused their hierarchical power by sexually abusing children. Governments have misused their power by fostering racism, apartheid, and ethnic hatred. Jesus' teaching about servanthood remains a salient reminder that where God's Word is heard, believed, and obeyed, there occurs a transfiguration of power (Mark 20:24-28; Matt 10:41-45; Luke 22:24-27).

♦ *Authoritarian and authoritative.* Since power is part of life, we need to distinguish between the legitimate and illegitimate use of power. Part of that distinction is to understand the difference between authoritarian and authoritative power. In an authoritarian use of power, the strong forces his or her will on the weak. In contrast, an authoritative use of power seeks the voluntary agreement of the other for the common good. Authoritative power uses talk and dialogue, not force or violence.

Power and Truth

Most social institutions in Western democracies are secular, especially national governments or global institutions like the United Nations. But this secularization does not mean that such institutions are absolute and can do what they like. They cannot be their own reference

Source

Universal Declaration of Human Rights Adopted by U.N. General Assembly Resolution 217A (III), December 10, 1948.

189

points, make their own rules, create their own morality, or demand blind obedience from their citizens.

There are intimations in our world that such institutions are held accountable to a truth that transcends them. Some countries include in their constitution a reference to "almighty God." In the context of the global community, universal human rights transcend the authority of the nation state. Indeed, each state promises to observe and implement these universal human rights, rights that are based on the reality that all human beings are "born free and equal in dignity . . . They are endowed with reason and conscience and should act towards one another in a spirit of brotherhood" (Universal Declaration of Human Rights). No country can grant these rights, and no one can take them away. They exist to be recognized and implemented. However, their very existence is a protest against a postmodern relativism that refuses to give credence to any truth that transcends the situation. As Christians, we claim that power is not identical with truth. Rather, power must echo truth, or else lose its credibility and authority.

The Biblical Texts

Our study will focus on the following biblical texts that deal with the problem of power:

♦ Session 1, "The Transfiguration of Power," examines Revelation 5, which emphasizes the crucified Christ as the revelation of God's plan for the world. This text helps us distinguish between the power of weakness and the weakness of power.

♦ Session 2, "Money is Power," looks to Mark 10:17-31 and Luke 19:1-10. These texts provide two paradigms of responses to the power of money and possessions.

Sessions 3, 4, and 5 address aspects of the relationship between Christians and government authorities in the New Testament.

♦ Session 3, "Christians, Government Authorities and Context," focuses on Romans 13:1-10.

♦ Session 4, "Christians, Government Authorities, and Obedience," studies Revelation 13.

♦ Session 5, "Christians, Government Authorities, and Conflict," examines 1 Peter 2:13-17, Mark 12:13-17, and Acts 5:17-42.

The Transfiguration of Power

Tears (Rev 5:1-4)

As the chapter begins, a weeping seer meets us (Rev 5:4). Because he is frustrated that he cannot reconcile his faith in God with the reality he experiences in the world, the seer believes that God has a meaningful plan for life and history. He sees a scroll held in the right hand of God, the place of authority, action, and power (Rev 5:1).

The scroll is sealed with seven seals (Rev 5:1) and nobody seems to be able to interpret God's plan for the world. This weeping seer says, ". . . and I began to weep bitterly because no one was found worthy to open the scroll or to look into it" (Rev 5:4).

The Lion (Rev 5:5)

Drawing from traditional messianic language, our attention turns to the lion of the tribe of Judah. He "has conquered, so that he can open the scroll and its seven seals" (Rev 5:5). This is familiar language; it is the language of force. Who can assail a lion? He has no enemies because he does not tolerate enemies. He will break the seals of the book with his strength and wipe the tears of frustration from the face of the seer.

In our world, the candles of peace marches and the prayers and demonstrations of Christians committed to nonviolence do not determine the plan of history. Rather, violence as a means of foreign policy and the force of the military machinery seem to determines history.

The Lamb (Rev 5:6-7)

The picture of the lion fades away and makes room for the lamb: "I saw a Lamb!" cries the seer. Not God and

Lectionary Loop

**Third Sunday of Easter, Year C
(Rev 5:11-14)**

Study Bible

See several meanings related to the use of the word *scroll* in the *NISB*, 2221.

Reflections

The Nature of God

If the crucified Christ defines the nature of God, what does that mean for our use of the word *God*?

Study Bible

See *NISB*, 2222 for the christological transfiguration of images of violence.

the lion, but God and the lamb. This is a new way of picturing God.

The description of the slaughtered lamb is clearly a reference to the crucified Christ. Here, the seer uses picture language to say what other early Christian theologians had also emphasized. Paul defines the center of his vision of reality to the Corinthian church when he writes, "For I decided to know nothing among you except Jesus Christ, and him crucified" (1 Cor 2:2). The Gospel of Mark climaxes in the Gentile centurian's confession made in the face of the crucified Christ: "Truly this man was God's Son!" (Mark 15:39). What the treasures of Greek philosophy could not convey, and what the heroes and heroines of the Jewish religion could not unravel, comes to fulfillment in the crucified Christ. The "seven horns" signify true power, and the "seven eyes" true insight. This is a picture of the enthronement of the crucified Christ as the center of reality.

The image of the lamb, rather than the lion, helps us to seek an alternative understanding of history, an alternative that is not a model of force and conquest. There are examples of the power of the lamb in human history. Consider the "velvet" revolution in Eastern Europe (1989). The visible symbol was the candle. The citizens of Leipzig, Berlin, and Dresden lit candles on their altars and then walked out into the streets. Many wore signs around their necks explaining, "Every Monday, without violence!" Eventually, there were tens of thousands of these peaceful protesters making their statement, softly at first, then more and more loudly, but always without violence. In this act of nonviolent protest, the world saw an eloquent symbol of the power of weakness.

In light of the slain lamb as the mysterious center of history, we can also appreciate the transforming power of the silent Jesus versus the mighty Pilate; of Rosa Parks versus the powerful structures of racism; of Dietrich Bonhoeffer versus Adolf Hitler; of Mahatma Ghandi versus the mighty British Empire; of Nelson Mandela versus the Apartheid regime.

By recognizing the crucified Christ as the center of history, we have hope that those who appear to be without power like Aung San Suu Kyi, under house arrest in

> ## Reflection
> ### The Lion and the Lamb
> Give examples from your experience of the power of weakness (lamb) and the weakness of power (lion).

Myanmar, or the peace movement around the world, will have the promise of truth on their side.

Singing a New Song (Rev 5:8-14)
The enthronement of the crucified Christ as the center of history gives rise to a new song, as seen in Revelation 5:9-10.

Throughout the ages, most Christians have never sung this song, just as the majority of Christians throughout the ages have supported slavery, apartheid, racism, women's subordination, nationalism, and imperialism. The song that should have been sung, the song about the lamb that was slaughtered, more often has been a whisper, drowned out by the celebrations of national, cultural, and military triumphs. But the whisper becomes louder crescendos because it is a song that cannot be quenched. It is grounded in the very heart of God.

The new song contains this message: Jesus Christ, by his life, death, and resurrection, has done for us what we could not do for ourselves. He has opened our way into God, here expressed in the word "ransom" (Rev 5:9). Also, God's love and salvation are all-inclusive. God's love covers "saints from every tribe and language and people and nation" (Rev 5:9). All believers are priests who give witness to the new song that God has composed and that God keeps alive. We are invited to sing along!

We Belong in the Message
Revelation 5:13 promises that one day all creatures in heaven and on earth will sing the song.

Will that song begin to shape our lives? It will be difficult, and we do not know what it will bring to us. The earliest opponents of slavery, apartheid, and violence lived in hope. Like Moses, they did not experience the fulfillment of their dreams. Did those who took the candles off of the altar and carried them into the streets know what the results of their risky action would be? Did Rosa Parks know what would happen when she breathed her tired "No"?

Sometimes, we have to do what our consciences tell us, even if we do not know where we will end up. As Christians struggling to remain faithful, we must not use

---

Reflections

Nonviolence
1. Are there other ways that New Testament authors express the same message as found in Revelation 5?
2. Is a commitment to nonviolence an act of courage or of cowardice? Explain.

God to justify our personal self-interests and national or cultural dreams. Instead, we begin to sing with our lives the song about the lamb that was slaughtered.

Conclusion

The picture of the lamb and the new song contain the following emphases:

God is different from the way we often think of God and wish God to be. The image of the slaughtered lamb tells us that God has revealed God's nature in the cross of the risen Christ. Pilate, Constantine, and the triumphant church that enjoyed the privileges of the state do not give witness to God's nature. The suffering prophets, Jesus, Francis of Assisi, and the discipleship movements through the ages are the true witnesses to God's nature.

Jesus' death and resurrection cannot be separated from his life. His commitment to God and his compassion for others remain the text of the new song.

Following Jesus implies a new understanding of power. The power of love, compassion, and service begins to replace the use of power for furthering one's own interests.

This new vision of reality calls for celebration. Our focus on the lamb who was slaughtered does not lead to a morbid mentality. Instead, it celebrates the reality that we can interpret history with a new understanding of power and engage our lives, not in that which is popular, but in that which is true.

Session 2

Mark 10:17-31, Luke 19:1-10

Money Is Power

"You cannot serve God and wealth" (Luke 16:13)
Money is power. We all know it! Those who have money have clout. This is true in our private lives, in the church, and on the international stage. The rich often use their power exclusively to further their own interests and convictions. There is no way for Christians to avoid the issue of money and power if we want to be serious about following Jesus.

The Markan text for our lesson is the only text in the Christian Bible where a person refuses to follow Jesus. The man in Mark's story refused to follow Jesus because he could not reconcile the liberating claim of Jesus with the power of money.

The Paradigm (Mark 10:17-22)
Jesus is on a journey. A man—any person; you, me—approaches Jesus with the question of ultimacy. His manner of running and kneeling, and his language when he says "Good Teacher," suggest expectancy. Jesus' presence gives the impression to some that he is able to deal with ultimate questions.

After acknowledging the difference between himself and God (Mark 10:18), Jesus gives the answer of traditional morality. His citations come from the second half of the Ten Commandments. The first five speak about God and God's liberating relationship to people, while the second five deal with the content of that relationship. As Christians, we know that faith and morality are related, but we also know that they are not the same.

The response of the inquiring man (Mark 10:20) is revealing. He has fulfilled the moral claims of his reli-

Lectionary Loop
Proper 23, Year B (Mark 10:17-31); Proper 26, Year C (Luke 19:1-10)

Teaching Tip
The Young Man
The man in Mark 10:17-22 is described as a "young man" in Matt 19:20 and a "ruler" in Luke 18:18.

Reflections
The Power of Money
1. Why is the choice of either God or money/property so stark and forbidding?
2. Would we have the courage and honesty to name the power of money and possessions in our own life? How does it compare with the power of faith and love?

gion, but his longing for eternal life and for God have not been satisfied.

Now comes the crunch point. Who or what will be the ultimate reality? Who or what will be "god" in his life? Before the challenge is posed, the text makes clear that not morality, but abundant life, is the driving motivation. "Jesus, looking at him, loved him" (Mark 10:21).

The challenge to "go, sell what you own, and give the money to the poor, and you will have treasure in heaven; then come, follow me" (Mark 10:21) touches the foundations of the man's life. The choice is clear. Will Jesus' invitation to "follow me" be more promising in the quest for eternal life than possessions?

This exchange also reveals Jesus' special provision for the poor. They are to be the benefactors of the man's turning to God.

One can feel the tension. The choice must be made. Unless he transfigures his dependence on possessions into a new lifestyle of relationships, the man will never understand what Jesus and God are about. Again, this is the only place in the Christian Bible where someone refused the invitation to follow Jesus, and the reason for the refusal is a preference for material possessions.

In a money-mad, consumer-crazy world, we must feel the shocking importance of this decision. Will Jesus or money be the focus of your conscience and mine?

The Paradigm Applied to the Church (Mark 10:23-27)
Jesus' invitation applies to the early church as well. From the encounter between Jesus and the man, the focus shifts to the disciples. In our post-Easter situation, where the horizons of Jesus and the church are interrelated, the word "disciples" refers to Christians.

The metaphor that points to the power of money is a potent one. Just as it is impossible for a camel to get though the eye of a needle, so it is impossible for a rich person to enter the kingdom of God (Mark 10:25). We do not like this picture. Many commentaries attempt to domesticate Jesus' words. The most popular interpretation explains that there was a gate in Jerusalem's wall called The Eye of the Needle. People used this entrance when the main gates were closed for the night, and there was just enough room for them to squeeze through with their camels. This explanation is attractive because it allows Christians to keep their riches and still squeeze into the kingdom. But such a gate is not known, and there is no basis for such an explanation. Therefore, the disciples respond appropriately, "Then who can be saved?" (Mark 10:26).

Again, the limits of morality are named (10:27). The power of money is strong. Only a divine act of grace, such as we know from the resurrection of the crucified one, can transfigure the power of money into an experience of liberation.

Transfiguration (Mark 10:28-31)
Peter gives voice to the human reaction of Jesus' followers through the ages when he says, "We have left everything and followed you" (Mark 10:28). What more can we do? We have burned our bridges behind us. We have left jobs and family. What more do you expect?

Jesus then introduces the disciples to a new way of being—a way of life where, not the world, but God, sets the standards. Earlier in the Gospel, Jesus spoke about his new family when he said, "Whoever does the will of God is my brother and sister and mother" (Mark 3:31-35). Natural family ties are transfigured to include the family of those who follow Christ.

Yet this new reality of God and of love still conflicts with the old ways of individualism and competitiveness. Therefore, persecution and suffering will accompany the Christian on her or his faith journey. Nevertheless, in God's plan, justice and salvation provide for a meaningful life here and now and the promise of eternity in the presence of God. Thus, Paul writes, "Therefore, my beloved, be steadfast, immovable, always excelling in the work of the Lord, because you know that in the Lord your labor is not in vain" (1 Cor 15:58).

A Counter Paradigm (Luke 19:1-10)
Zacchaeus was also rich (Luke 19:2). His riches had come from a tax collecting business that he had leased from the government. There were many opportunities

---

Reflection
The New Family
If the Christian community forms a new "family," what consequences does this have for waging war with countries where there are Christians?

Reflection
The Micah Declaration
Read and discuss the "Micah Declaration" (issued by Evangelical Mission and Aid organizations. See **www.canbap.org** and **www.micahnetwork.org**).

197

to overcharge people and pocket the surplus. In addition to the moral suspicion that arose, the people did not like tax collectors because they collected taxes on the soil that God had given to the Jewish people, and then gave the taxes to a Gentile government. Some people, the Zealots, refused to pay taxes and openly fought those who compromised with the Romans.

People were suspicious when Jesus gave special attention to this despised tax collector. Jesus calls to him, saying, "Zacchaeus, hurry and come down; for I must stay at your house today" (Luke 19:5). Note the urgency of the invitation. For Zacchaeus, this encounter became a joyous surprise. Rather than turning away, he turned to Jesus and joyously accepted the consequences or his repentance, saying, "Look, half of my possessions, Lord, I will give to the poor; and if I have defrauded anyone of anything, I will pay back four times as much" (Luke 19:8). This is salvation: turning to God and loving one's neighbor.

Session 3   Romans 13:1-10

Christians, Governing Authorities, and Context

A s human beings, we live within given structures. We live in accordance with standards set by such authorities as family, church, school, and government. In a democratic society, we vote those who govern in and out of power, and, although we may feel that our influence is limited, each of us participates in shaping the structures of our societies.

The relationship to government has been a challenge for Christians since the early days. Should we be uncritical of government, accepting it as God-given, and therefore obeying it without question? Or should we be prophetic and denounce or even resist government when its attitudes and actions are against what we understand to be God's way?

In this and the next two sessions, we will analyze our relationship to governing authorities in light of important biblical texts. Although our situation is very different from that of the early Christians, there are important principles that we can glean from these texts as we shape our own attitudes toward the governing authorities in our respective countries.

Romans 13:1-10 has been one of the most controversial texts in the history of Christianity. Using this text, Christian theologians have argued that the government is part of the "orders of creation" or "orders of redemption," implying that it must be obeyed under any circumstances. In countries that have professed to be Christian through the ages, politicians and judges have used this text to call for obedience to the law and, at the same time, to deny citizens the rights of civil disobedience and conscientious objection.

> **Lectionary Loop**
> **Proper 18, Year A**

This text, like every biblical text, must be carefully interpreted in its context. It is important to remember that Paul was not composing an abstract theory of the state. Rather, he was addressing a particular situation in Rome where political unrest may have been in the air. How Christians were to relate to governmental authorities was a part of everyday life in Paul's setting.

The state institution of Paul's day and the state institution of today differ greatly. In a democratic society, the limitations of the government and the influence of citizens on their governments are much greater than in ancient times. We normally have a separation of powers that provides checks and balances. Also, most democratic constitutions are aware of the danger of the state's demanding absolute obedience of its citizens and therefore provide ways to protect the freedom of conscience. When we compare the situations, then and now, we must be suspicious of our human tendency to use biblical texts in support of our own human, national, and cultural biases.

In Romans 12:1-2, Paul begins the pastoral and ethical section of Romans. He emphasizes that Christians worship God with their bodies, with their whole lives. This includes involvement with the life of the church (Rom 12:3-8) and with the life of society (Rom 12:9-21). Then the apostle names the measure for the Christian conscience (Rom 13:5). That measure is love (Rom 13:8-10, see also Rom 12:9-21).

Paul speaks about the end of human history and its imminence when he says, "Salvation is nearer to us now than when we became believers" (Rom 13:11); therefore "put on the Lord Jesus Christ, and make no provision for the flesh, to gratify its desires" (Rom 13:14). This awareness of an imminent end has led some theologians to understand Paul's ethics as "interim ethics." What is meant by this designation is that Paul's instructions were only meant for a short time, until the imminent return of Christ. Therefore, Paul's instructions are no longer relevant and valid, since the Lord did not come and indeed has not returned. But that is not Paul's message. Besides emphasizing that we worship God with our whole selves, and that the content of our being and acting is love, Paul

Reflections
Loyalty and Obedience

1. What would you say to a politician or a judge who says that, in light of Rom 13:1-7, Christians must show unquestionable loyalty and obedience to their governments?
2. In light of information from the study material, compare Rom 13:1-10 and Rom 12:1-2.

Reflections
Functions of Government

1. To what does the state's "bearing the sword" refer?
2. What are the central functions of government?
3. What is meant by the use of the word "conscience" in Romans 13: 5?

wants to remind his readers that our relationship to the government has a different quality than our relationship with God. Relationship with God is exclusive. Relationship to the government, while important, is not ultimate. When the apostles were accused of disobeying the authorities, they reminded the authorities that their consciences were bound to Jesus Christ, and that they had to "obey God rather than any human authority" (Acts 5:29-31).

Study Bible

Compare Rom 13:1-7 to 1 Tim 2:1-2, Titus 3:1 and 1 Pet 2:13-17. See the "Excursus: Christians and Government," *NISB*, 2029.

- ♦ Verse 1 exhorts the Christian citizen to "be subject to the governing authorities" (Rom 13:1, 5). To "be subject" does not mean uncritical obedience. Paul uses the same verb to describe the relation of the wife to the husband (1 Cor 14:34) and of the Christian church member to a church leader (1 Cor 16:16). It is relational language, describing the voluntary acceptance of an authority that one recognizes and gives to a person or an institution for the common good.

In the text, Paul asserts that people should subject themselves to governing authorities because God institutes and appoints these governments (Rom 13:1-2). Governments serve God (Rom 13:4, 5). In the ancient world, it was not uncommon to believe that rulers and authorities were appointed by God and were used by God to fulfill God's purposes. However, even if that were the case, the state was not divine; it was divinely appointed. It was not an order of being that existed independently of God. It was a functional institution that existed to serve the purposes of God.

- ♦ Verse 2 draws the conclusion that resistance against the authorities is resistance against God, which God will punish in the last judgment. The state's "bearing the sword" (Rom 13:4) does not refer to the military, or even the right to exercise capital punishment, but to a legal system that seeks to implement justice, order and peace.

Since the text has often been used by governing authorities to demand obedience from their citizens, and since even theologians have counseled churches not to oppose their respective national governments, we must raise this question of whether or not there are limits to

Christian submission to the state. Note the following:

- Verse 4 states that the government "is God's servant for your good." The government, therefore, has certain functions it must fulfill. Government should provide order, peace, and social security for its people.
- Verse 5 introduces an important alternative to the use of fear (Rom 13:3-4) and wrath (Rom 13:5), by which governments seek to maintain order. That alternative is conscience. Conscience signifies the fact that we humans can have an ultimate focus that provides us with the possibility of analyzing and evaluating our lives both individually and communally.
- Verses 8-10 provide the content by which the Christian conscience monitors life, that content being love. (Rom 13:8, 10).

Paul resisted political authorities and had to flee from them (2 Cor 11:32-33). Also, in the wider context, we must not forget that in Revelation 13 the same Roman government affirmed by Paul is unmasked as an instrument of Satan that must be resisted at all costs.

Therefore, in this particular situation, Paul admonishes the Christians in Rome to be responsible citizens and to see societal structures as part of the economy of God for the common good. Christians are to observe the law and pay the required taxes. Meeting this obligation is part of their worship of God with their bodies (Rom 12:1-2). At the same time, the content and context of the text make it clear that obedience to the state must be seen in the context of one's relationship to Christ. Any obedience to the law and to the government is not blind and is not absolute. Obedience must spring from the human conscience that is focused on the love of God as expressed in Jesus Christ.

Christians, Governing Authorities, and Obedience

This text was written during the reign of the Roman emperor Domitian (81-96 CE), who ruled toward the end of the first century in Asia Minor. The Christians experienced opposition and persecution (Rev 2:13; 6:9-11; 17:6; 18:24; 19:2; 20:4) because they had separated from the protecting ties of the Jewish religion. Also, these Christians refused to accept the emperor's absolute authority or to worship him by the means required for all.

John of Patmos communicates his message in pictures that have given rise to much speculation. We will not join the throng of apocalyptic speculators, but simply mention what our text clearly affirms and denies.

The first beast is the Roman Empire. It encircles parts of the Mediterranean Sea (Rev 13:1). This empire is described as the incarnation of evil. It embodies the evil characteristics that Daniel 7 had previously ascribed to four beasts (Rev 13:1-2). The empire is seen as the manifestation of Satan on earth. (The dragon in Rev 13:2*b*, according to Rev 12:9, is "the Devil and Satan.") The beast, the Roman Empire, is the Antichrist.

It is not surprising that this chapter was composed in close connection to Revelation 5, where Jesus Christ, as the slain Lamb of God, is enthroned as the secret ruler of the world. Phrases and pictures originally used with reference to Christ are applied here to the beast, including:

♦ Diadems as signs of Christ's lordship (Rev 19:12).

Reflections

Human and Divine Authority

1. How would you deal with the different evaluations of the government in Romans 13 and Revelation 13?
2. Are there limits to our obedience of the government and the law? (See Mark 2:23—3:6)
3. Should our society allow for conscientious objection?
4. Should Christians engage in civil disobedience?

♦ The dragon giving "his power and his throne and great authority" to the empire, a reference to the enthronement of Christ by God (Rev 3:21).

♦ Reference to the wound (Rev 13:3) caused by the sword (Rev 13:14), and yet that he was healed and lived (Rev 13:3, 12, 14), are allusions to the death and resurrection of Jesus Christ.

What is the basic criticism against the Roman Empire? There is no abstract, generalized criticism of the state as such; rather, this particular state is called satanic because it absolutized itself and demanded complete obedience from its citizens. The Roman Empire claimed to be divine and consequently expected people to worship it. Although most people were willing to do so (Rev 13:3b, 4, 8a), our author calls this blasphemy (Rev 13:1, 5, 6). The state is blasphemous when it makes divine claims and demands what only God can demand—namely, worship and complete obedience. The Roman state expected total obedience in all realms of life, even the buying and selling of goods (Rev 13:17). Where such a total claim is resisted, persecution will follow (Rev 13:15).

Even such an evil and powerful state, however, is not outside the realm of the providence by which God sustains, guides, and accompanies human history. The mouth of the beast, though uttering blasphemies against God, "was given" to him (Rev 13:5, note the passive voice), and even the beast's war against the saints is waged within the limitations of the world that God has created (Rev 13:7, passive voice; Rev 13:5b, divine time limit set). In this light, Christians are called to endurance and faith (Rev 13:10).

The second beast (Rev 13:11) serves the first beast, and gives it divine validation. The fact that it rose out of the earth (Rev 13:11) refers to its presence in Asia Minor. It symbolizes the priests of the emperor cult who led people to divine adoration of the Roman emperor and his empire. The image in Rev 13:14-15 refers to the representation of the emperor, who is so closely identified with his representation that it even speaks. The priests try to demonstrate their divine power by performing great miracles (Rev 13:13-14). Those who accept the authority of the emperor show their allegiance by wearing his official seal (Rev 13:16), and those who refuse allegiance are persecuted and economically boycotted (Rev 13:15, 17).

The beast is identified with the number 666. This symbol has exercised the minds of theological speculators for centuries. Protestants have found ways to relate it to the Catholic Church, Catholics have found ways to relate it to the Lutheran Church, Christians have related it to Muhammad, and others have related it to Napoleon or Hitler. The number may refer to the Roman emperor who enforced the cult and demanded the people's absolute obedience, but we cannot be sure.

Christians cannot fulfill a government's demand for total obedience. Fulfilling such an expectation would not only go against the first commandment, but also deny the lordship of Christ over all realms of life. Government is not intrinsically evil, but it can become evil. When that happens, Christians know where their first allegiance lies, whatever the cost may be.

Session 5 1 Peter 2:13-17, Mark 12:13-17, Acts 5:17-42

Christians, Governing Authorities, and Conflict

1 Peter 2:13-17

This text was composed in the context of a church that lived in a hostile environment. In such a situation, the important question becomes: what attitude will Christians adopt toward a hostile government? To answer this and other similar questions, the early churches followed social customs and lists of ethical instructions were composed to provide guidance for the people. These ethical lists dealt with questions such as relationships within the family, between slaves and masters, within the church, and the church's relationship to society.

Since we are interested in what is specifically Christian, it is important to identify where early Christians modified the structure and content of such given ethical instructions. In 2:13 we read, "For the Lord's sake accept the authority of every human institution." Accepting the authority of social, political, and economic institutions is part of our faith in Christ.

The important center of our lesson is in 1 Peter 2:16. Commitment to Christ as Lord implies freedom and responsibility. Christians are free because they have been set free from focusing their ultimate concern on worldly institutions and ideologies. Out of this freedom, they can subject themselves to worldly structures because, in a fallen world, life is not possible without such structures. We need governments, police, and a legal system. However, such subjection can never be given uncritically. We cannot surrender our freedom to an institution. We must remain committed to Christ and act responsibly in our relationship to institutions. Christian freedom should

Lectionary Loop

Proper 24, Year A (Matt 22:15-22)

Reflections
Freedom

1. Compare 1 Pet 2:13-17 with Col 3:18-4:6; Eph 5:22-6:9; 1 Tim 2:8-3:13; 1 John 2:12-17.
2. Explain the different verbs in 1 Pet 2:17: "Honor everyone. Love the family of believers. Fear God. Honor the emperor."
3. What does freedom mean as you understand it? (1 Pet 2:16)

not be used as a pretext for evil. How much selfish ideology is spread under the banner of freedom! Freedom is here defined as the freedom to serve responsibly.

The authorities to which we must relate are not called God's servants or ministers who are instituted by God (as in Romans 13:1, 4, 6), but rather are called human creatures, not institutions. In our worldly lives, we relate to human and finite beings, whose function is to order human life (1 Pet 2:14). If they fulfill that function, they should be supported and obeyed. By supporting and obeying properly functioning authorities, Christians fulfill the will of God (1 Pet 2:15).

The final verse emphasizes again the constructive and critical relationship of Christians to the world. While many ancient and modern theologians have tended to put obedience to God and obedience to political, economic, and social authorities on the same level (see Prov 24:21), our text makes clear distinctions. Only God is to be feared, revered, and worshipped! Political authorities, and indeed all human beings, should be honored and respected, and brothers and sisters in Christ should be loved.

The text makes clear that the world and its authorities are neither divine nor satanic. Worldly authorities function to assure peace and justice, and to protect the rights of the weak against the strong. Insofar as they fulfill these functions, they are to be supported and obeyed. Yet such support and obedience must always be critical, because support and obedience arises from a primary commitment to Christ. Support and obedience can change to criticism and resistance if the authorities no longer fulfill their appointed functions. To show that such a possibility was also experienced by biblical Christianity, we turn to consider Mark 12:13-17.

Mark 12:13-17 (par. Matt 22:15-22, Luke 20:20-26)
This story is a story of conflict. It comes to us from the church out of which the Gospel of Mark was written. With this story, Christians wanted to define their attitude toward the governing authorities. They did so by asking, "What would Jesus do if he were in our situation?"

Study Bible

For more information about the Pharisees, see *NISB,* 1809.

For more information about the Herodians, see *NISB,* 1810.

The Pharisees and Herodians confront Jesus with the question. They ask, "Is it lawful to pay taxes to the emperor, or not?" (Mark 12:14). It was a loaded question. Many people were poor and exploited by the Roman occupation forces. The head and land tax, introduced in 6 CE, was an added financial burden for the poor. More important, however, was the theological problem. The people understood themselves as God's chosen people, living on the soil God had given to them. Were they not, in fact, betraying their God and giving allegiance to the Gentile emperor by paying this tax? Was this not a direct transgression against the first commandment? The radical Zealots believed this and therefore refused to pay this tax.

What should Jesus answer? If he said "Yes," then he would be called a friend of Rome and a betrayer of his own people and their God. If he said "No", he would be identified with the Zealot cause and their desire to overthrow the Roman occupation forces including the use of violent means.

Jesus asks for a denarius. On the front of this Roman coin was the image of Emperor Tiberius, bearing a laurel wreath and symbolizing his divine claim. The inscription read, "Tiberius, Caesar, blessed Son of the blessed God." On the back of the coin was the picture of the Emperor's mother, seated on a divine throne. In her left hand she held an olive branch, and in her right hand she held the Olympic scepter, symbolizing heavenly peace. The inscription read, "High Priest." The implication was clear: this coin symbolized the emperor's divine claim. Zealots considered touching such a coin, or even looking at it, idol worship and blasphemy.

Jesus takes the coin. In doing so, Jesus acknowledges political reality. You cannot escape such reality. You must live in it. Living in the reality of the world does not mean conforming to it, but transforming it (cf. Rom 12:1-2.). That is the meaning of Jesus' verdict, "Give to the emperor the things that are the emperor's, and to God the things that are God's." The people were utterly amazed at this response. The emphasis clearly falls on the second half of the saying. The coin has the picture and the inscription of the emperor. It belongs to him. As

> ## Reflection
> ### Jesus' Alternative
> In your own words, state Jesus' alternative to that of the Zealots and the Essenes.

part of political reality, even the faithful can pay taxes. But the faithful also bear the image and inscription of God (Gen 1:26-27). They belong to God alone.

The text does not support the idea that Jesus accepts the emperor as God's divinely appointed ruler. Instead, Jesus counsels responsible, critical involvement in the world. Jesus does not support any division between the religious and the worldly realm. Our allegiance must be to God. We belong to God. But God has created the world and loves it. Therefore, our attitude toward the world must be positive and constructive. Perhaps the issue can best be understood in terms of critical participation and critical cooperation. Jesus neither identifies with the status quo, nor does he counsel withdrawal from the world, as the Essenes did in the Qumran community. Neither does Jesus support the Zealot cause, but out of a primary commitment to God, Jesus expects us to discern the will of God in each situation, and then try to act on it.

Acts 5:17-42
This text portrays the ministry of the apostles in the Jerusalem temple. They are opposed by the religious and political authorities of the day, which include the High Priest, other members of the Sanhedrin, and the temple police. Despite this opposition, and motivated by the conviction that God exalted Jesus as Leader and Savior, the apostles fearlessly proclaimed: "We must obey God rather than any human authority" (Acts 5:29).

Summary and Conclusions
From these texts, guidelines emerge as to how Christians should understand their relationships to institutions such as the government, the law, and the police.

We live in a world where we experience not only beauty and generosity, but also selfishness and greed. In such a world, institutions such as the state, the church, the family, and the economic structure are necessary to maintain order and to protect human life. Governments, for instance, have the function of providing peace, order, justice, and social security for their citizens.

Revelation 13 is the constant reminder that governments can fail to fulfill their function and become instruments of evil.

Teaching Tip
Visualize Church and State Relations
Have class members draw and later discuss how they visualize the relationship between church and state today (e.g., lion and lamb image, priest consecrating a naval aircraft carrier, doomsday prophet in front of the White House).

When a government fulfills its function, Christians should support, obey, and pray for it. At the same time, power can corrupt. If a government demands total and absolute obedience, or if it fails to honor human dignity, then Christians "must obey God rather than men" (Acts 5:29).

As Christians, we are called not to withdraw from the world, but to worship God by living in the world in a responsible manner. We honor all people and the governments. We love the members of the family of faith. But our worship and reverence are directed to God.

Reflection

Obedience to God

What does it mean in our situation to "obey God rather than any human authority"?

LIBERATING DISCIPLESHIP

A STUDY BY

THORWALD LORENZEN

Thorwald Lorenzen, a native of Germany, is pastor of the Canberra Baptist Church in Canberra, Australia, following many years as a professor of systematic theology and theological ethics at the International Baptist Seminary in Rueschlikon, Switzerland.

LIBERATING DISCIPLESHIP
Outline

I. Introduction
  A. Christian Faith Defined
  B. Distortions of Faith
  C. Faith as Discipleship
  D. Liberating Faith
  E. Interpreting Biblical Texts

II. Session 1: The Call to Discipleship—Mark 1:14-20
      (Mark 2:13-14; Luke 19:1-10; Exodus 3)
  A. God Takes Initiative
  B. God Elects
  C. The Call
  D. The Response
  E. Do Not Miss the Moment of Truth
  F. Invitation

III. Session 2: No Cheap Grace—Mark 8:27-38
  A. Cheap Grace Defined
  B. Who Is Jesus and What Does It Mean to Believe?
  C. Responses to the Question
  D. Identifying Disciples
  E. The Secret of the Christian Life
  F. Consequences of Discipleship

IV. Session 3: Radical Discipleship—Luke 9:57-62 and
      Matthew 8:18-22
  A. The Context of the Study
  B. Transfiguring the Security of a Home
  C. Transfiguring the Imperative of Culture
  D. Transfiguring the Affection of Family
  E. Beyond Legalism, Moralism, and Liberalism
  F. Icons of Discipleship
  G. Who Is Jesus?

V. Session 4: The Lord's Supper—1 Corinthians 11:17-34
      (Matthew 25:31-40)
  A. Celebrating the Presence of Christ
  B. Coming Together in Corinth
  C. Problems in the Church
  D. Paul's Response
  E. The Crucified Christ as Host at the Lord's Supper

VI. Session 5: Christian Worship—Romans 12:1-2
      (Amos 5:21-24; Micah 6:6-8)
  A. What Is Christian about Worship?
  B. Jesus and the Prophets
  C. The Mercies of God
  D. The Will of God
  E. Conclusions on Liberating Discipleship

Introduction

Liberating Discipleship

Faith

"Liberating Discipleship" seeks to describe what Christians mean when they speak of "faith." Paul Tillich, in his *Dynamics of Faith* (1957), wrote:

> There is hardly a word in the religious language . . . which is subject to more misunderstandings, distortions and questionable definitions than the word 'faith.' It belongs to those terms that need healing before they can be used for the healing of [persons]. Today the term 'faith' is more productive of disease than of health. It confuses, misleads, creates alternately skepticism and fanaticism, intellectual resistance and emotional surrender, rejection of genuine religion and subjection to substitutes.

In these Bible studies, we discuss what it means to believe in Jesus Christ. The biblical texts tell us how the early Christians addressed that question for their situation. But then each of us must become part of the answer. After hearing the message of the texts, we must then ask how that message affects our lives and the world around us.

We do so with the conviction that the world belongs to God and that we are important to God. What God said to Jacob applies to all of us: "Do not fear, for I have redeemed you; I have called you by name, you are mine" (Isa 43:1). Not only do we believe that God created the world, but also that God loves the world (John 3:16) and has reconciled with the world (2 Cor 5:17-21). "The earth is the Lord's and all that is in it, the world, and those who live in it" (Ps 24:1).

Sources

Paul Tillich, *Dynamics of Faith* (New York: Harper & Row, 1957), p. ix; also found in: Carl Heinz Ratschow, ed., *Paul Tillich: Main Works/Hauptwerke*. Vol. 5 (Berlin/New York: De Gruyter, 1988, 231-290), 231.

Study Bible

"Faith" in Scripture

See Gen 15:6; Isa 7:9; 28:16; Hab 2:4; 2 Chron 20:20. Before the resurrection, Jesus did not call for faith in himself, but interpreted people's coming to him and relying on God as "faith" (Mark 2:5; 5:34; 10:52; 11:22). For faith in the risen Christ, see Rom 10:9-10; Gal 2:16; Acts 16:31. Gospel texts that advocate belief in Christ before the resurrection (Matt 18:6; Mark 9:42; John 11:25; 12:46) reflect the specific christologies of the evangelists who wrote them. See Special Note on Hab 2:2-4 in *NISB*, 1324.

In the Scriptures, faith means trusting God, relying on God, and obeying God. But it was not until Jesus was raised from the power of death that the language of faith exploded, and faith was experienced as faith "*in* Jesus Christ."

So when we as Christians speak of faith, it must become clear that we do not speak of a general religious sentiment, but of *faith in Christ*. This point raises the question of what we mean by "faith" and "Christ." Our studies seek to address these and related matters.

Through our faith and baptism we have become part of the grand story of faith in Christ. We have focused the center of our personality, our conscience, on Jesus as the one who has made God known to us as a good and liberating personal reality.

Nevertheless, this free and voluntary commitment to Christ comes into conflict with the way *we* want to understand and interpret life. This conflict between our way of seeing things and what God has made known in the story of Jesus must be admitted and constructively addressed.

One important way of addressing this conflict is to study the Scriptures together with other Christians. In open and honest dialogue with biblical texts and with each other, we open our beings to God's Word and allow the Spirit to transform us so that our lives may echo today the ways of God expressed in Jesus.

Distortions of Faith

Faith is a fragile plant that can easily get bruised or broken. It is so easy to take our eyes off Christ and focus on ourselves. We are constantly tempted to use God for our own interests. The following are some fairly common distortions of faith.

♦ By *politicizing faith*, Christians have fought crusades, burned heretics, blessed weapons of war, and used the word *God* to justify and further their own national, political, economic and other ideological causes.

♦ By *individualizing faith*, believers have failed to recognize that, although faith comes to individuals, it does not individualize people. Faith takes place

Teaching Tip
Theological Guidelines

Have the class formulate its own paradigm (similar perhaps to the Wesleyan "quadrilateral" of Scripture, Tradition, Experience, and Reason) as theological guidelines for overcoming distortions of faith.

How might discipleship, following Jesus, work in such a paradigm?

within a community, and it calls and shapes people into a community of faith.

♦ Then there is the *emotional distortion of faith*. Faith has, of course, emotional elements, but faith must not be reduced to human experience.

♦ Even the *church* can get in the way of faith by claiming to become the object of worship and obedience. Not the church, but Christ, is the ground and object of faith.

♦ Faith must also not be confused with *reason*. For the Christian, reason is a servant of, not a master over, faith. Faith is not against reason, but it is much more encompassing than reason.

♦ There is also a *moralistic distortion of faith*. Faith includes obedience. Faith entails content and structure.

But both the Ten Commandments ("I am the Lord your God, who brought you out of the land of Egypt . . . ." Exod 20:2) and the Sermon on the Mount ("Blessed are you . . . ." Matt 5:3) teach us that obedience and morality are grounded in the liberating activity of God.

In trying to avoid these distortions, we join a number of theologians (Dietrich Bonhoeffer, Karl Barth, Jürgen Moltmann, and various advocates of liberation theology) who have sought to interpret faith as the biblical expression of "following Jesus."

Faith as Discipleship

A key example of a holistic understanding of faith as liberating discipleship is the *Micah Declaration* (2001). With it a global network of evangelical churches and Christian aid agencies commit themselves to a praxis of "integral mission":

Integral mission or holistic transformation is the proclamation and demonstration of the gospel. It is not simply that evangelism and social involvement are to be done alongside each other. Rather, in integral mission our proclamation has social consequences as we call people to love and repentance in all areas of life. And our social involvement has evangelistic consequences as we bear witness to the transforming grace of Jesus Christ. If we ignore

Source

See Tim Chester, ed., *Justice, Mercy and Humility. Integral mission and the poor. The Papers of the Micah Network International Consultation on Integral Mission and the Poor (2001)* (Carlisle, Cumbria, United Kingdom; Waynesboro, Georgia, USA: Paternoster Press, 2002).

This resource is also accessible on the Internet: www.micahnetwork.org; www.canbap.org.

217

the world we betray the word of God, which sends us out to serve the world. If we ignore the word of God we have nothing to bring to the world. Justice and justification by faith, worship and political action, the spiritual and the material, personal change and structural change belong together. As in the life of Jesus, being, doing and saying are at the heart of our integral task.

Let us summarize why the concept of "discipleship" is significant for clarifying what we mean by Christian faith.

♦ It is a biblical concept, deeply engraved in the Gospel narratives where Jesus called people to follow him and share his vision of God and of life (e.g., Mark 1:16-20, 2:14, 8:27-9:1, 10:17-31; Matt 8:19-22; Luke 9:57-60).

♦ It maintains the divine initiative and the christological content, because it is *Jesus* who calls people, and he calls them to follow *him* as friends on a journey of personal allegiance.

♦ Faith as discipleship features highly in those great theologians of modern times who have emphasized the prophetic and transforming power of faith (for instance Dietrich Bonhoeffer, Karl Barth, Jürgen Moltmann, Elisabeth Schüssler Fiorenza, Dorothee Sölle, Gustavo Gutiérrez, Jon Sobrino and Robert McAfee Brown).

♦ It is relevant in that it insists that faith must display creative solidarity with the downtrodden of the earth and become involved with their struggle for justice.

♦ It is kept alive today by committed and prophetic Christian groups inside and outside the established churches.

Liberation

Discipleship can easily lead to burnout. I know many people who attempted to take their faith in Christ seriously, but left the cause because it was too stressful. Or they became disillusioned or cynical with a church that was in the mode of comfort, convenience, and compromise. Or they became disheartened when Christians found ingenious ways to avoid the claim of Christ on their

> ## Teaching Tip
> ### Balanced Faith
> Discuss the importance of focusing on discipleship as the corrective to two extremes: faith as emotional conviction or an intellectual assent to a creed. Mention how the "hands and feet" (service) assist the "heart" (passion) and "head" (reason) in living the Christian faith.

lives. Or they came to the conclusion that intentional and serious faith simply does not work in our complicated world.

Our focus on Christ addresses these questions. There is nothing more important and more liberating than discovering and knowing the meaning of life. It is that knowledge that faith brings into our life. And faith in Christ is intimately interrelated with "freedom," "love," "joy," and what in the New Testament is called *paressia* (openness, courage, boldness, confidence, fearlessness). The call to follow Jesus is a call to freedom. The challenge of discipleship cannot be sustained by command, duty, and will. Faith introduces us into the liberating passion of God for God's world. All the resources of God's grace will sustain disciples on this road.

Interpreting Biblical Texts

All Christian churches acknowledge the authority of biblical texts. They do so because they recognize the need for an authority to measure and evaluate their faith and practice. An important reason for studying the Bible is to keep our praxis of faith in continuity with its origin and content.

The biblical texts come to us through communities of faith. They were written to address questions and challenges that communities faced. They received their authorization in communities, and they were passed on through communities from generation to generation.

It is a privilege and task of every church to teach the biblical stories and join the process of tradition. None of the New Testament writings, however, were intended for or written to us. They are *situational*. They were written to meet specific needs in the early church. It would have been disastrous, for instance, if Paul had sent his Letter to Galatians to Corinth instead. The same is true for the Gospels. The authors of Matthew and Luke knew the Gospel of Mark, but they must have thought that for their situation the Gospel of Mark was inadequate. In the introduction, Luke writes the following:

> Since *many* have undertaken to set down an orderly account of the events that have been fulfilled among us, just as they were handed on to us

Teaching Tip

Practices That Discourage

Have the class do a roundtable discussion on behaviors and practices in a church setting that discourage sincere followers of Christ: personnel squabbles, money issues, doctrinal debates, activity program overload, volunteer burnout. What are some behaviors and practices to encourage and activate the faith of the members?

219

by those who from the beginning were eyewitnesses and servants of the word, *I too* decided, after investigating everything carefully from the very first, to write an orderly account for you, most excellent Theophilus, *so that you may know the truth* concerning the things about which you have been instructed (Luke 1:1-4, italics added by the author, here and throughout).

So as we engage with biblical texts, remember that they have their own settings in the lives of their writers and the original audiences. The message of these texts, however, has remained relevant and authoritative for Christians through the ages.

I have chosen the following texts for five Bible studies on liberating discipleship:

1. Mark 1:14-20 (compare also Mark 2:13-14; Luke 19:1-10; Exodus 3) will set the scene by narrating the divine initiative and our human response.

2. Mark 8:27-38 (parallels in Matt 16:13-27 and Luke 9:18-26) warns against the intellectual distortion of faith and spells out clearly what it means to know Christ.

3. Luke 9:57-62 (parallel in Matt 8:18-22) illustrates how life becomes transfigured when God becomes its determining center.

4. Romans 12:1-2 (compare Amos 5:21-24, Mic 6:6-8). Public worship is important for us. It is also one of the more controversial topics in church life. A study of these verses will help us to discern what Christian worship really means.

5. First Corinthians 11:17-34 (Matt 25:31-40). The Eucharist, Holy Communion, the Lord's Supper are central to the church's worship life. This study will help us to evaluate our present practice in light of the biblical message.

Session 1

Mark 1:14-20 (Mark 2:13-14; Luke 19:1-10; Exodus 3)

The Call to Discipleship

Texts as Windows

These discipleship stories are windows into the being of God. The church has been retelling these stories because preachers found them to be word-pictures demonstrating the journey of faith and illuminating the elements that shape Christian discipleship.

God Takes the Initiative

The stories are simple but profound: "And *passing along* by the Sea of Galilee . . . . [Jesus] entered Jericho and was *passing* through it." Jesus is frequently portrayed as traveling *on the road*. He walks by the lake. He walks from village to village. He walks through the streets of Jericho and Jerusalem.

That is a picture of God. The Bible therefore speaks of God in *participles*. God is the one who creates—loves—liberates—judges—comforts—empowers—encourages. God is not a static deity who lives in splendid isolation. God is active, dynamic, and on a mission. God is on the move to help, save, liberate, comfort, and challenge.

God Elects

Our stories continue: He "*saw* Simon and Peter, the fishermen." He "*saw* James and John, mending their nets." He "*saw* Levi, the tax collector." Even Zacchaeus, the little man who was a despised tax collector, wanted to see Jesus, but nobody allowed him room to stand. He, therefore, climbed up a sycamore tree and hid in its heavy branches. Jesus comes. He *sees* Zacchaeus and receives him joyfully.

God sees. That is what theologians refer to when they speak of God *electing*. God does not simply watch our

Lectionary Loop

Third Sunday after Epiphany Year B

Teaching Tip
Pictures of God

What picture of God emerges in these stories?

Pass out colored pens or crayons and paper. Have each class member draw a picture illustrating God as an active participant in the lives of God's people. Have each member display and describe what he or she drew.

Study Bible

See notes on Jesus and Zacchaeus (Luke 19:1-10) *NISB*, 1889–90.

world and merely observe how we mismanage the creation. God *sees*, and, in seeing, relates the divine self to us and wants to share the divine life with us.

It is good to know that God moves toward us. We may flee from God, but God will never flee from us. A new day dawns after every night. Simon and Peter, James and John, Levi and Zacchaeus did not expect that Jesus would *see* them. So also we may be surprised by joy in the midst of our everyday life.

The Call

God's election reaches us in the call. Since it is Jesus as God's man who sees, the call is already implied: "Follow me!" We are reminded of the story when God *saw* the affliction of the people of Israel, when God *heard* their cries. This activity does not imply merely watching or observing. It means that "I *know* their suffering, and I have *come down to* deliver *them* out of the hands of the Egyptians" (Exod 3:7-8). For God, seeing means personal involvement and liberating praxis, not merely watching, but acting compassionately.

The Response

The response is *immediate* and *holistic*. How shall people respond when it is God, and not the projection of our religious imagination, who calls? The stories say: "And *immediately* they left their nets and followed him." What else could they do? "Immediately"—they set out for a new adventure. A new vision of life begins to shape them.

Let us not try to romanticize the story, although the bold actions of the fishermen to leave their busy tasks and follow Jesus throughout Palestine were courageous. Also, the women who joined them were probably kind and caring. Does it not correspond to a longing within all of us to get away from the complicated structures and ambiguities of life, and to embark on an outdoor adventure? But the story of Jesus does not refer to that eternal longing for a "back to nature" experience. It is an invitation to a new way of life, a new vision of reality. Not only the ordinary fishermen—Simon and Andrew, James and John—but also the rich capitalists Levi and Zacchaeus follow Jesus. What they do for a living is not important.

> ## Reflections
> ### Holistic Responses
> In which sense was the response of the people in these stories holistic? What can we do to make a holistic response?
>
> Why did the evangelists describe the response as immediate? (See Mark 1:18; 2:14; Matt 4:20, 22; Luke 19:6).

What is important here is that regardless what they do, they follow Jesus!

This response is not the grudging response to a "must" invading their life. It is not like going to school or to military service because the law demands it. It is God who calls, and God is the source of life and freedom!

We must recall, however, that whenever people have taken God seriously as God, it was not a call to a life of ease. Remember Moses and Jeremiah and Paul. But it is *God's* call; therefore, it would be an offense against the rules if we treat such a call in the same way as the invitation to a football game, rock concert, or cocktail party.

When *God* calls, then we can only respond *holistically*. We cannot hold anything back. We know this from life's experiences. When we really love someone, the response can only be holistic, involving all areas of life.

Do Not Miss the Moment of Truth

God is love, and love cannot rape. Therefore, the call can be missed or it can be refused. The New Testament relates only one occasion when Jesus' call, Jesus' invitation to life, was refused. Christians in the so-called "first world" find this difficult to hear. It was because the man was rich. Jesus had reminded him that God is not of material worth, and therefore it is not possible to worship God and mammon at the same time (Mark 10:17-31).

Invitation

These discipleship stories are windows, word-pictures, into the nature of God. There may be times when it is good to know that God cares and that God is there to share our burdens. It is good to know that God's invitation to life is always there. It is there even when we have become lukewarm in our faith, when a cloud has descended upon our hearts, when we have not kept our promises, when we have become too comfortable, and perhaps even too lazy. God will not force us to respond. God will become personal to us when we open our hearts, minds, and lives. Let us hear the call of Christ and then follow!

Reflections
Call and Response

1. What are the ways in which God's call comes to us? (Friends, people in need, sermon, Bible, books, reliable information about hunger, poverty, torture, loneliness).
2. How can we respond in a way that honors God and brings fulfillment to ourselves? (Let our words and deeds echo the story of Jesus; love God and people with a special regard for those in need.)

Teaching Tip
Asking for a Response

Bible studies (in addition to sermons) can become effective moments for response, for change of heart or mind, especially when the group is smaller and there is more opportunity to listen to the participants.

No Cheap Grace

Cheap Grace

Dietrich Bonhoeffer coined the helpful distinction between "cheap" and "costly" grace. He named cheap grace "the deadly enemy of the church. . . . Cheap grace means grace as a doctrine, a principle, a system . . . . Cheap grace is grace without discipleship, grace without the cross, grace without Jesus Christ . . . . The word of cheap grace has been the ruin of more Christians than any commandment of works."

The Question

Theology begins with the experience of faith. Faith then seeks words to understand this newly found, this strange, this mysterious yet liberating and life-enhancing reality. So, "on the way" with Jesus—an important phrase in the Gospel of Mark—the question becomes inevitable: Who is this Jesus whom I have believed?

The *people* in our narrative stand for those who want to explain Jesus within the limitation of their culture. From their religious traditions they knew about the promised return of John the Baptist, Elijah, or other prophets. For us the question arises: Are the categories "John the Baptist," "Elijah," "prophet" (Matt 16:14 adds "Jeremiah") adequate to capture the reality of "Jesus Christ"?

There is no doubt that Jesus was a follower of John the Baptist and that he stands in the tradition of Israelite prophecy. But can the relationship with John the Baptist or with the prophets capture his distinctiveness? While John the Baptist proclaimed God's imminent judgment that can only be escaped by repentance and baptism, Jesus announced the nearness of God's liberating pres-

Lectionary Loop
Lent 2, Proper 19, Year B

Sources

Dietrich Bonhoeffer, *The Cost of Discipleship,* trans. R. H. Fuller and Irmgard Booth (New York: McMillan, 1963 [1937]) 45-47, 59.

See also: Dietrich Bonhoeffer, *Discipleship,* Dietrich Bonhoeffer Works, Vol. 4, trans. B. Green and R. Krauss (Minneapolis: Fortress, 2001) 43-44, 55.

Reflections

Count the Cost

1. Can you give concrete examples of how grace becomes cheap?
2. How can we avoid cheapening God's grace? What Christian practices will help us consider the cost?

ence and invited people to celebrate life by following him. To understand Jesus only as a follower of John the Baptist would make him into a prophet of judgment and a preacher of repentance. Jesus, however, as representative of the "ways of God," brought joy, peace, and liberation. The prophets spoke the word of the Lord, they committed their lives to truth and justice. They were revered by the people of God. But many still waited for another one to come, someone who could and would do "more" than the prophets have done.

The Response

Perhaps the "disciples," the followers of Jesus, know more! Peter, answering on behalf of the church, seems to get it right: "You are the Messiah." Is the mystery now solved? Has the adequate designation for Jesus been found?

Words of caution follow. Jesus "sternly ordered them not to tell anyone about him." Where is the problem? What more can you do than confess Jesus as the Christ, "the Messiah"?

Jesus "began to teach them," and he did so "quite openly." These are important words in the Gospel of Mark. The evangelist wants to lift the mystery that surrounds Jesus: "The Son of Man must undergo great suffering, and be rejected by the elders, the chief priests, and the scribes, and be killed, and after three days rise again." Here we have all the elements of a holistic christology.

Christians tend to focus on *one* aspect of christology. If, for instance, Jesus' *life* becomes the focus, then Jesus may be admired as a courageous hero, an ethical teacher, or a moral example, but his saving and liberating reality is forfeited. If, on the other hand, his *death* becomes the center of attention, then Jesus may be regarded as an abstract God-man who is necessary for a theory of atonement to bridge the gulf between a holy God and a sinful humanity, but the particularities of his life, his poverty and his prophetic critique are lost. If, to use a further example, his *resurrection* is the focal point, then Jesus may be understood as a "superman" or a miracle worker, but the offence that his life provoked and the subsequent way to Gethsemane and Calvary become

---

Reflections
Who Is This Jesus?

1. Let's talk about Jesus. Whom do we have in mind when we say "Jesus Christ"?
2. Is he the *historical Jesus* whom scholars try to reconstruct from the biblical and extra-biblical sources?
3. Is he the *biblical Christ* of whom we encounter different portrayals in the Gospels?
4. Is he the Christ who lives in the heart of believers (the so-called *Christ of faith*), or who encounters us in the *Eucharist?*
5. Is he the Christ who has promised to meet us in the *poor and oppressed?*

Reflections
Knowing Jesus?

1. How can Christ be known in a way that is fair to him, the object of our knowledge?
2. Do we know Christ primarily with our *intellect,* so that knowing him means essentially accepting as *true* what the Bible or the church teaches about him?
3. Or is our *will* the most adequate way to respond, so that knowing Christ means to make a *decision* to believe in him and follow him?
4. Or does knowing Christ mean to *worship* him, or *be engaged for justice* in a needy world?

---

theologically irrelevant. The theological challenge is to develop a *holistic* christology in which the *life*, *death*, and *resurrection* of Jesus are essentially inter-related, and complement each other.

Will Peter—will we!—understand? Will we accept Jesus on his own terms? Or will we want to decide what God can and cannot do?

"Peter took him aside and began to *rebuke* him." Peter had confessed Jesus as the Christ. Jesus had interpreted Peter's confession, but Peter did not like Jesus' interpretation. Peter had his own theology, and God was supposed to fit into it. There is a *human* way to talk of God. It is the way church, society, politics, and business would like it. The word *God* is then used to validate our ideas and interests. Consequently, we have fought wars, blessed weapons of destruction, have tortured, and killed —each in the name of God. We have used the word *God* to justify our denominational preferences. Where is the "dangerous memory" of Jesus (Johann Baptist Metz) and "costly grace" (Dietrich Bonhoeffer) in the church today? We have all joined Peter and expected God to dance according to our tune.

Jesus turned and looked at his disciples; then he rebuked their leader and said, "Get behind me, *Satan*! For you are setting your mind not on divine things but on *human things*." Those are harsh words for the one who had just confessed Jesus as the Christ. But sometimes a frank and honest language is needed. Peter's confession is named satanic and human, rather then divine and revelatory, because he refuses to listen. Satan is the absolute individualist. Satanic is the attempt to claim autonomy over against God and refuse to accept God on God's terms.

Will Peter change his theology to integrate what he has learned from Jesus, or will he expect Jesus to fit into his theology? For the church this means: 1) Will we understand God in terms of the story of Jesus, or 2) Will we shape our knowledge of God according to our needs and interests? With his orthodox confession of Jesus as the "Christ," Peter fared no better than the demons who confessed Jesus as the "Son of God" (Mark 3:11-12; cf., 5:7).

Teaching Tip
Wanted: A Holistic Christology

Have class members share their experiences with other Christians who may focus on the resurrected life of Christ, or his radical teachings, or his sufferings and death. How does the focus on a particular aspect of Christ influence their faith and spiritual practices? Have someone who enjoys drawing sketch the different ways that Christ might be visualized by each distinct viewpoint. Have the artist share his or her work.

Sources

Johann Baptist Metz, a Roman Catholic diocesan priest from Auerbach, Bavaria, is an advocate of responsible Christian social and political practices. He wrote *A Passion for God* (New York: Paulist Press, 1997), and *Faith and the Future: Essays on Theology, Solidarity, and Modernity* (Maryknoll, N.Y.: Orbis Books, 1995).

See also Ekkehard Schuster, *Hope Against Hope: Johann Baptist Metz and Elie Wiesel Speak Out on the Holocaust* (New York: Paulist Press, 1999).

Study Bible

Why did Jesus call Peter's first response "satanic"? See also the discussion of Mark 8:32-33 in *NISB*, 1824-25.

The evangelist now invites us to listen to Jesus. The problem is clearly stated. Will our theology reflect and validate our own or the church's needs and interests? Will we listen before we speak, and will we accept God on God's terms, based on revelation?

Discipleship

Jesus "called the *crowd* with his *disciples*, and said to them, 'If any want to become *my followers*, let them *deny themselves* and *take up their cross and follow me*'." This is decisive, yet it has remained controversial in the church to the present day.

Denying ourselves, and taking up our crosses, and following Jesus—that seems to be a tall order in a world where self-realization and self-fulfillment, rather than self-denial is in fashion. This is a touchy point. But truth may begin to dawn at the point of pain. Is not sin the severing of self from God, neighbor, and environment, and thus claiming autonomy? Does not faith open the door toward God in prayer and worship, toward the neighbor in love, and toward the environment as channels of life?

The Secret of the Christian Life

We are touching here the very secret of the Christian life. Jesus in Mark 8:35-36 declares:

> For those who want to save their life will lose it, and those who lose their life for my sake, and for the sake of the gospel, will save it. For what will it profit them to gain the whole world and forfeit their life?

The call to discipleship is an invitation to a life of helping people. Life, joy, and celebration are its ingredients, not morality. Why is this so? Because it is *Jesus* who is calling and inviting, and Jesus is the way, the truth and the life (John 14:6). He lived and died for the vision that God is a liberating God who shares his life with all persons who are weary and tired, for those who are not given a chance to shape their own destiny. God has transfigured Jesus' death into a new invitation of life by raising him from the dead.

Consequences

Who then is Jesus? He is God's unconditional and lib-

Reflection
Faith and Praxis

What does the confession of Jesus as Christ imply in light of Mark 8? (Not only right doctrine but right living.)

Reflections
Cross Bearer

1. Can we give some examples of what it means now for us to take up our cross and follow Jesus?
2. How are autonomy or independence evidence of sin?

Study Bible

Suffering for Jesus or working to alleviate suffering? See Special Note on Mark 8:35 in *NISB*, 1825.

erating *yes* to us. How can he be known? By following him and thereby becoming servants of life. The great philanthropist, theologian, organist, and medical doctor Albert Schweitzer concludes his book on Jesus with these words:

> Jesus comes to us as One unknown, without a name, as of old, by the lake-side, He came to those men who knew Him not. He speaks to us the same word: 'Follow thou me!' and sets us to the tasks, which He has to fulfill for our time. He commands. And to those who obey Him, whether they be wise or simple, He will reveal Himself in the toils, the conflicts, the sufferings which they shall pass through in His fellowship, and, as an ineffable mystery, they shall learn in their own experience Who He is.

Teaching Tip
Right Belief or Right Practice?
Have the class do a short dramatic piece on the Parable of the Good Samaritan (Luke 10:25-37), focusing on the deeds of the religious priest and Levite who both ignore the injured man on their way. See also: James 2:14-17. Use the skit as the basis for discussion on the importance of right belief plus right practice.

Sources
Albert Schweitzer, *The Quest of the Historical Jesus: A Critical Study of its Progress from Reimarus to Wrede,* Trans. W. Montgomery from the first German ed., *Von Reimarus zu Wrede,* 1906; with a Preface by F. C. Burkitt, first English ed., (N.Y.: Macmillan, 1910), 403.

See also Albert Schweitzer, *The Quest of the Historical Jesus* (rev. and enl. ed.) trans. J. Bowden (Minneapolis: Fortress Press, 2001), 487.

Session 3   Luke 9:57-62; Matthew 8:18-22

Radical Discipleship

Context

These brief narratives come from a *source* ("Q" from the German *Quelle*, meaning "source") that the evangelists Matthew and Luke used to write their Gospels. Both evangelists highlight the importance of these discipleship stories. For Luke it introduces a special section (Luke 9:51—19:27) where Jesus is traveling, setting "his face to go to Jerusalem." For Matthew this call to discipleship is intimately interlocked (Matt 8:18 anticipates Matt 8:23) with the narrative of stilling the storm (Matt 8:23-27). Discipleship does not seek the comfort and safety of the harbor. It dares the storms of life, because even they cannot separate the follower from the authority and the protecting care of Jesus.

We shall follow Luke's version of the narrative, but also consult Matthew. It is therefore desirable that *Gospel Parallels* are used to teach these stories. We can easily identify with Luke. He was a probably a Gentile Christian of the second or third generation. His skilled use of Greek showed that he was fluent in language and culture. He made full use of the Greek version of the Scriptures (the Septuagint, or LXX).

"Someone"

In Luke three persons are involved in the encounter with Jesus, while Matthew has only two. Either Matthew omits one of the encounters, or he had a different version of the Q-Source.

The persons who seek the encounter, or who are called to follow Jesus, are not named. They are "someone" or "another." Leaving the identity open invites

Lectionary Loop

Proper Eight, Thirteenth Sunday, Year C

Sources

Gospel Parallels: A Comparison of the Synoptic Gospels, 5th ed., ed., Burton H. Throckmorton, Jr. (Nashville: Thomas Nelson, 1992), 111-12, uses the NRSV.

Synopsis of the Four Gospels: Greek-English Edition of the Synopsis Quattuor Evangeliorum, 6th ed., ed. Kurt Aland (Stuttgart: United Bible Societies, 1983), 164-65, uses the RSV.

231

every listener, including each of us to occupy a place in the narrative.

Transfiguring the Security of a Home (vv. 57-58)

When you ask persons what are the basic goals that motivate them, one of the answers will be to own a home. So when we say: "I will follow you wherever you go," and many of us have voiced such an intention, we still have our home, or money in our retirement fund to buy it when we need it.

Therefore Jesus' answer hurts: "Foxes have holes, and birds of the air have nests; but the Son of Man has nowhere to lay his head." We are similar to foxes that have holes that provide shelter for them, or birds that have nests, and in our case comfortable nests, for rest and relaxation.

Jesus is a wandering prophet. Liberated by the Spirit to be the man with others and for others; passionate in his concern to make human life human. The designation "Son of Man" is elusive. It carries the connotations of being one of us, truly human, and at the same time, being God's man for us, truly divine.

The response that is called for is not doctrinal orthodoxy (saying the right words). It is not withdrawal from the world for mystical experiences, or well-constructed liturgies, or eucharistic celebrations. It is the invitation to follow Jesus, share in his passion, and become, as the apostle Paul says, "God's servants, working together" (1 Cor 3:9).

The response is left open! It needed to be left open, because each of us needs to decide for ourselves, whether we shall risk that journey.

Transfiguring the Imperative of Culture (v. 59)

Another strong influence upon us is our culture, its norms and expectations. We become defensive when someone questions the norms and values we live by. You can take any issue—refugee policy, abortion, the war in Iraq, and the place of the flag in our self-understanding—and we have an opinion. And often it is fairly difficult to decide what is *Christian* about our opinion.

In those days—and it is still largely true for us today—to bury one's father was considered a noble religious

Study Bible

Matthew specifies and defines: a "scribe" and one "of the disciples." Thereby Matthew applies the story to a specific situation. Since it is not reported that the scribe actually follows Jesus, Matthew wants to emphasize how hard it was for scribes to become Christians. With the disciple it is clear that he will follow, yet he first wants to meet his family obligation. But even that is denied. Christians here are confronted with the radicalness of discipleship. See *NISB*, 1760-61.

duty. It was expected from heritage, tradition, and culture. It was part of respecting their Scriptures and obeying the fourth commandment. The many burial sites in the ancient Near East show the reverence people had for a proper burial. This duty is also reflected in our Christian Bible when Joseph of Arimathea "went boldly to Pilate and asked for the body of Jesus" in order to give him a dignified burial (Mark 15:42-46). In the culture of the day, attending to a dead relative was more important than fulfilling such essential religious duties as "reciting the Shema, . . . the Eighteen Benedictions, and . . . all the commandments stated in the Torah." (Ber 3:1*a*)

It seems decent, pious, and moral that you would "first" bury your father and then respond to the invitation to follow Jesus. Some interpreters have therefore tried to explain away the radicalness, or at least the apparent insensitivity. They say that there must have been a brother, who could have performed the duty, or that the father was not really dead and that the aspirant to discipleship wanted to wait until he was dead. But all of these attempts to take the sting out of Jesus' verdict are unconvincing.

In the prophetic tradition there are intimations of this radicalness, when God commanded the prophet Ezekiel not to mourn or weep at the funeral of his wife (Ezek 24:15-24), and when God forbade Jeremiah to "enter the house of mourning, or go to lament, or bemoan them" (Jer 16:5-7). In cultural terms such divine demands are offensive. In the prophets they served as prophetic symbols to announce, "I have taken away my peace from this people, says the Lord, my steadfast love and mercy" (Jer 16:5).

Jesus' challenge transcends what God is expecting from the prophets. While individual prophets were expected to carry out certain symbolic functions, Jesus expects every follower to transfigure cultural claims and expectations in order to be a witness to the ways of God (the "kingdom of God").

Those who do not tune into the reality of the kingdom are already "dead." They have cut themselves off from the source of life. Let them bury those who have come to the end of their physical life.

Sources

On Matt 8:21-22 (par. Luke 9:59-60), see W. D. Davies and Dale C. Allison, *The Gospel according to Saint Matthew.* ICC. Vol. II (Edinburgh: T.&T. Clark, 1991), 56-58.

On burial according to *Berakoth* 3:1*a* and in the time of Jesus, see: M. Hengel, *The Charismatic Leader and His Followers.* Trans. J. C. Greig. Ed. J. Riches (Edinburgh: T.&T. Clark, 1981), 9.

Reflections
Hymns on Discipleship

In a church hymnal, find and discuss several hymns that deal with discipleship and service: e.g., Take Up Thy Cross; Forth in Thy Name; O Master, Let Me Walk with Thee.

1. What does Jesus require of his followers?
2. What do the followers owe to Jesus? What kind of loyalty is mentioned?
3. What is to be renounced or surrendered?
4. What assurances are given for following Jesus? What benefits or rewards are offered?

Transfiguring the Affection of Family (vv. 61-62)

A third potential follower of Jesus wants to do the decent thing and say good-bye to those at home. Saying farewell acknowledges the importance of family in one's life. In ancient Mediterranean culture it seems to have been more important than in our Western individualistic culture. The individual was part of the family unit and could not survive apart from it. We remember Jesus' parable of the Prodigal Son (Luke 15:12-24). The son who left the father's house is described as "dead." It seems to be entirely reasonable and moral to say farewell to one's family before one would embark on a new and strange way of life.

Again, Jesus' response comes as a shock. He interprets saying farewell to one's loved ones as "looking back" and being unfit "for the kingdom of God."

At another occasion we read:

> Whoever comes to me and does not hate father and mother, wife and children, brothers and sisters, yes, and even life itself, cannot be my disciple. Whoever does not carry the cross and follow me cannot be my disciple (Luke 14:26-27; see also Matt 10:37-38, similar but less offensive).

Radicalness and Transfiguration

What do we do with this radicalness? Is it possible to take these radical demands seriously? In fact none of us really do. We have our homes to go to after work, whether we own them or not. We observe basic cultural norms and see no reason not to follow them. We are grateful and kind to our families and certainly would not think of leaving them without saying farewell when we go on a journey. So what do we do, especially if we want to be sincere and credible with regard to our faith?

We need to find a way beyond legalism, moralism, and liberalism.

Beyond Legalism, Moralism, and Liberalism

Legalism does not motivate people. It stifles the soul. You can't compel people by laws to commit their lives to God. The ways of God cannot be fitted into a *legalistic* framework. Jesus means freedom (which is not to

---

Reflections

Discipleship and Procrastination

What is your best or favorite excuse for putting off something? If Jesus were to say to you today, "follow me," what excuse would you use and what might happen?

Reflections

What Drives and Hinders Us?

1. What are the basics of life that motivate and drive us? Family? Home? Culture?
2. Can we imagine what life would be without them? How might they prevent us from responding positively to God's claims on our lives? Why?

be mistaken for autonomy). In sovereign freedom and authority he exalted the dignity of human life beyond the expectation of laws, norms, and institutions. "The Sabbath was made for humankind, and not humankind for the Sabbath" (Mark 2:27). When the church in Galatia was falling back into legalism, the apostle Paul echoed the freedom of Christ by calling the Christians in Galatia back to their roots: "For freedom Christ has set us free" (Gal 5:1). It is true, of course, that freedom includes responsibility: "Do not use your freedom as an opportunity for self-indulgence, but through love become slaves to one another" (Gal 5:13). But we must avoid legalism and ask for the structure and discipline of freedom.

We must also avoid *moralism*. Jesus' love is unconditional. When the church after the resurrection sought to find words to capture the unconditional nature of love they said that we are saved by grace *alone* through faith *alone*: "We know that a person is justified not by the works of the law but through faith in Jesus Christ" (Rom 3:28; Gal 2:16). This liberating reality of unconditional love must not be lost.

Liberalism is the attempt to understand faith within the parameters set by science and culture. The *newness* and the *otherness* of the gospel are difficult to express in these terms. Jesus turns out to be a sophisticated teacher, rabbi, or wise man rather than the person through whom God wants to shape and transform the world.

Icons of Discipleship

A recommended approach to these invitations to follow Jesus is to appreciate their representative nature. They are *icons of discipleship*. In each new situation and historical context they illuminate our decisions and our lifestyle.

They therefore place a lot of responsibility on the individual believer. Such responsibility must not be avoided by expecting church authorities to make rules and regulations as to what it means to be a Christian. The church is the place where people hear the radical claim of the gospel and are then encouraged to ask how that claim impinges on their life.

Reflections
Fanaticism and Discipleship

Have the class discuss what motivates a religious fanatic to do extreme actions (e.g., terrorism) in the name of a cause? Then have them discuss the differences between fanaticism and discipleship as taught by Jesus. What motivates a follower of Jesus? *Read also Luke 10:25-37.*

Sources

See the following by Eduard Schweizer, *Luke: A Challenge to Present Theology* (Atlanta: John Knox, 1982).

Lordship and Discipleship, SBT 28 (London: SCM, 1960).

The Good News According to Matthew (Richmond: John Knox, 1988).

Jesus: The Parable of God (New York: Continuum, 1997).

Who Is Jesus?

It all comes back to the one point! The question must be asked! If the claims are so radical, by what *authority* does Jesus issue those claims, and why does the church through the ages continue to proclaim those claims?

During his *life* it was already obvious that Jesus was the man "who fits no formula" (Eduard Schweizer). In sovereign *freedom* and *authority* he suspended the law, healed the sick, preached good news, and demonstrated divine presence wherever human need was felt. When this Jesus was raised from the dead, the *newness* of being a witness to the ways *of God* was confirmed. In Jesus, then, we meet more than a teacher, wise man, or rabbi. Here something new has broken into our history.

This newness has led to language like "savior," "Lord," "Son of God," "truly divine," "begotten, not made." If we realize that our religious instincts tend to functionalize God for our convenience, then these discipleship stories invite us to get our priorities right. What determines our conscience? From where do our words, thoughts, and deeds flow? And at that point even the best—like home, culture, and family—can get in the way.

Our text does not say that a break with home, family, and culture leads to Christian discipleship. Our text also does not mean that Christian discipleship in every situation and for every person implies the break with what is natural and important to us. But our text does point out that there are moments of truth when the natural allegiances are transfigured into the setting of new priorities.

Reflections

More About Following Jesus

1. How does following Jesus affect your lifestyle? Relationships? Priorities?
2. When does Jesus' way still conflict with your way?

Session 4

1 Corinthians 11:17-34
(Matthew 25:31-40)

The "Lord's Supper"

Celebrating the Presence of Christ

The "Lord's Supper" (11:20) is the time and place when churches most visibly celebrate the presence of Christ in their midst. It is a tragedy that here, where the churches celebrate Christ's presence, they

♦ often do not invite;

♦ validate injustice by allowing oppressor and oppressed, torturers and their victims, to sit at the same table, as long as they are believers and have been baptized;

♦ intentionally exclude the world from the celebration.

Can that be in harmony with "following Jesus," the Messiah of the poor and the Savior of sinners? Our text will help us to examine that question.

"Coming Together" in Corinth (1 Cor 11:17-22, 33-34).

The best description for what we mean by "church" is Paul's naming of the church in Corinth as "coming together" (vv. 17-20) for a meal, fellowship, or worship, and in that context to observe the Lord's Supper. The early church did not withdraw from life, but were in the midst of it, cherishing community, and celebrating the presence of Christ.

Paul implies that the Christians in Corinth gathered regularly for meetings (1 Cor 14:23, 26). In the late afternoons the Christians—rich and poor, home owners and slaves, widows and wharf laborers, parents and children

Lectionary Loop

Holy Thursday,
Years A, B, C (1 Cor 11)

Study Bible

The Lord's Supper (1 Cor 11:20) is also called Eucharist and connected with the "giving thanks" at the meal (1 Cor 11:24; Matt 26:27). It is also called Holy Communion from the Greek koinonia or "a sharing in," (1 Cor 10:16). On 1 Cor 10:16-18 and 11:17-34, see *NISB*, 2050-52.

Reflection
Word

Seminary professor Ted Runyan said in a lecture that "the church is that body created by the Word for the world." What does that statement mean to you?

237

—would come together for a common meal, and in its context to celebrate the presence of Christ and be spiritually nourished.

The people would bring their own food and, remembering that "the earth is the Lord's and the fullness thereof" (Ps 24:1), they consecrated the food to the Lord. With this act of consecration they showed their desire to share. The food now belonged to the whole community. Their primary intention was not to eat their *own* meal, but they wanted to *share* and then eat *together*. By doing that, they manifested the church *of God* (1 Cor 11:22), and they demonstrated their *unity* in Christ (10:16). Then they ate and drank. At least here at the community meal —later called "agape" ("love": Jude 12; Ignatius, *To the Smyrnaeans* 8:2;)—all the members of the community would get enough to eat! They would eat, sing, pray, and listen to a sermon. In that context, probably toward the end of the gathering, they would also celebrate the "Lord's Supper" (so called in the New Testament only in 1 Cor 11: 20).

Problems in the Church

A discord must have begun to spoil the atmosphere in the church. Paul speaks of "divisions" and "factions" among them (vv. 18-19); and he distinguishes between their own meals (v. 21) and the "Lord's Supper" (v. 20). What had happened?

Most likely, those who were rich and had more leisure time came earlier than the rest (implied in vv. 21, 33) and brought some extras like fish, meat, and wine for themselves. They began to eat before the slaves and laborers had arrived. As a result there was not enough food left for the latecomers (v. 21), and some of those who had come early were already drunk.

The problem was twofold.

♦ *Individualism.*There were those in the church who thought that they had already arrived (1 Cor 4:8). It was neither the welfare of the whole community nor the mission of the church that mattered; only the benefit of the individual or of the faction to which he or she belonged (1 Cor 1:12).

♦ *Lack of concern for the "latecomers."* They knew

Study Bible

The same togetherness of meal and sacrament is suggested in the Synoptic accounts: Mark 14:17-25, par. Matt 26:20-29, Luke 22:14-20. The phrase "after supper" in 1 Cor 11:25 suggests that at first the elements of bread and wine were separated by the full meal. However, for reasons that we shall mention below, the church probably soon placed the "sacrament" toward the end of the meal. See *NISB*, 1794, 1838, 1896.

Teaching Tip
Sacramental Security

In 1 Cor 10:1-5 Paul warned the church against a theology of sacramental security. Participating in the sacraments of baptism and the eucharist does not automatically assure God's pleasure and divert divine judgement. With class input, list the different types of behavior and practices motivated or inspired by a theology of sacramental security or entitlement in churches today (e.g., poor church attendance, indifference to the poor and needy).

of the latecomers. But they probably thought that "after supper" (v. 25) everyone would then have the opportunity to participate in the "cup." Is the sacrament not more important than a simple meal? Does not the sacrament feed the soul, while food and wine only provide pleasure for the perishing body? This was probably the rationale of those who had enough to eat!

But how did the apostle come to know about these problems? It is unlikely that those who had plenty to eat, and who did not wait for the latecomers, would have informed the apostle. The information must have come from those "latecomers" themselves.

Now the apostle was challenged. Should he take this matter seriously? Did this complaint affect the identity and relevance of the church? Does this criticism deserve or even demand theological attention? Is this only a question of morality, or is this a question of faith? Whom should he believe, and with whom should he side? In those days they did not have church buildings; he therefore needed the larger homes of the rich people for church gatherings. But then, the "latecomers" also belonged to the community of faith. How will the apostle rank the importance of those who have houses and food, on the one hand, and the slaves and servants and laborers, on the other? In what way does his theology, centered in cross and resurrection as spelled out in 1 Corinthians 1–2; 15, become relevant in a concrete church situation?

Paul's Response

Paul takes the information "from below" seriously. Indeed, he hurls at the church in Corinth the unbelievable verdict: "when you come together, it is not really to eat the Lord's supper" (1 Cor. 11: 20). Given the importance of the Lord's Supper, Paul seems to question the church's *Christian* identity. Had the church become another religious club, of which there were many in Corinth? How shall we understand such a harsh criticism?

A social problem had gained theological significance! Paul does not criticize the spiritual experiences of the Christians. He does not question the legitimacy of their

> ### Reflection
> #### A Club
> In what way does your congregation seem at times to be a religious club? Be brave and give examples.

singing, preaching, healing, and praying. His scathing criticism is directed against a church that claims to celebrate the *Lord's* Supper, but at the same time fails to display a social conscience. For him it was an intolerable contradiction that they met for the *Lord's* Supper but failed to fully integrate the servants, and the laborers in the community meal: "Do you show contempt for the church of God and humiliate those who have nothing?" (v. 22) With this question he suggests an essential inter-relationship between the nature of the church, as the church of God, and the mission of the church in the world.

Was it not the central passion of Jesus to share his life with the outsiders, the "latecomers"? Did Jesus not eat with tax collectors and sinners (Mark 2:15-16), and as a result of such bold practices was criticized, opposed, arrested, and killed? Indeed, did his opponents not call him "a glutton and a drunkard, a friend of tax collectors and sinners" (Matt 11:19 par. Luke 7:34)? How then can the church celebrate the *Lord's* Supper and not give equal status to the lower social classes? That, for Paul, was a denial of the lordship of Christ and therefore a negation of their Christian identity.

Nevertheless, Paul could a not imagine that a church could exist without celebrating the Lord's Supper. Was the church in Corinth not part of the "church *of God*" (1 Cor 1:2)? Could God's creation be annulled by human disobedience? Paul finds this difficult to imagine. Therefore, as a *compromise*, he suggests that in the future they should eat their family meal at home (v. 22), and then meet together for a separate "Lord's Supper."

The Crucified Christ as Host at the Lord's Supper (1 Cor 11:23-33)

At the beginning of his letter Paul reveals his theological passion: "I decided to know nothing among you except Jesus Christ, and him crucified" (1 Cor 2:2). He now applies his theology to the situation in Corinth. He does not preach morality. He simply reminds them that the Lord's Supper is not the church's meal. Perhaps, if the Christian leaders in Corinth realize who the host at the Lord's Supper is, they would change their ways.

> ## Reflection
> ### When He Was Betrayed
> What is the implication for you in the phrase, "the Lord Jesus on the night when he was betrayed"?

"The Lord Jesus on the night when he was betrayed took bread . . . as often as you eat this bread and drink the cup, you proclaim the Lord's death until he comes" (11:23, 26). By participating in the Lord's Supper the church is intimately interwoven with the *passion story* of Jesus. It is the Crucified One who is host at the Lord's Supper.

And why was Jesus crucified? Because he practised solidarity with the "latecomers" in his society. The Lord's Supper is therefore not a religious liturgy that separates the church from the world. Rather, it is the intensive recalling and reassuring that the church is the "body of Christ" and as such must minister to the world's needs. The church's privilege and responsibility is to let its life and its worship be shaped by the crucified Christ and thereby create analogies to him. If and when that happens, then they "proclaim the Lord's death until he comes."

By understanding the death of Jesus as being for us— "This is my body that is *for you*" (v. 24)—the story of Jesus becomes intimately interwoven with our own story. It is this story, the passion-story of Jesus that the church must re-live and re-present in each new situation.

Ideally, therefore, the whole meal, including the breaking of bread and, "after supper" (11:25), the drinking of wine, should be the Lord's Supper. The often repeated "this" in the Lord's Supper tradition—"*This* is my body that is for you. Do *this* in remembrance of me . . . . *This* cup is the new covenant in my blood. Do *this* in remembrance of me" (11:24-25)—does not refer primarily to the elements of bread and wine, but it applies to the whole meal, the whole Lord's Supper, which, if it is to be the *Lord's* Supper, must include the servants, laborers, and slaves. In Corinth, however, modifications in the celebration of the Lord's Supper must have taken place. At first, the sacramental action was placed toward the end of the meal, so that those who came too late for the meal could at least partake in the sacrament; and then, finally, the sacrament was separated from the meal altogether. For Paul this was a *compromise*. The church has institutionalized that compromise and kept it to the present day.

Teaching Tip
Finding Christ's Presence

Where may we look for the presence of Christ in our life and world? Have the class make suggestions, e.g., Lord's Supper, community, prayer, Scripture, preaching. Then have the class read Matthew 25:31-46. Why are these places of christophany often overlooked by Christians today?

241

In the celebration of the Lord's Supper, the church is defined as the *community of the* "new covenant" (v. 25). The *newness* of the eschatological community consists in the fact that in and with its life and celebration it *anticipates* the ultimate victory of the crucified Christ—"until he comes" (v. 26; see also 16:22: "Our Lord, come!"). It anticipates the future of the crucified Christ by creating *analogies* in which the content of their faith comes to expression. Social, racial, and sexual barriers are relativized. The church understands itself as the community of the friends of Jesus who are liberated by the power of the gospel to provide an alternative to the encroaching selfishness and individualism. Faith in Christ and the love implied therein create community, while selfishness and individualism destroy it. And since human beings are relational beings who need fellowship and friendship as much as they need air to breathe, water to drink, and food to eat, the destruction of community has consequences that affect the health of the participating members (1 Cor. 11:30).

When the church "remembers" Christ in the celebration of the Lord's supper (vv. 23, 25) the passion story of Jesus merges with the life of the community of believers, so that the church can no longer *be* the church apart from remembering at the same time the people with whom Christ lived and for whom he died. The church cannot "remember" Christ, worship him and, at the same time, block out those with whom Christ shared his life. The Lord's Supper tradition therefore reaches its aim when it kindles within each successive generation the question as to who the late-comers in our community and in our world are. The Eucharist as the *Lord's* Supper is therefore not only concerned with the identity of the church, but also with its relevance.

By eating the bread and drinking the cup worthily the church is proclaiming "the Lord's death until he comes" (v. 26). *Unworthy* participation in the Lord's Supper manifests disobedience to Christ: "Whoever, therefore, eats the bread and drinks the cup of the Lord in an *unworthy manner* (*anaxios*) will be answerable for the body and blood of the Lord" (v. 27). What does "unworthy" mean in this context? It can only refer to the indi-

Reflection
Wisdom from Bonhoeffer
Dietrich Bonhoeffer said: "Only those who cried out for the Jews have the right to sing the Gregorian chant." What does that analogy mean for our celebration of the Lord's Supper?

See The Wisdom and Witness of Dietrich Bonhoeffer, *ed. W. W. Floyd (Minneapolis: Fortress Press, 2000).*

Reflections
Communion Queries
1. Who should be invited to attend the Lord's Supper?
2. How can the church keep an "open" Lord's Supper without validating injustice?
3. Who can and should officiate at the Lord's Supper?

vidualism and the selfishness that destroys community. Paul is reminding the Christians in Corinth that it is possible to participate in the Lord's Supper in a manner that is *inappropriate* to the occasion. The reference point for "unworthy" is not one's private morality, or the liturgical way in which the sacrament is administered. The reference point is given with verses 17-22 and 33-34. In Corinth it was simply unfitting to the occasion, to celebrate the *Lord's Supper*, and then by-pass the concerns of the late-comers. Had not Jesus, the host at the Lord's Supper, shared his life with those who were morally and religiously suspect? Not private morality but concrete social concern is at the heart of the matter. When Paul writes those strong exhortations in verses 27-30 and even intimates that weakness, illness, and death are the result of an unworthy participation in the Lord's Supper, then this signifies that one cannot and must not separate spiritual welfare from the bodily, social, or historical dimension of human life. "Discerning the body" (v.29) refers therefore to the failure to recognize the nature of the community meal as the *Lord's Supper*.

Paul's plea becomes very personal: "examine yourself" (v. 28, cf. v. 31)! Self examination is an implicit aspect of faith in Christ. By examining, evaluating, and judging oneself in light of the passion story of Jesus, the believer and the believing community recognize their humanness and their selfishness. They begin to realize that the way of the cross is a process of continual repentance and renewal. It is the church's theological function to constantly evaluate its faith and practice in light of the story of Jesus.

Teaching Tip

Food for the People

Read from Dom Helder Camara of Recife, Brazil: "When I give people food, they call me a saint. When I ask why there is no food, they call me a communist." Have the class interpret the statement. See also by Helder Camara, *The Church and Colonialism* (London/Maryknoll, N.Y.: Sheed & Ward, 1969); *The Desert is Fertile* (Maryknoll, N.Y. Orbis, 1974); and *Hoping Against All Hope* (Maryknoll, N.Y.: Orbis, 1984).

Session 5

Romans 12:1-2
(Amos 5:21-24; Micah 6:6-8)

Christian Worship

What is Christian about Worship?

Since worship is a universal religious practice, Christians need to ask whether there is anything specific about *Christian* worship, and what that *Christian* dimension might be.

When we think of worship, our first thoughts are probably of "Sunday morning," "church," "hymns," "sermon," "prayers," "liturgy," "eucharist." The text for this study questions whether that is the essence of *Christian* worship.

Spiritual Worship

In our text, Romans 12:1-2, the apostle Paul uses traditional religious words such as *spiritual*, *holiness,* and *sacrifice*, but then transfigures their meaning to bring out the Christian understanding of worship. He does it by interrelating "spiritual worship" with "body."

Bodies

I appeal to you therefore, brothers and sisters, by the mercies of God, to present your bodies as a living sacrifice, holy and acceptable to God, which is your spiritual worship.

Christian worship is our human response to God's mercies. But such response is not merely with our minds or our souls, and it is certainly not the offering of dead animal sacrifices. It is the presentation of our "bodies as a living sacrifice."

Bodies here do not refer to the believers' flesh and bones at a certain period of time. *Bodies* speaks of "our being in relation to the world." *Body* stands for our whole life as it relates to God in prayer and worship, to

Lectionary Loop

**Proper 16 or Thirteenth Sunday after Pentecost, Year A
(Rom 12:1-8)**

Study Bible

On Romans 12:1, see Ernst Käsemann, *Commentary on Romans*. Trans., Geoffrey W. Bromiley (Grand Rapids: Eerdmans, 1980) 327-30 and *NISB*, 2028.

245

others in love and service, to nature and history through work, culture, and politics.

The "living" sacrifice is our *voluntary* response to God with our whole lives. We do so in gratitude for the fact that God has defeated the estranging powers of death by raising the crucified Jesus from the dead.

This response is *holy* not in a religious sense of being removed from the world. It is holy by being open to God and to God's activity in the world. The holy life is the life that is intentionally lived by being aware of the liberating claim of God in all areas of life. As such it is "acceptable to God!"

Jesus and the Prophets

With these emphases the apostle picks up a central concern of Jesus and the Hebrew prophets. He joins them in being critical of an understanding of worship that compartmentalizes life into sacred and secular, holy and profane. Such division of life tends to limit worship to what we do Sunday mornings in church, and as such excludes our life in family, business, and politics from our worship life.

Both Amos and Micah give us the prophetic critique of worship without social conscience.

> I hate, I despise your festivals, and I take no delight in your solemn assemblies. Even though you offer me your burnt offerings and grain offerings, I will not accept them; and the offerings of well-being of your fatted animals I will not look upon. Take away from me the noise of your songs; I will not listen to the melody of your harps. But let justice roll down like waters, and righteousness like an ever-flowing stream. (Amos 5:21-24 NRSV)

> "With what shall I come before the Lord, and bow myself before God on high? Shall I come before him with burnt offerings, with calves a year old? Will the Lord be pleased with thousands of rams, with ten thousands of rivers of oil? Shall I give my firstborn for my transgression, the fruit of my body for the sin of my soul?" He has told you, O mortal, what

---

Reflections

Worshiping with the Prophets

1. In what way are the texts from Amos and Micah related to Romans 12:1-2?
2. Are there examples today where worshipers have compartmentalized worship and social responsibility?

is good; and what does the Lord require of
you but to do justice, and to love kindness,
and to walk humbly with your God? (Micah
6:6-8 NRSV)

Jesus was crucified because he took this kind of
worship seriously. His celebration of God and his obedience to the first commandment included fellowship
with those who were considered religiously suspect
(tax collectors and sinners). He suspended traditional
Sabbath laws and religious rules of fasting, claiming a
higher authority than that of the law and the temple
cult. Jesus was critical of the traditional separation of
life into holy and profane, sacred and secular, by
claiming all of reality for God, with a special leaning
for those who were religiously suspect or unqualified:
lepers, sinners, people of the land, prostitutes, tax collectors, women, children. In direct consequence of
fleshing out this new view of God and of life, Jesus
was declared guilty of blasphemy and of leading people astray. He was captured, tortured, sentenced, and
executed. Nevertheless, God confirmed and enacted
this new view of reality by sharing his life with the
dead Jesus and raising him from the dead.

The Mercies of God
The reshaping of religious worship in the Christian
community is grounded in the mercies of God. Not a
religion of law, where God can be pleased by obeying
certain moral rules. Not a religion of temple cult,
whereby God can be pleased by rituals and sacrifices.
Rather God's freely given grace to be received by faith
is the ground of Christian life and worship.

The "spiritual" worship, therefore, the worship that
most adequately responds to God as God, happens in
the everyday life of our world, our marriage, our work,
our politics. Ernst Käsemann comments: "Christian
worship does not consist of what is practiced at sacred
sites, at sacred times, and with sacred acts . . . . It is the
offering of bodily existence in the otherwise profane
sphere. As something constantly demanded this takes
place in daily life, whereby every Christian is simultaneously sacrifice and priest" (*Romans,* Commentary

247

on Romans, trans G. Bromiley, Grand Rapids: Eerd-mans, 1980).

The Will of God

The Christian is therefore called to be both the salt of the earth and the light of the world. The Christian community is the *body* by which Christ in the power of the Spirit ministers his liberating grace to a needy world. Christian worship brings the world before God and thereby transforms it.

> Do not be conformed to this world, but be trans-formed by the renewing of your minds, so that you may discern what is the will of God—what is good and acceptable and perfect.

Worship cannot merely be a church or private matter: "When God claims our bodies, in and with them he reaches after his creation" (Kasemann, *Romans,* 330). The "renewed" mind of the Christian is grounded in the "mercies of God," not in the "world." But Christians live in the world. They know that, however cruel and ghastly its distortion and estrangement, this is God's world and God's creation. Through divine grace and faith Christians have become part of God's passion to liberate the world from sin and selfishness. Christians echo the being of God by being a transformative presence in the world.

The "will of God" is neither derived from the world nor our culture, character, or disposition. It arises from God's revelation in the life and death of the risen Christ. By saying that the "will of God" is related to "what is good and acceptable and perfect," grounded in the "mercies of God," and connected with the response of our "bodies," the apostle wants to fend off a number of positions that have been popular in the Christian church from the beginning:

♦ spiritual *enthusiasm* that is mainly concerned with personal edification and therefore assigns a secondary place to our responsibility for the world;

♦ spiritual *abstraction* that adheres to the humanistic and idealistic split between matter and spirit, body and soul, and therefore tends to focus wor-

---

Teaching Tip

Discerning God's Will

Leslie Weatherhead gives us some guidance for discerning God's will: intimacy with God, reading Scripture, the voice of the church, the advice of friends, using common sense. Discuss these guidelines and others with members of the class.

See Leslie Weatherhead, *The Will of God* (Nashville: Abingdon Press, 1944, 1972), 46-53.

Reflections

Religionless Christianity

In his letters from prison, Dietrich Bonhoeffer made a distinction between religious activity that was partial or incomplete and dynamic faith that involved the whole of one's life.

Ask the class: Is it possible to be a Christian without being religious? Discuss the difference between "religious" and "Christian."

See Dietrich Bonhoeffer, Letters and Papers from Prison *(New York: Macmillan, 1972), 279-80 and* Wisdom and Witness of Dietrich Bonhoeffer, *114-15.*

ship on private and communal devotion, on church, rather than on all areas of life

♦ spiritual *conservatism* that does not sufficiently recognize the tension and possible conflict between the "world" and the "cross."

The "minds" that are focused on Jesus Christ and renewed by the Holy Spirit will distinguish what in the world can and must be affirmed, and what in the world can and must be resisted, opposed, or transformed.

Worship, therefore, cannot be limited or reduced to certain times, places, and rituals. It happens *all* the time with our *whole* life in our *everyday* world. A religion focused on "law" (i.e., morality or doctrine) tends to reduce the radical claim upon *all* of our lives. A religion focused on "cult" tends to *compartmentalize* life and reduce worship to certain religious exercises, holy places, liturgies, sacrifices, often performed by a priestly class. It must therefore be emphasized that for Christians: 1) there are no special holy places, but the whole creation is the theater of God's glory; 2) there is no priestly class, but all believers are "priests"; 3) there are no holy actions but all that we do has the dignity of service to God. What we do on Sunday mornings in church is the communal celebration and confession that this is God's world and that we have the honor of witnessing that God loves the world and seeks reconciliation with it.

Conclusion

The question raised in these studies is how Jesus Christ, the foundation and content of our faith, can be known in a way that honors him. We have studied representative texts from the Gospels and Epistles, with some references to the prophets. As this short-term Bible study concludes, consider the following:

1. Our response to Christ should be holistic. Doctrinal correctness, personal piety, and liturgical sophistication are important, but they must aid a holistic response, not replace it or divert from it.

2. God in Christ and through the Spirit takes the initiative by calling us to the life of a disciple, and at the

---

Reflection

Romans 12 and Worship

The remaining verses in Romans 12 provide a good illustration about what it means to worship God with our whole lives. In what particular practices do we worship God at work, in our marriage, in politics, at the close of the day?

Sources

From Miroslav Volf, *Exclusion and Embrace: A Theological Exploration of Identity, Otherness, and Reconciliation* (Nashville: Abingdon, 1996), 40.

same time providing the spiritual resources to sustain us on the journey.

3. The call to discipleship is an ultimate concern which relativizes reasonable, but penultimate obligations. Miroslav Volf comments appropriately:

> At the very core of Christian identity lies an all-encompassing change of loyalty, from a given culture with its gods to the God of all cultures. A response to a call from that God entails rearrangement of a whole network of allegiances. As the call of Jesus' first disciples illustrates, 'the nets' (economy) and 'the father' (family) must be left behind (Mark 1:16-20). Departure is part and parcel of Christian identity. Since Abraham is our ancestor, our faith is "at odds with place."

4. For the life of discipleship it is determinative that the call to follow Jesus is a call to freedom. The challenge and the hardship of discipleship cannot be sustained by command, duty, and will. The Christian view of reality is therefore characterized by words like *freedom*, *love*, *joy*, and *parresia* (openness, courage, boldness, confidence, fearlessness).

5. Discipleship is lived and exercised in community. Although faith comes to each individual, and therefore each individual is called to discipleship, faith in Christ does not individualize people. It creates a community. The community of faith is necessary for our spiritual survival.

6. Our response and obedience to God is given theological dignity because we are called God's co-workers (*synergoi* in 1 Cor 3:9).

7. The call to follow Jesus also gives special attention to the needs and rights of those who are disadvantaged as a result of oppression and discrimination.

8. Christian discipleship feeds on the promise that "in the Lord your labor is not in vain" (1 Cor 15:58).

9. Since discipleship has to do with following Jesus, the willingness to suffer is part of the journey.

Reflection
The Call to Suffer

There is no virtue in suffering for its own sake, and Christian faith must be carefully distinguished from a martyr's complex. Yet the Christian must be mindful that Jesus' messianic journey was from its beginning met by opposition and within a reasonably short time ended in capture and crucifixion. Whatever christology we adopt, we cannot overlook the fact that Jesus did not die of natural causes. He was "executed as a political subversive and crucified between two social bandits. It appears that Jerusalem elites collaborating with their Roman overlords executed Jesus because he was a threat to their economic and political interests." There is no doubt that if Christians resist the racism, violence, militarism, ethnic hatred, and ecological exploitation of our time, the willingness to suffer must be part of being friends with Jesus.

On Jesus as a threat to the authorities, see William R. Herzog, Parables as Subversive Speech: Jesus Pedagogue to the Oppressed *(Louisville: Westminster/John Knox, 1994), 9.*

SOURCES

SOURCES

The Gospel of Matthew

Carter, Warren. "The Gospel According to Matthew." In *The New Interpreter's Study Bible: New Revised Standard Version with Apocrypha,* edited by Walter J. Harrelson. Nashville: Abingdon Press, 2003.

————. *Matthew and Empire: Initial Explorations.* Harrisburg, Penn.: Trinity Press International, 2001.

————. *Matthew and the Margins.* Maryknoll, N.Y.: Orbis Books, 2000.

First Isaiah

Silverman, William B. *Rabbinic Stories for Christian Ministers and Teachers.* New York: Abingdon Press, 1958.

Healing and Grief

Bartocci, Barbara. *From Hurting to Happy: Transforming Your Life After Loss.* Notre Dame, Ind.: Sorin Books, 2002.

Bassler, Jouette M. "Cross." In *The HarperCollins Bible Dictionary.* Rev. ed. Edited by Paul J. Achtemeier. San Francisco: HarperSanFrancisco, 1995.

Boss, Pauline. *Ambiguous Loss: Learning to Live with Unresolved Grief.* Cambridge, Mass.: Harvard University Press, 1999.

Brueggemann, Walter. *First and Second Samuel.* Interpretation, a Bible Commentary for Teaching and Preaching. Louisville: John Knox Press, 1990.

————. "The Formfulness of Grief." *Interpretation* 31, no. 3 (1977): 263–75.

————. *The Message of the Psalms: A Theological Commentary.* Augsburg Old Testament Studies. Minneapolis: Augsburg Fortress Press, 1984.

Cone, James. *Black Theology and Black Power.* New York: Seabury Press, 1969.

Hawkins, Peter S. "Flannery O'Connor." In *Listening for God: Contemporary Literature and the Life of Faith,* edited by Paula J. Carlson and Peter S. Hawkins. Minneapolis: Augsburg Fortress Press, 1994.

Keck, Leander E. "The First Letter of Paul to the Thessalonians." In *The Interpreter's One-Volume Commentary on the Bible: Introduction and Commentary for Each Book, Including the Apocrypha with General Articles,* edited by Charles M. Laymon. Nashville: Abingdon Press, 1971.

Kushner, Harold S. *When Bad Things Happen to Good People.* New York: Schocken Books, 1981.

Meeks, Blair Gilmer. *Standing in the Circle of Grief: Prayers and Liturgies for Death and Dying.* Nashville: Abingdon Press, 2002.

Meyer, Lester. "A Lack of Laments in the Church's Use of the Psalter." *Lutheran Quarterly* 7, no. 1 (1993): 67–78.

Mitchell, Kenneth R., and Herbert Anderson. *All Our Losses, All Our Griefs: Resources for Pastoral Care.* Philadelphia: Westminster Press, 1983.

Moe, Thomas. *Pastoral Care in Pregnancy Loss: A Ministry Long Needed.* Binghamton, N.Y.: Haworth Press, 1997.

Moloney, Francis J. *The Gospel of John.* Sacra Pagina Series 4, edited by Daniel J. Harrington. Collegeville, Minn.: Liturgical Press, 1998.

Moore, James W. *When Grief Breaks Your Heart.* Nashville: Abingdon Press, 1995.

O'Collins, Gerald, and Edward G. Farrugia. *A Concise Dictionary of Theology.* New York: Paulist Press, 1991.

Park, Andrew Sung. *The Wounded Heart of God: The Asian Concept of Han and the Christian Doctrine of Sin.* Nashville: Abingdon Press, 1993.

Pretzel, Paul W. "Suicide (Ethical Issues)." In *Dictionary of Pastoral Care and Counseling,* edited by Rodney J. Hunter. Nashville: Abingdon Press, 1990.

Rando, Therese A. *Parental Loss of a Child.* Champaign, Ill.: Research Press Company, 1986.

Stone, Howard W., and James O. Duke. *How to Think Theologically.* Minneapolis: Augsburg Fortress Press, 1996.

Suchocki, Marjorie Hewitt. *In God's Presence: Theological Reflections on Prayer.* St. Louis: Chalice Press, 1996.

Sullender, R. Scott. "St. Paul's Approach to Grief: Clarifying the Ambiguity." *Journal of Religion and Health* 20 (Spring 1981).

For examples of Greco-Konran consolation literature cited by Sullender, see Seneca, "On Consolation to the Bereaved," vol. 3, *Ad Lucilium Epistulae Morales* (Cambridge, Mass.: Harvard University Press, 1962) and "Moral Essays," vol. 2 (Cambridge, Mass.: Harvard University Press, 1965).

Sunderland, Ronald H. *Getting Through Grief: Caregiving by Congregations.* Nashville: Abingdon Press, 1993.

Switzer, David K. "Grief and Loss." In *Dictionary of Pastoral Care and Counseling,* edited by Rodney J. Hunter. Nashville: Abingdon Press, 1990.

Thurman, Howard. *Jesus and the Disinherited.* Richmond, Ind.: Friends United Press, 1981.

————. *With Head and Heart: The Autobiography of Howard Thurman.* San Diego: Harvest Book / Harcourt Brace, 1979.

Tuttle, Kate. "Soweto, South Africa, South African Township Near Johannesburg." In *Africana: The Encyclopedia of the African and African American Experience,* edited by Kwame Anthony Appiah and Henry Louis Gates, Jr. New York: Basic Books, 1999.

Wallace, Richard. "Racism, Grief, Chemical Abuse and Dependency, and African-American Males: Towards A Conceptual Model of Pastoral Care." Ph.D. diss. Luther Seminary, 1996.

————. "The Theological View of Aging that Permeates the African American Experience." Vol. 2, *Aging, Spirituality, and Religion: A Handbook,* edited by Melvin A. Kimble and Susan H. McFadden. Minneapolis: Augsburg Fortress Press, 2003.

Weaver, Andrew J., Laura T. Flannelly, and John D. Preston. *Counseling Survivors of Traumatic Events: A Handbook for Pastors and Other Helping Professionals.* Nashville: Abingdon Press, 2003.

Weems, Renita. *Battered Love: Marriage, Sex, and Violence in the Hebrew Scriptures.* Minneapolis: Augsburg Fortress Press, 1995.

Weiser, Artur. *The Psalms: A Commentary.* Philadelphia: Westminster Press, 1962.

Westburg, Granger E. *Good Grief: A Constructive Approach to the Problem of Loss.* Minneapolis: Augsburg Fortress Press, 1979.

Young, Fredricka A., arr. "Plenty Good Room." In *Songs of Zion,* edited by J. Jefferson Cleveland and Verolga Nix, 99. Nashville: Abingdon Press, 1981.

Unselfish Prayer

Coleridge, Samuel Taylor. "Hymn before Sun-Rise, in the Vale of Chamouni." In *Selected Poetry and Prose of Coleridge*, edited by D. A. Stauffer, 104–5. The Modern Library. New York: Random House, 1951.

Foster, Richard J. *Prayer: Finding the Heart's True Home.* San Francisco: HarperSanFrancisco, 1992.

Job, Rueben P., and Norman Shawchurch. *Guide to Prayer for All God's People*. Nashville: Upper Room, 1994.

Merton, Thomas. *Praying the Psalms.* Collegeville, Minn.: Liturgical Press, 1956.

Steere, Douglas V. *Dimensions of Prayer.* Nashville: Upper Room, 1962.

Suchocki, Marjorie Hewitt. *In God's Presence: Theological Reflections on Prayer.* St. Louis: Chalice Press, 1996.

Wainwright, Geoffrey. *Doxology: The Praise of God in Worship, Doctrine, and Life*. New York: Oxford University Press, 1984.

Faith and Power

Craig, Mary, ed. *His Holiness the Dalai Lama: In My Own Words.* London: Hodder & Stoughton, 2001.

United Nations General Assembly. "Universal Declaration of Human Rights." Resolution 217 A (III) of 10 December 1948. http://www.un.org/Overview/rights.html.

Liberating Discipleship

Aland, Kurt, ed. *Synopsis of the Four Gospels: Greek-English Edition of the Synopsis Quattuor Evangeliorum.* 6th ed. Stuttgart: United Bible Societies, 1983.

Bonhoeffer, Dietrich. *The Cost of Discipleship*. Translated by R. H. Fuller and Irmgard Booth. New York: McMillan, 1963.

——— . *Discipleship: Dietrich Bonhoeffer Works*. Vol. 4. Edited by John D. Godsey and Geffrey B. Kelly. Translated by B. Green and R. Krauss. Minneapolis: Augsburg Fortress Press, 2001.

——— . *Faith and the Future: Essays on Theology, Solidarity, and Modernity*. Maryknoll, N.Y.: Orbis Books, 1995.

Chester, Tim, ed. *Justice, Mercy and Humility: Integral Mission and the Poor*. Carlisle, Cumbria, U.K.: Paternoster Press, 2002.

Davies, W. D., and Dale C. Allison. *A Critical and Exegetical Commentary on the Gospel According to Saint Matthew*. International Critical Commentary on the Holy Scriptures of the Old and New Testaments 2. Edinburgh: T. & T. Clark, 1991.

Hengel, M. *The Charismatic Leader and His Followers*. Edited by J. Riches. Translated by. J. C. Greig. Edinburgh: T. & T. Clark, 1981.

Metz, Johann Baptist. *A Passion for God*. New York: Paulist Press, 1997.

Ratschow, Carl Heinz, ed. *Paul Tillich: Main Works/Hauptwerke*. Vol. 5. Berlin: De Gruyter, 1988.

Schuster, Ekkehard. *Hope Against Hope: Johann Baptist Metz and Elie Wiesel Speak Out on the Holocaust*. New York: Paulist Press, 1999.

Schweitzer, Albert. *The Quest of the Historical Jesus*. Rev. ed. Translated by J. Bowden. Minneapolis: Augsburg Fortress Press, 2001.

———. *The Quest of the Historical Jesus: A Critical Study of Its Progress from Reimarus to Wrede*. Translated by W. Montgomery from the first German ed. *Von Reimarus zu Wrede* published in 1906. Preface by F. C. Burkitt from the first English ed. published in 1906. New York: Macmillan, 1910.

Schweizer, Eduard. *The Good News According to Matthew*. Richmond: John Knox Press, 1988.

——— . *Jesus: The Parable of God*. New York: Continuum, 1997.

——— . *Lordship and Discipleship*. Studies in Biblical Theology 28. London: SCM Press, 1960.

————. *Luke: A Challenge to Present Theology*. Atlanta: John Knox Press, 1982.

Tillich, Paul. *Dynamics of Faith*. New York: Harper & Row, 1957.

Throckmorton, Burton H., Jr., ed. *Gospel Parallels: A Comparison of the Synoptic Gospels*. 5th ed. Nashville: Thomas Nelson, 1992.

Volf, Miroslav. *Exclusion and Embrace: A Theological Exploration of Identity, Otherness, and Reconciliation*. Nashville: Abingdon Press, 1996.

LECTIONARY

LECTIONARY

Year A

Year B

Year C

SCRIPTURE INDEX

Scripture Index

Notes

Notes

How to Use the Compact Disk

The compact disk located in the back of *The Pastor's Bible Study: Volume One* may be used to supplement and enhance the study experience. The disk includes:

♦ A QuickTime® video introduction to *The Pastor's Bible Study: Volume One* by general editor David Albert Farmer

♦ The full text of *The Pastor's Bible Study: Volume One* in Adobe Reader® (.pdf) format, plus several versions of Adobe Reader® software

♦ PowerPoint® presentations containing outlines for each study within the volume, in both PowerPoint® Presentation (.ppt) and PowerPoint® Show (.pps) format

♦ Background projection images (.jpg) portraying underlying themes for each of the six studies

♦ Study outlines and reflection questions in rich text file (.rtf) format that may be edited, printed, and given to group participants

To access any of this material, insert the compact disk into the CD-ROM drive of your computer and browse to the item(s) you wish to select using your PC Windows Explorer, or your Macintosh Browser.

Viewing the QuickTime® Introductory Video

To view the QuickTime® introductory video of *The Pastor's Bible Study: Volume One*, you must have QuickTime® software installed on your computer. If you wish to install this free software, download it from the web at www.apple.com/quicktime/download/.

> *Note: The QuickTime® program is not included on* The Pastor's Bible Study: Volume One *disk. Technical support for QuickTime® is available at www.apple.com.*

Once QuickTime® is installed on your computer, browse to the file named **Video** on the disk and double click on it to play it.

Using the Adobe Reader® Book

To use the Adobe Reader® book containing the full text of *The Pastor's Bible Study: Volume One*, you must have Adobe Reader® software installed on your computer. If you wish to install Adobe Reader®, browse to the **Adobe_Installation** folder on the disk and select the correct version.

Make your selection by referring to the chart below. Once you have determined the corrected version to install, double click on the file and follow the onscreen instructions for installation.

> *Note: Technical support for installation of the Adobe Reader is available at www.adobe.com.*

Once Adobe Reader® is installed on your computer, browse to the file named **PBS_Vol_1.pdf** on the disk and double click on it to open it. After opening the **PBS_Vol_1.pdf**, you may search on any keyword or phrase in *The Pastor's Bible Study: Volume One*.

Another useful feature of the Adobe Reader file is the addition of links to other resources on the supplemental disk. These links are at the beginning of each of the six studies at the bottom the study's outline page. Clicking on a link will open the selected resource on your computer in its default program. Just be sure that *The Pastor's Bible Study: Volume One* compact disk is in your CD-ROM drive.

Platform	OS	Acrobat Reader® Version	Acrobat Reader® File
Windows	XP	6.0.1	AdbeRdr60_enu.exe
	2000	6.0.1	AdbeRdr60_enu.exe
	ME	6.0.1	AdbeRdr60_enu.exe
	NT	6.0.1	AdbeRdr60_enu.exe
	98SE	6.0.1	AdbeRdr60_enu.exe
	98	5.05	rp505enu.exe
	95	5.05	rp505enu.exe
Palm	1.1		accrreadpalmosv11.exe
	2.0	English Windows	arpos_winv20enu.exe
	2.0	English Mac Palm Desktop 2.6.3	arpos_macv20pd263enu.sit
	2.0	English Mac Palm Desktop 4.0	arpos_macv20pd40enu.sit
	3.0	English Windows	AdobeReader305-PalmOS.exe
	3.0	English Mac Palm Desktop 4.0	AdobeReader305-PalmOS.dmg
Pocket PC	2002		acrobatreader-ppc2002.exe
	English ARM		acrobatreader-ppcarm.exe
	English MIPS		acrobatreader-ppcmips.exe
	English SH3		acrobatreader-ppcsh3.exe
Mac	10.2.2-10.3	6.0.1	AdbeRdr60_enu.dmg
	9.1-10.2.1	5.1	AcroReader51_ENU.bin
	8.6-9.0	5.05	ar505enu.bin
	8.1-8.5	4.05	rs405eng.bin
	7.5.3	4.05	rs405eng.bin

Viewing PowerPoint® Presentations

There are twelve PowerPoint® files on the disk, two for each of the six studies. These two PowerPoint® files contain presentations of study outlines. All PowerPoint® files are in a folder named **PowerPoint**. To view the PowerPoint® files that accompany *The Pastor's Bible Study: Volume One*, you must have Microsoft PowerPoint® software or PowerPoint® Viewer installed on your computer.

.PPT files: The .ppt files are files associated with the full version of Microsoft PowerPoint®. If you have the full version of PowerPoint® software installed on your computer, you may double click on the .ppt files to open them in PowerPoint® and customize your study presentations.

> Note: The Microsoft PowerPoint® program is not included on The Pastor's Bible Study: Volume One disk. Technical support for PowerPoint® is available at www.microsoft.com.

.PPS files: The.pps files are "stand alone" files that may be viewed using the PowerPoint® Viewer, which is installed on most computers. If you wish to install this free software, download it from Microsoft at www.microsoft.com/downloads/ details.aspx?FamilyID=7C404E8E-5513-46C4-AA4F-58A84A37DF1&displaylang=EN.

In most cases, using the .pps files will be the best choice for presenting the outlines to study participants. To begin the presentation:

♦ Place the disk in your computer's CD-ROM drive.

♦ Click on the link found on the appropriate study outline in Adobe Reader$^{®}$ to start the presentation. (Or, you may open the .pps file by browsing to it on the disk and double-clicking it.)

♦ Click anywhere on the slide, or use the Page Down button, to move through the presentation.

> *Note: If you click past a point in the outline and wish to go back, use the backspace or Page Up button on your computer's keyboard.*

Using Backgrounds for Projection

To view the images from the PowerPoint$^{®}$ presentations, browse the on the disk to a folder named **Images**. Double click on the .jpg images to open them in your computer's default image viewer.

Using Study Outlines

Study outlines for all six sections are in a folder named **Study_Outlines**. Double-click on an outline to open the rich text format (.rtf) file in your computer's default word processing program. You may then customize your study experience by making changes to the outline. You may also access these files by clicking on the links provided in the study outline in Adobe Reader$^{®}$.

> *Note: At the end of each session outline, Participant assignments for the upcoming sessions are noted, including scripture reading assignments and* New Interpreter's Study Bible *references. Providing the outlines to participants will enhance their study experience.*

Using Reflection Questions

Reflection questions for all six studies are in a folder named **Reflection_Questions**. Double click on an outline to open the rich text format (.rtf) file in your computer's default word processing program. You may then customize your study experience by making changes to the reflection questions. You may also access these files by clicking on the links provided in the study outline in Adobe Reader$^{®}$.

Contacting Technical Support

To contact one of our Technical Support Representatives, call: **1-615-749-6777, Monday through Friday, 8:00 A.M. to 5:00 P.M.**, central time.

Notes

Notes

Notes

Notes